GOOD OLD
Sussex by the Sea

GOOD OLD
Sussex by the Sea

**A SIXTIES CHILDHOOD
SPENT WITH
HASTINGS UNITED,
THE ALBION AND
SUSSEX COUNTY CRICKET**

TIM QUELCH

First published by Pitch Publishing, 2020

Pitch Publishing
A2 Yeoman Gate
Yeoman Way
Worthing
Sussex
BN13 3QZ
www.pitchpublishing.co.uk
info@pitchpublishing.co.uk

A CIP catalogue record is available for this book
from the British Library.

ISBN 978 1 78531 619 7

Typesetting and origination by Pitch Publishing

Printed and bound in India by Replika Press Pvt. Ltd.

Contents

A tribute to my family

Thank you, mum and dad for such a happy adolescence, for fostering and supporting my passion for football and cricket and for helping me achieve ambitions I once thought were beyond me. Thank you, Liz and Lydia, my wife and our daughter, respectively, for your constant love, care and encouragement in all aspects of our happy lives together, tolerating, supporting and sometimes sharing my passion for sport. I hope that in time our grandchildren might discover such joys for themselves.

Tim Quelch, September 2019

Thanks

I WOULD like to thank everyone who has helped me in writing this book. If I have overlooked anyone please accept my apology I am deeply grateful to former professional footballers who gave me generous amounts of their time, notably Ken and Alan Ballard, and Keith Tucker, all of whom played for Hastings United. I am very appreciative of the support I have received from other authors, namely Dave Thomas, who allowed me to use extracts from his biography of Willie Irvine *Together Again*; Ivan Ponting, who encouraged me to write this book as well as granting me usage of his eloquently written obituaries; Roger Sinden, for allowing me generous access to both of his lovingly assembled histories of Hastings United, including use of his captivating interviews with former Hastings United players; Paul who gave me access to his absorbing interviews with ex-Brighton players. Thanks are due to both the original Hastings United and Brighton & Hove Albion for use of material from their historic match programmes. Thanks go to Daren Burney and his colleagues at the current Hastings United who have shown great interest in this book, offering to play an active role in its marketing and sales, and assist with its charitable fund-raising objective. National and local newspapers have provided rich sources of material. Thanks go to the *Hastings & St Leonards Observer*, whose editor kindly permitted me to use extracts from their coverage of the original Hastings United including use of six atmospheric images from the 50s and 60s. Thanks go to the *Brighton Argus*, who have previously, kindly granted me permission to use material from historic interviews with former Brighton players, which are replicated in this publication; and to the national press for supplying material, rediscovered in unattributed cuttings in my boyhood scrapbooks of over 50 years ago. The references listed at the end of this book have helped improve my understanding of past times, enabling me to present a more rounded portrait, not only of the football and cricket, but also of life in Britain and elsewhere, during the last 70 years. If I have inadvertently breached copyright anywhere in this book, I hope that the copyright owners will please accept my profound apology. This book is being written to raise funds for the British Lung Foundation. All my royalties will be donated to this important cause. However, if any copyright owners wish to pursue their concerns, would they please address these first to my publisher, Pitch Publishing at Yeoman Gate, Yeoman Way, Worthing BN13 3QZ. Last, but not least, I would like to express my gratitude to my friends, notably Roger King, who carefully proofread my earlier drafts, suggesting helpful amendments and supplying copious memories and statistics; and to my publishers Paul and Jane, and their assistants, Michelle, Dean, Duncan and Graham for their experienced guidance and high quality assistance.

Tim Quelch, October 2019

Introduction

AFTER MOVING North in 1968, I began watching my dwindling local side, Burnley FC, suggesting, perhaps, that tough love is sometimes the more captivating kind. Yet my interest in football and cricket started in East Sussex, where I was born and bred. Here, I supported Hastings United, Brighton & Hove Albion and Sussex County Cricket Club, learning quickly the harsh price of loyalty. For soon after I had resumed watching Hastings United in August 1960, the U's dropped like a stone. They fell out of the Southern League Premier Division in 1961, and kept falling, careering to the bottom of the league below 12 months later, forcing the club to seek re-election in the chilly summer of 1962. While Brighton narrowly clung on to their Second Division status in 1961, they, too, were relegated a year later, and after enduring the harsh winter of 1962/63, the coldest I can remember, they continued to drop, finding themselves in the Football League basement in May 1963. Conversely, Hastings were then embarking upon an unexpected, if short-lived, revival.

Sussex County Cricket Club was afflicted by a similar malaise. After gaining fourth spot in the dank summer of 1960, helped by the 3,086 runs plundered by Ted Dexter and Jim Parks, they subsequently slumped into mid-table mediocrity. And despite enjoying a brief reversal of fortune, when they won the new Gillette Trophy in 1963 and 1964, they lost their 'one-day' crown a year later and completed the 1965 County Championship season next to bottom.

It may seem a contrived virtue summoned by necessity, but I remain fonder of underdogs who scrap for mere morsels and strive to punch above their weight, than the giants accustomed to wealth and glory. This predisposition is derived from my deceased father. He never hitched his wagon to big names. He supported Brentford, then in the third tier. His message to me was not to expect too much. Not that I drool over failure. For while my love of modest causes often leaves me disappointed, the unexpected triumphs seem so much sweeter. Sometimes I wonder whether I could have sustained my support of Burnley as they hurtled towards oblivion in 1987, without this sturdy Sussex education.

Coincidentally, both Brighton and Burnley have faced identical catastrophes –Burnley ten years before Brighton. And both clubs were rescued by their loyal fans, whether in the boardroom, on the pitch, on the terraces or beyond. Both clubs endured existential traumas, and both have survived triumphantly. And now both fly the flag of the 'small guys', determined to lower the colours of the opulent fraternity in a league bloated by obscene wealth and greed. So, while I continue to be an ardent supporter of Burnley, I remain fond of Brighton, having watched them during the intervening years, in triumph and woe, at the Goldstone, Gillingham, Withdean and the Amex. Regrettably, no one could rescue the original Hastings United in 1985.

I have an abiding loyalty to Sussex CCC, too, while being a well-wisher for the club that now bears Hastings United's name. In fact, I extend similar goodwill to many 'underdogs', from Barrow to Aldershot; from Accrington to Torquay; from Morecambe to Hartlepool, all of whom I have watched in the last 60 years. If this is brazen promiscuity, it's a perverse kind.

Tim Quelch, June 2019

1953 New Elizabethans

'The Black Hills of Dakota'

MY EARLIEST memory of East Sussex is of the stunning view from the hilltop council house estate where my parents and I lived for most of the 1950s. The newly built, white stippled houses were formed into a tight circle, as if defying a marauding Sioux war party. From this lofty Wealden ridge, the view extended over the undulating pastures and woodland below to the distant whale-backed downs and the glimmering sea. Had Satan chosen this spot to tempt Jesus, he might have succeeded. As beautiful as this location was, it gave little protection against the buffeting gusts of wind which would blast through our cracked walls and ill-fitting window frames with ghoulish shrieks. As for the established villagers, our reticent hosts, their frosty reception matched the elements.

But with their musty grocery store rejuvenated by our custom, the villagers' antipathy turned to tolerance, and eventually acceptance. This reconciliation allowed us, the invading 'townies', to take our place in village society, helping at its fetes, swelling its harvest festivals and participating in its sporting activities. Dad played both football and cricket for the village, but his early attempts at enticing my interest fell on muddy ground.

Dad introduced me to football in the year of Queen Elizabeth's coronation. He bought me a leather football for my fifth birthday. On a glowering winter afternoon, we tried it out in a soggy recreation field. The ball became impossibly heavy with excess moisture, barely trickling away from my flailing kicks. This was not fun.

More to my taste then was bubbly, boisterous, buckskinned Doris Day, the star of the Hollywood musical of that year, *Calamity Jane*. With her jauntily placed US Cavalry cap and her thigh-slapping androgyny – such an alluring 'pop' commodity – she exuded high-octane fun, gymnastically belting out rowdy numbers such as 'The Windy City' and 'The Deadwood Stage'. But it is her wistful version of 'The Black Hills of Dakota' which stands my test of time, perhaps possessing greater poignancy because it signified that the heyday of the Western was passing.

In our crowded, smoky cinemas, the sweeping western panoramas of Monument Valley, Montana and the Great Plains provided a perfect antidote to grey, rationed lives. But in the brighter, more prosperous years that followed the coronation of our new Queen, we had less need of vicarious horizons.

Not that the Coronation Day weather gave any cause for encouragement. After watching, in grainy monochrome, a heavily bejewelled Elizabeth solemnly dedicate herself to a life of regal duty, we trudged in bedraggled procession towards the village hall, waving our miniature flags determinedly in the persistent June rain, and hungrily anticipating the feast being laid out on the trestle tables inside. For this was our celebration, too, of an end to austerity, as plates were piled high with sandwiches and bridge rolls bulging with scrambled egg, ham and cheese and tomato, not forgetting the abundance of jelly, fairy cakes and the ever-serviceable Victoria sponges. Our garish coronation mugs ensured it was a day we would never forget.

With the nation pumped up with patriotic pride it was entirely fitting that Len Hutton's England cricket team should defeat the mighty Australians for the first time since 1933. At a sun-drenched Oval in August I was told that the winning runs were hit by 'pin-up' boy Denis Compton, who swivelled on Arthur Morris's wayward long-hop and smacked it joyfully to the long-leg boundary. As the ball raced towards its triumphant destination, Brian Johnston can be heard shouting, on the surviving footage: 'It's the Ashes! The Ashes!' Thousands of men and women can be seen swarming all over the turf, racing one another to embrace the not-out batsmen, 'Compo' and Bill Edrich, while women planted fat kisses on their heroes' burning cheeks. Apparently, BBC radio commentator, Bernard Kerr, found difficulty in restraining his euphoria, reporting: 'This is staggering. In fact, it's rather moving. From the broadcasting box, you can't see any grass at all, there's just a whole carpet of humanity. It really is just a wonderful sight!'

Appearing on the pavilion balcony, England's captain Len Hutton addressed the tumultuous crowd in a pastiche of Oxford diction, so different from his uninhibited, Yorkshire accent, adopted when interviewed after his record-breaking innings at the Oval in 1938. The Australian captain, Lindsay Hassett, seemed much more at ease, amiably extending his congratulations to his victorious rival. However, at the post-match party, Hassett confessed that his speech had been more sporting than he felt, remarking: 'Yes, I think it was pretty good considering Lockie threw us out.' In the maelstrom of patriotic fervour prevalent in 1953, his accusation of cheating was brushed aside. After all, a Commonwealth team had just conquered Everest and the three-year Korean War had ended with tales of British valour at the Battle of the Imjin River. But the collective euphoria was upset by a fatal crash of our pioneering De Havilland Comet, the world's first jet airliner. And the England football team's supremacy at home was shattered by the technically and tactically superior Magyars.

Hastings United v Norwich City

FA CUP Third Round, 9 January 1954

'Who Killed Cock Robin?'

UNDETERRED BY my initial resistance, Dad tried once more to convert me to football. On a gloomy 9 January 1954, Dad took me to the Pilot Field to watch Hastings United take on Third Division Norwich City in the third round of the FA Cup.

Semi-professional Hastings United were still in their infancy in 1954, having been formed only six years before. Their birth, like mine, in that hot summer of 1948, was set against a backdrop of massive war debts, ration cards and grim austerity. Despite the welcome 'Welfare State' reforms introduced by Clem Attlee's Labour government, 'mend and make do' was a phrase of choice. But while Bradman's 'Invincibles' crushed England's cricket team in that summer of 1948, our bankrupt country laid on a cheap, cheerful, yet undeniably successful Olympic Games. Public entertainment had never been so popular, particularly professional football.

During the 1948/49 season the average crowd at a Football League game was 22,300, with attendances regularly in excess of 60,000 at top clubs. Even county cricket registered almost two million admissions during the long hot summer of 1947.

This level of popularity could not be sustained, though. Once television ownership expanded prodigiously during the mid-50s, providing an absorbing hearth-side alternative, there was a sharp drop in custom for other public entertainments, notably the cinema. But in 1948 the voracious appetite for football was such that 2,000 turned up at the Pilot Field on 14 August to watch a pre-season trial match.

According to the *Hastings & St Leonards Observer*, Hastings United were created in a rush. A successful application was made by its ambitious board to join the Southern League, arguably the strongest competition outside the Football League, but by July 1948 the newly formed club had yet to secure a ground and a team. Their choice of ground was the council-owned Pilot Field, situated in an elevated position on the Eastern edge of town. However, it was occupied by amateur club Hastings and St Leonards FC, who asked the council to renew their tenancy at a previously agreed rent of £300 per year. The Hastings United board, led by chairman George Steel, offered twice that figure. *The Hastings & St Leonards Observer* reported on its front page, 'After a lively debate, the Town Council decided by a narrow margin of 18 votes to 17 to grant Hastings United use of the lower Pilot Field pitch on Saturday and Wednesday afternoons, during the 1948/49 season. The rent was set at £750 a year, inclusive of rates and maintenance.' Although the amateur club belatedly matched the United bid of £600, it was to no avail. The debate had been as heated as the outside temperature of 90°F.

The lower Pilot Field was also then the venue for speedway motorbike racing, attracting crowds of 9,000 or more. However, the objections of wealthy and influential neighbours, on grounds of noise, were sustained by the council. For 15 years after, the football pitch remained surrounded by a cinder track and 30 short floodlight pylons.

In mid-August 1948 the *Hastings & St Leonards Observer* reported that Hastings United had received 14 applications from professional footballers. While the remuneration on offer was frugal, the Hastings directors attempted to mitigate any deficit by offering part-time work in the town. Amateur players were also signed to supplement the thin first-team squad. The amateurs were signified on the team sheet by their initials preceding their surnames, mirroring the traditional differentiation of 'gentlemen' and 'players' adopted in English first-class cricket.

Councillor Frank Oak became the club's full-time secretary, while George Skinner, a former Spurs player and qualified coach, was appointed as player-manager. Somehow, Skinner cobbled together a team for the opening fixture at the Angel Ground, Tonbridge, on 21 August 1948, although his final selection, George Milton, was signed just minutes before kick-off. Amazingly, Hastings won 2-1 after coming from behind. With the Tonbridge team also thrown together in great haste, the game was hardly a classic. However, the game was watched by a large crowd of 5,800, 200 of whom were from Hastings, transported in coaches organised by the club. The inaugural supporters' club chairman, Chas Harris, wished the new squad 'Good luck, good shooting and a very successful season,' while Skinner urged the fans to give his players 'throaty encouragement'.

As encouraging as the Tonbridge result was, the going became a lot tougher thereafter. Hastings did not win again until October, when they were fortified by the signing of Bernard Moore, a fine striker from Brighton. His superior technique and potency in front of goal kept the turnstiles clicking, taking the club to mid-table security in its first two seasons. But with Hastings's financial situation deteriorating, Moore was sold to Luton in 1950 for £4,000. This fee probably represents around £1million in today's hyper-inflated transfer market. The Hastings directors had underestimated the costs of running a semi-professional club. The overheads, comprising rent, rates and maintenance, amounted to £150 per year, on top of the £600 rent. This combined liability would represent around £28,000 today.

Then there were the staff costs to meet, the utility bills, catering, transport, and Southern League fees, too, plus medical and accounting expenditure. According to the *Hastings & St Leonards Observer*, rent debts were mounting and the tax man had been alerted. Playing standards fell alarmingly. Over 500 goals were conceded in Hastings's first four seasons. They completed the 1949/50 season in bottom place. With the club on its knees, George Skinner resigned at the start of the following season. His successor, Bill Spencer, hung on for just over one year before resigning because of poor health. In December 1951 59-year-old Jack Tresadern came to the club's rescue.

Tresadern had been an artillery officer in World War One. He was accustomed to strife. Between the wars he had been a half-back with West Ham and Burnley, good enough to represent England twice in 1923, although he thought little of his performance against Scotland, remarking, 'I was the best player Scotland had on the field.' He was an FA Cup finalist in 1923, appearing in the first Wembley final. Here, thousands broke through the barriers and engulfed the pitch, requiring a mounted policeman on a white horse to restore a semblance of order. With hundreds of fans still crowding the touchlines, the game went ahead, Bolton winning 2-0. Tresadern recalled that after two minutes' play, he became entangled in the converging crowd while taking a throw-in, allowing Bolton's David Jack the freedom to blast Bolton in front. Apparently, Jack's shot was so fierce that it knocked out a supporter who had his head pressed against the back of the net!

Having played in 279 league games for West Ham, Tresadern was transferred to Burnley in October 1924, where he played 22 times before moving to Northampton in May 1925. Here, he completed his playing days. His transfer from Burnley was facilitated by Louis Page moving in the opposite direction. Predatory Page would become an all-time hero at Turf Moor, scoring 115 goals, including a double hat-trick. Tresadern's impact at Northampton's County Ground was also considerable.

After his playing career was ended by injury, Tresadern became Northampton's manager in 1927, guiding his third-tier side to a runner-up position a year later, and helping raise their average gate from 7,000 to 16,000. Tresadern then became Crystal Palace's secretary and manager in October 1930, helping the financially troubled south London club to evade bankruptcy. His achievements here earned him a plum post as Spurs' manager in 1935.

His subsequent managerial career at Plymouth, whom he joined in 1938, was cut short by the Second World War. Tresadern once again served in the army. However, after being demobbed in 1945, he returned to Argyll for two more years, assisting Home Park's recovery from wartime devastation. He also discovered several young talented players whose sales realised £20,000 for his club.

His success at scouting attracted the interest of Aston Villa, whom he joined as a scout in 1947. Ambitious Southern League club Chelmsford City then persuaded him to take over their managerial reins in June 1949, but, having resigned in November 1950, he looked for a similar opportunity elsewhere. It is unclear, though, why Tresadern chose to leave his native Essex in December 1951 to join a listing ship at Hastings. If he was in any doubt about the task facing him, his new side lost 7-0 at Kettering upon his arrival. But Tresadern's magic had not deserted him. In his first home game Hastings beat the famous FA Cup giant-killers Yeovil 3-0, who were pressing for the Southern League championship. Although United finished the 1951/52 season bottom again with only 11 points, a miracle was about to unfold.

At the end of Tresadern's first full season in charge, in 1952/53, Hastings had returned to mid-table respectability, despite the manager being heavily preoccupied with his club's debt crisis. Tresadern was not fazed by this responsibility – after all, he had faced similar difficulties at Crystal Palace in the 1930s. He immediately launched a 'tanner fund', requesting the Hastings public to make donations of sixpence or more, stating, 'There are 65,000 inhabitants in Hastings. Now, if each were to give 6d to a 6d Appeal Fund it would save professional and Southern League football for Hastings.' He set up a weekly lottery, too, albeit illegally. He targeted friends and supporters for additional donations and invited those attending home games to toss loose change into a sheet carried around the Pilot Field at half-time.

While the light from the former speedway pylons was later deemed too dim for Southern League football, Jack Tresadern believed it was strong enough for another of his fundraising exercises. Capitalising upon his many Football League contacts, Tresadern staged a series of floodlit friendlies against Spurs, West Ham, Brentford, Gillingham and Charlton. These games attracted crowds of over 2,000, providing essential revenue for his cash-strapped club. The first floodlit Football League match did not take place until 22 February 1956, when Portsmouth played Newcastle at Fratton Park. Here, though, Tresadern was ahead of his time. His buoyant enthusiasm and innovative ideas were irrepressible.

Board members chipped in too. Director and garage owner Cecil Catt acquired a decrepit coach which he renovated to be fit for transporting the players to away games, thereby saving on hire bills. One of the players, Sammy Booth, drove it. The season ended satisfactorily, with Hastings accumulating 41 points from their 42 games. Their leaky back door was sealed, helped by Bill Griffiths's imposing displays at centre-half. The number of goals conceded was reduced by half while the number of goals scored had risen by 83 per cent. Things were looking up. The brilliant FA Cup runs of the next two seasons provided a seismic uplift, though.

In the 1953/54 FA Cup qualifying rounds Hastings were unstoppable. They disposed of Shoreham (3-0), Horsham (4-1) and Eastbourne (7-2) with ease. Although Ashford (Kent) and Hounslow provided stiffer opposition, the U's won both games 2-1. Keeping his beady eye on the bottom line, Jack Tresadern was delighted that the BBC chose to televise the

Hounslow tie in full, a pioneering decision by the station. This earned each club £75, around £2,000 each in present values. Hastings then faced Southern League rivals Guildford City in the first round proper. Hastings made the most of the home advantage, winning 1-0.

Almost another 60 years would pass before a team known as Hastings United would experience live TV coverage again. This was when Hastings Town, renamed as Hastings United, beat Harrogate Town at the Pilot Field in an FA Cup second round replay in December 2012 in front of a 4,000-plus crowd. This unexpected victory set them up with a third-round tie with Middlesbrough at the Riverside, earning the club around £50,000 from their cup run.

Hastings's next opponents were Third Division South side Swindon in the second round and once again they had the home advantage. According to the *Hastings & St Leonards Observer*, manager Jack Tresadern ordered 'a pre-match diet of sherry and oysters'. It worked a treat! Swindon were thrashed 4-1, with Hastings snatching a three-goal lead inside the opening 18 minutes. The *Hastings & St Leonards Observer* reporter added, 'Tresadern believed Burton, the Swindon goalkeeper, was suspect with low shots, so told his players, "Keep them down boys." They followed his instructions. Two of their goals came from fierce ground shots.'

The *Hastings & St Leonards Observer* correspondent reported that, 'The Hastings United forwards broke quickly and decisively while their defenders tackled with gritty determination.' Hastings's sturdy centre-forward, Tommy Huckstepp, bullied the hapless Swindon defenders throughout, while his strike partners, Asher and Parks, led them a merry dance. Although a defensive error allowed Swindon to reduce the deficit, flying winger 'Dickie' Girling quickly restored Hastings's advantage with a penetrative pass that Hillman latched on to and put away with aplomb. The *Hastings & St Leonards Observer* reporter concluded, 'It was an incredible feat for a side that had managed only six wins so far in 18 Southern League fixtures.'

Given that the Norwich game took place 65 years ago, my memories are shaped by the *Hastings and St Leonards Observer's* coverage and what my now deceased parents subsequently told me. Apparently, I had not been keen to go, especially after Mum pinned a claret-and-blue rosette on my winter coat. But once I was on the green-and-cream Maidstone & District bus, Dad said my mood changed. There were many family groups aboard, in their claret-and-blue bobble hats, scarves and, yes, rosettes. I no longer felt a fool. Apparently, one grinning chap leaned across me and said loudly, 'Up the U's!' as Dad and I found our seats upstairs. It seemed that at every village stop more supporters joined the throng. Their excited chatter became intoxicating. Dad told me we were going to see a battle between 'David' and 'Goliath', a stirring biblical story I knew from Sunday school. By the time the packed bus had growled along the wet, deserted seafront and reached the centre of Hastings, my appetite was sharpened.

Many years later I heard an Everton fan recount his first experience of going to Goodison Park with his grandfather. He said that despite the excited chanting inside the ground, his granddad would not quicken his slow, measured stride. He later realised that he was being initiated into the foreplay of football. Without having any comprehension of this term, then, years later, I realised so was I.

Having left the bus in Wellington Square we joined a large queue outside the Central Cricket Ground waiting for the special buses to take us to the Pilot Field. I hadn't realised that 'Pilot' was a distortion of an Old English term 'Pilate' meaning hair oats. I had wrongly assumed that we were going to an airfield. As the special bus laboured up the hill out of town, I could see other supporters emerging from the side roads. Some had large bells which they were ringing with gusto. Others had huge wooden rattlers that required a two-handed grip to turn. Even above the noise of the straining bus engine I could hear what a din they made. Dad told me that the rattlers were originally used as a wartime warning against gas attack. I was in no doubt then that this was a much bigger event than the town's annual carnival procession, which attracted thousands to its promenade.

With the approach road blocked by converging fans and the lengthening queues for the turnstiles, we had to leave the bus and walk the final 100 yards to the lofty ground. On a better day than this, its long-side grassy bank afforded panoramic views of Pevensey Bay and Beachy Head. Dad was keen that we obtained stand seats, though, as he was doubtful that I would see much of the game from below. Fortunately, the queue for the more expensive stand was less congested. But had we not arrived so early we would have been forced to make for the grassy bank.

The attendance was 12,527, a club record, smashing the previous one of 9,917, set in the preceding Swindon tie. The gate for the Norwich game represented almost one fifth of the town's population, bearing in mind that many of those there came from outlying villages, such as ours, and local towns including Bexhill, Rye and Battle, and possibly Eastbourne too. Looking back, there seemed to be something reverentially ceremonial about this occasion, a massive coming together of local people in shared parochial celebration. How quaint that seems when compared with what happens now. As LP Hartley wrote, 'The past is a foreign country; they do things differently there.'

On the crackling loudspeaker a song was played repetitively. I asked Dad what it was. He said, 'Who Killed Cock Robin?' The *Hastings & St Leonards Observer* reporter informed us later that Tresadern wanted it played loud and often so that it might disconcert the Norwich players in their dressing room, given that Swindon's nickname was the Robins. Tresadern told the *Hastings & St Leonards Observer* reporter, 'I hope we knock the feathers out of the Canaries.' Norwich were formidable opponents. They were then the leaders of the Third Division South. They posed a much harder test than Swindon.

The teams came out to a ferocious roar, the PA system blasting out 'Sussex by the Sea', sung ardently by thousands of home fans. This was football at its tribal best.

'Oh Sussex, Sussex by the Sea!
Good old Sussex by the Sea!
You may tell them all we stand or fall,
For Sussex by the Sea.'

Hastings won the toss and chose to attack the Elphinstone Road End. The pitch was like a ploughed field with both goalmouths engulfed with cloying clay, sand and sawdust. With the Hastings boys high on adrenalin and driven on by savage support, they poured forward immediately. After only four minutes Hastings went in front. A glorious move resulted in Parks hooking the ball past Oxford in the Norwich goal. It was as if a powder keg had been ignited. But Norwich were not easily subdued. Even on this sludgy surface they were frighteningly fast, producing a succession of rapier-like thrusts, which left the Hastings defenders hot in pursuit. Against Swindon, Hastings's canny positioning, timely tackling and decisive interceptions kept the Football League side at bay. Here, Norwich fomented indecision and distributional error. It was no surprise when, in the 23rd minute, Brennan – a star in Archie Macaulay's heroic giant-killing side of 1958/59 – nipped in as Barr and Griffiths dithered, and calmly equalised. Then nine minutes before the interval, Hansell escaped the attentions of three hesitant Hastings defenders, and nonchalantly slotted in Norwich's second. Norwich were clearly in charge at this point, but on the stroke of half-time the nimble Parks was chopped down in the box. Alas, Asher's penalty was a poor one, allowing Oxford to save easily.

Recharged by the half-time break and the huge reception they received at their re-appearance, Hastings pinned Norwich back, forcing successive corners, one of which resulted in a frantic goalmouth tussle. It seemed sure to yield a goal, only for a Norwich defender to block a goal-bound effort on the line.

Nevertheless, Parks eventually found a way through Norwich's stonewall defence, smartly heading a crisp cross past Oxford. Driven on by the febrile crowd, Hastings sensed that the tide had turned and committed themselves to all-out attack. But Norwich ruggedly defied them before producing a brilliant breakaway that resulted in Gavin putting the Canaries 3-2 ahead. There were only 12 minutes left. Although dismayed by this sucker punch, Hastings girded themselves for a final push. With just five minutes remaining, Parks, who had a grand game, carved out a decisive opening. Having received the ball from a throw-in, taken deep inside Norwich's half, he beat his marker and instantly struck a teasing cross towards the near post. The fleet-footed Dickie Girling confounded both mud and the Norwich defence with a diving header that found goal to the left of the statuesque Oxford. The Pilot Field erupted. Minutes later, a blistering drive from wing-half George Peacock smacked against the Norwich crossbar, leaving a muddy stain as proof of how near Hastings had been to a fifth-round tie at Highbury. What a game! Tresadern's reaction was, 'Worth a Guinea a Box. The Canaries were so lucky to hop away on level terms.'

I could not recall experiencing anything quite as exciting as this. My parents said I chattered obsessively about the game for weeks afterwards. Dad had achieved his purpose. On this dank, grey afternoon, spellbound by the game's switchback fortunes, the never-say-die determination of the Hastings players, and deafened by the unrelenting roar of a huge, partisan crowd with their horns, bells, rattlers and firecrackers, I had been turned on to football forever. Moreover, I had been baptised in claret and blue, directing my allegiance not only to Hastings but, in time, to Burnley, too.

Hastings were defeated 3-0 in the replay at a sopping Carrow Road. Their pride was undiminished, though. 17,027 fans were there, lifting the aggregate attendances for Hastings's brave cup run to 71,543, the proceeds of which were shared with their opponents. Alby Parks (7) and Syd Asher (6) had been Hastings's principal goalscorers, followed by Phoenix (4), Girling (3) and Hillman (2). Asher, like Bernard Moore, would later play league football, in his case for Northampton.

Sheffield Wednesday v Hastings United

FA CUP Third Round, 8 January 1955

'Shake, Rattle and Roll'

THE 1954/55 season brought outstanding success for Tresadern and his team. They made a terrific start, reaching top spot in the opening weeks, and embarked upon another stirring FA Cup run. Due to his side's magnificent efforts in the previous season, they entered the 1954/55 competition at the fourth qualifying stage, where they once again beat Guildford City at home by a single goal. Having beaten Hounslow (4-2), where Tresadern admitted that 'his ticker shifted about two feet', Hastings then defeated Selby Town (2-0) in the second round proper, earning themselves a third-round tie at First Division Sheffield Wednesday. Tresadern urged the committed U's fans to buy their tickets promptly so that they didn't lose out to the 'lukewarm once-a-year supporters'! In order to stop these 'Johnny-come-latelys' from snaffling the ticket allocation, Tresadern imposed a limit of two tickets per applicant. In keeping with the practice adopted by much bigger clubs, Tresadern arranged for his players to spend two days in York prior to the Selby tie, obtaining permission from York

City, another 'giant-killer', to train on their Bootham Crescent pitch. To rouse his players' spirits, Tresadern requested leave to play 'Sussex by the Sea' on the York PA system while they trained. Adept at team motivation and mind games, he skilfully utilised his many inside contacts for his side's gain.

Although the Owls reached the FA Cup semi-final in 1953/54, losing to Tom Finney's Preston, their league form had been abysmal, not helped by the tragic loss of their free-scoring centre-forward Derek Dooley. Wednesday were the ultimate 'yo-yo' side during the 50s. They were promoted to the First Division four times and relegated thrice. They would complete the 1954/55 season at the bottom of the First Division, nine points below Leicester, who would also go down.

The Owls' star man was brilliant 21-year-old inside-forward Albert Quixall. He had already been capped by England, playing alongside Stanley Matthews. Three years later 'Golden Boy' Quixall joined Manchester United, who were still struggling to recover from Munich. His £45,000 fee was huge, equating to around £45m today. Despite winning an FA Cup-winner's medal in 1963, Quixall did not do justice to his talent there. Hastings faced a daunting task for the Owls were at least 50 rungs above them.

Jack Tresadern decided his lads deserved a pre-match meal in keeping with their rising status, prime beefsteak. Trainer Sammy Booth maintained, 'Those steaks give the boys extra vim.' Sadly, the travelling Hastings fans were without Dad and me. A special steam train was laid on. The journey took longer than planned, though, the game having started by the time they arrived.

The teams lined up as follows:

Sheffield Wednesday: McIntosh, Conwell, Curtis, Gannon, McEvoy, Turley, Marriott, Quixall, Shaw, McAnearney, J. Greensmith.

Hastings United: Ball, Crapper, Chadwick, Peacock, Griffiths, Girling, Hillman, Burgess, Asher, Parks, Robinson.

Hastings started well. Spluttering Wednesday seemed more troubled by nerves than their plucky opponents. Their passing was poor, and their defenders were not in tune. Hastings took heart from this, pouncing quickly on a litany of errors. With Wednesday unable to make much progress, Hastings pushed forward. Burgess was on target with a leaping header from Parks's cross, while Parks troubled McIntosh with a firm, low drive. It was no surprise when Hastings took the lead after 25 minutes. Redoubtable centre-half Bill Griffiths had been giving an exemplary display of composed defending. Here, he showed he could sting as well as tame. Intercepting another sloppy pass, he pinged the ball immediately to unmarked left-winger Robinson. He pushed the ball deftly into the path of Parks, who scampered to the byline before crossing for the in-rushing Asher to head home. With the ground hushed with humiliation, some Owls fans actually joined the U's celebrations.

Smarting at this setback, Wednesday sprung into life and began attacking with greater menace. Wednesday right-winger Marriott had too much skill and pace for Chadwick, leaving the left-back floundering in his wake. But with Hastings keeper Jack Ball in sensational form, the hosts could not convert their increasing dominance into goals. However, McAnearney shamefully squandered a one-on-one opportunity. This was not one-way traffic, though. Just before the interval, Burgess produced a sizzling drive that skimmed the top of Wednesday's crossbar.

After sharp words were exchanged at the break, Sheffield Wednesday returned to the pitch in determined mood. Hastings's defence came under extreme pressure, with Quixall belatedly justifying his illustrious reputation. While Griffiths, Crapper and Peacock scrapped for their lives, poor Chadwick continued to be run ragged by Marriott. On the hour, Marriott skinned the bemused left-back once more and crossed for Shaw to head in. But Hastings were not prepared to capitulate. With everyone summoned to the pump, sheer cussedness and gritty defence kept Wednesday at bay. It was heart-breaking, though, that with only two minutes left, and a lucrative replay in sight, Wednesday found a way through. Or did they? After successive shots were blocked by the heroic Hastings defenders, one from Greensmith was adjudged to have crossed the goal-line. Chadwick contested the referee's decision, vociferously protesting that he had prevented Greensmith's effort with his chest. The watching pressmen agreed. George Peacock joined the chorus of disapproval, demanding that the referee consult with his better-placed linesman. When the referee refused, Peacock retorted angrily, 'That was because you did not want to come to Hastings for the replay.' Whereupon the referee reached for his notebook, insisting that Peacock gave him his name. According to the *Hastings & St Leonards Observer* reporter, 'Peacock replied: "My name's George, what's yours?" It was the first and last time that Peacock was booked. After the game the linesman admitted that, had he been consulted, he would have confirmed that the ball had not crossed the goal-line. It was a deeply exasperating end to a courageous display.

In reflecting upon the game many years later, former Hastings player Alan Burgess speculated whether Tresadern made a rare error in his team selection, after first-choice left-back Joe Thompson was ruled out with a leg strain. Tresadern chose to replace him by moving left-half Chadwick into an unaccustomed role. Chadwick was out of his depth contending with Wednesday's Marriott. Tresarden also decided to move flying winger Girling into Chadwick's wing-half position, bringing in Robinson on the left wing. Burgess argued that, 'There was probably too much disruption to our familiar formation.'

Many Owls fans were embarrassed by their side's fortuitous victory. The *Hastings & St Leonards Observer* reported, 'Some Wednesday fans were heard to say, "The better team lost"; and "Hastings deserved a replay at least".' There was little doubt that this was the original Hastings United's greatest performance.

The 50s were 'golden years' for the underdog. In 1953/54 Third Division Port Vale reached the FA Cup semi-final, putting out holders Blackpool before being eliminated by the eventual winners, West Bromwich Albion. In 1954/55 Third Division York City followed suit, as did Third Division Norwich City, under Archie Macaulay, in 1958/59. But Hastings's achievements in 1953/54 and 1954/55 deserve special mention in the annals of spirited underdogs. Hastings's consolation was that it took home an equal share of the £2,810 receipts from the 25,965 attendance. Hastings United would never play in front of so many again. The renamed Hastings United side came closest when they played in front of 12,579 fans at Middlesbrough's Riverside stadium on 5 January 2013.

The 1954/55 season was a particularly memorable one for Hastings United. In finishing third, they also achieved their highest position in Southern League football, just four points behind champions Yeovil.

The original Hastings United reached the FA Cup first-round proper on eight occasions, four times under Tresadern, during the five full seasons he was in charge at the Pilot Field. His other FA Cup runs included a second-round proper defeat at his former club Northampton in 1955 and a first-round defeat at Ipswich in 1956/57. The calibre of Tresadern's staff management was self-evident, while his relationship with supporters was courteous and remarkably inclusive. His programme notes opened with the greeting 'Dear partners'. Tresadern hoped that some supporters might be willing to accommodate unmarried players signed from distant clubs. Like Ted Ballard, who became the U's manager four years later, Tresadern wanted his players to be based locally.

The Hastings players' contracts during Tresadern's time at the club specified that 'part-timers living away from HQ must arrange with the manager for facilities to train at the nearest club ground to where they reside'. All players were expected to comply with clearly articulated club rules, including, 'The player hereby agrees to play in an efficient manner to the best of his ability' and 'do everything necessary to get and keep himself in the best possible condition so as to render the most efficient service to the club, and will carry out all the training and other instructions of the club through its representative officials. The player shall not engage in any business or live in any place which the Directors or Committee deem unsuitable.'

Tresadern was aware of his club's community responsibilities. In 1957 he and the directors donated all proceeds from two pre-season games to a local charity, a sum of almost £182, worth over £4,000 today. He revolutionised the club, improving its calamitous finances to the extent that, by 1953, he could employ 22 full-time professionals and three part-timers. To ensure high playing standards were maintained throughout his squad, he entered a reserve side in the Metropolitan League, comprising second- or third-string teams of several top Football League clubs such as Chelsea and Arsenal. In 1956 a Hastings reserve team pipped Chelsea to the Metropolitan League title, also winning its Professional Cup. During Hastings's famous FA Cup run of 1953/54, Tresadern boasted that within 12 months, he expected to have scouts in every English county. Full-back Crapper was the first Hastings player to be recruited via this comprehensive scouting network. Tresadern was extraordinarily committed, innovative, astute and ambitious.

It is unclear why the Hastings board of directors decided not to renew his contract for the 1958/59 season, despite the club's satisfactory mid-table position. In five full seasons at Hastings, Tresadern had a win ratio of 41 per cent, better than that of current Burnley manager Sean Dyche at 39 per cent. The next two Hastings managers, Bill Corkhill and Tim Kelly, managed only 24 per cent between them. Tresadern and his assistant, Harry Haslam, a former Hastings player, left for Tonbridge. He wanted to take Peacock with him, but the wing-half had already decided to move to Rye. Tresadern said to him, 'Make sure they know and match what I was going to offer you at Tonbridge and ask for a three-year contract. Sadly, Tresadern died there a year later. Whereupon, Haslam took over the reins. Haslam was so successful that he was subsequently offered management posts at Luton Town and Sheffield United. Bill Corkhill, who succeeded Tresadern, ably kept the show on the road, with the reserves continuing to enjoy prestigious success. But once Corkhill was replaced by Tim Kelly, the wheels fell off, with Hastings careering to the bottom of the lower Southern League division by May 1962. Hastings's recovery from this fall was led by another inspirational manager, Ted Ballard, in 1962/63. Ballard underlined the foolishness of Kelly's 'clear out' policy in 1960 by re-employing several players Kelly had discarded, including Gerry Boon, who would become Hastings United's last manager in the mid-80s.

1956 My first date with Elvis

'Heartbreak Hotel'

THE SUMMER of 1956 was largely cold and wet. As a child of the 50s I still bear the watermark of my formative years. But on one blue remembered evening, the sun beamed on the lush recreation ground where long shadows were cast by the pines and elms at its northern perimeter. I was kitted out in my green-and-khaki Cub uniform, with my yellow scarf neatly held in place by a leather woggle. While waiting for the village hall to open and the other Cubs to arrive, I became aware of a scowling teenager perched defiantly on the crossbar gate. He was wearing heavy duty jeans – coarse, prickly and sweaty. I knew that after mistakenly borrowing a pair to play in. His greased quiff tapered at the back into a DA – a 'duck's arse'. He was affecting a sneering lip curl as he tunelessly murmured the mordant opening lines of a song that I came to know as 'Heartbreak Hotel'. The lyrics were lifted from a suicide note, but that wasn't why the song had so much edge. This was down to the singer – Elvis Presley.

Elvis, the man, entered my life via a friend's TV. I gawped at what I saw. His legs shimmered with restless energy; he shook, twitched and rolled his hips, with what I would later understand to be combustible sexuality. His wide pants showcased every pelvic thrust. The adulatory crowd was frenzied. Young women were screaming their heads off. Meanwhile Elvis's bassist was whooping it up, riding his instrument, and hitting double licks.

Elvis Presley was a call to arms, 'a rebel without a pause' – a hiccupping, gyrating Brando or Jimmy Dean. He conflated hoarse, visceral, black rhythm 'n' blues with ecstatic, wailing gospel, and yet he was a white Dixie boy. Little Richard squared the circle, explaining, 'Elvis was an integrator. He opened the door to black music.' Elvis's view was more emotive: 'Rock and roll music, if you like it, if you feel it, you can't help but move to it, rhythm is something you either have or don't have, but when you have it, you have it all over.'

By 1956 The Comets had begun to splutter out, exposing Bill Haley, their avuncular-looking, middle-aged vocalist, as no more than a 'great pretender', an improbable adolescent hero, whereas Elvis not only sounded but also looked like the real deal. So did the gender-bending Little Richard, with his raunchy shrieks and key-bashing excitability; the leathered Gene Vincent, with his sultry Virginian whispers; and the manic, deranged, piano-pummelling Jerry Lee Lewis. This insurgent quartet blasted a giant crater in the grey conformity of the times.

1956 was the year of the 'angry young man', when, with a growing swagger, restless adolescence barged into the narrow confines separating childhood from adult life; when the British working class flexed its muscles in response to rising prosperity; and when their children began seizing the educational opportunities granted by the Butler Education Act. It was when the despotic Soviets crushed the Hungarian Revolution and when Britain's status as a world power was lost at Suez, where the USA called, or, more correctly, stopped, the shots. This ill-planned campaign ended less like the growl of a bulldog and more like the yap of a poodle. British Prime Minister Sir Anthony Eden never recovered from this humiliation.

Brighton & Hove Albion v Watford

Football League Third Division (South), 30 April 1958

'A Thorne in the Side'

WITH THE break-up of our family in the summer of 1957, not long before Jack Tresadern's senseless severance, football was not only an obsession, it was my sanctuary, too. With my kind if eccentric aunt in Windsor taking over my care, I had to move to a new school. Here, I found many of my new classmates doting on football. To become accepted, it was not enough to profess interest. I had to 'talk the talk' accurately, reciting the names of the top players, their clubs and major achievements.

Chix bubble gum football cards were hard currency. These could be swapped, bought or won in a card-flicking game, in which, by turn, a child flicked a card hoping to cover one previously flicked by his opponent. In my many solitary moments at my aunt's tiny house, I created a large store of scrapbooks made up of cards and press cuttings. I soon became knowledgeable about all four divisions of the Football League, the progress of the clubs and that of their stars. A more testing challenge was to name the Real Madrid and Barcelona forward lines.

I then discovered *Charles Buchan's Football Monthly*, which I often bought with my pocket money when meeting Mum at Waterloo. At our awkward access meetings, she would begin by asking me how I was. I was evasive, uncertain of where this might lead, but I was content to talk about football. As an eight-year-old, I had rarely been any further than Hastings, a mere ten miles from our former home. Places such as Newcastle, Burnley and Sheffield seemed as exotic as the 'Black Hills of Dakota'.

Christmas seemed strange without Mum. Dad stayed with me for a couple of days, though, bringing me *The Big Book of Football Champions* as my present. Its photos seemed quite different from what I found on the Chix cards. Here was drama aplenty. There were shots of the ball bursting the net amid broken-tooth celebrations. There were lunging, muscular tackles by beefy defenders with furrowed expressions, while slight forwards writhed in pain at their feet. There were ballistic Brylcreemed goalkeepers, clad in thick, roll-neck jerseys, their flat caps dislodged by their frozen acrobatics. Thick, cloying mud was everywhere as if football was a form of trench warfare. I was so entranced by these still moments of high drama that I emulated them alone in my aunt's ramshackle garden. Dad realised it was time he took me to another game, although I would have to wait until August for that to happen, when we watched Chelsea thrash Football League champions Wolves.

Knowing Dad had been a Brentford fan before he met Mum, I took an interest in their fortunes. I discovered that in their 1957/58 promotion push, Brentford, Swindon, Reading, Plymouth and Brighton vied for the Third Division (South) top spot, which would guarantee Second Division football.

I was intrigued by Brentford's so-called 'Terrible Twins', George Francis, who would later play for Hastings, and Jim Towers, who would not, despite Ted Ballard's best efforts. Between them this pair scored 51 league goals during the 1957/58 season, but due to the brilliant form of Brighton the

Sussex club managed to stay in front of the pack. However, Brighton experienced a wobble in April 1958 when they lost 4-2 at home to Northampton, and 2-0 at languishing Torquay, while only drawing 2-2 with second-from-bottom Millwall. These setbacks threatened to derail their championship bid. This presented me with a dilemma about who I should support, given that Brighton represented my much-loved home county.

As the season approached its climax, Brighton were left with three games to ensure promotion: two against Watford, and one against Brentford at Griffin Park. I read the match reports avidly. At Watford, Brighton grabbed the points with a last-minute goal from South African winger Denis Foreman, who was also a Sussex county cricketer. This took Brighton to pole position. But Brentford could overtake them if the Bees beat the Albion at Griffin Park. 25,720 fans turned up, Brentford's biggest gate for six years. Although Brentford battered Brighton, the Albion held firm with Eric Gill pulling off several spectacular saves. Brighton midfielder Glen Wilson also marshalled his besieged defence expertly. However, in the 51st minute Brentford wing-half Bill Goundry, who later played for Hastings, blasted Brentford into the lead, although Brighton were incensed that their late 'equaliser' was disallowed for offside.

The destination of the Third Division (South) championship trophy hinged upon the outcome of Brighton's final home game with Watford. The Albion did not choke, thrashing the Hornets 6-0 in front of a capacity crowd of 31,038. Their hero was 20-year-old local lad Adrian Thorne, who scored five times. Adrian later recalled to Paul Camillin, in the book *Brighton: Match of My Life*, 'I could sense the determination in the team. Glen Wilson was a superb skipper: a hard, efficient, tireless worker in midfield. He, with Don Bates – another Sussex county cricketer – and Kenny Whitfield formed a superb midfield trio throughout that season and stopped any sort of attacks from Watford that night. Up front we tore them apart, annihilating them with three quick goals. Bang, bang, bang. Effectively the game was over. I happened to get on the end of everything that came my way. In other matches you get the same number of chances, but don't put them away.'

Adrian thought Brighton's genial manager, Billy Lane, protected him at the start of his professional career. He explained to a Brighton *Evening Argus* reporter, 'I had come from a sheltered environment and when I first went into the senior dressing room and heard all the swearing I thought what have I got into? Billy was aware of this and would ask the players not to use bad language when I was there. That was rather embarrassing for me, but Billy could be a bit touchy about language. I thought he did a good job for the club and was the first manager to get them promotion.'

On an evening of jubilation, the ecstatic Brighton fans were unaware of the dark mutterings among Brentford players and fans. For the Bees alleged that both Watford games had been 'fixed'. In Brentford's 1989 centenary publication *A Hundred Years of Brentford* it is said that, despite the lack of concrete evidence at the time, there was a suspicion that both Watford games were not won legitimately. It was alleged that in October 1960 Brighton's Glen Wilson, then the manager of Exeter City, revealed to a *Daily Mail* reporter that some of the Watford side had agreed to 'lie down' in exchange for a small inducement. Of course, it is open to conjecture whether this alleged inducement changed the course of the games, but the matter left the Brentford players and fans with 'a sour taste in the mouth'. The Brentford fans' resentment found expression many years later when naming their new, glossy fanzine *A Thorne in the Side*.

Such allegations were not uncommon then. In his biography, *Greavsie*, Jimmy Greaves alleged that two unidentified Nottingham Forest players offered Chelsea captain, Peter Sillett, a £500 bribe in April 1960, worth £11,000 today, to 'throw' a game at Stamford Bridge. Relegation-threatened Forest were supposedly desperate for points. The bribe was offered on the basis that it was shared equally among the Chelsea players. Peter Sillett, a later Hastings United manager, rejected the offer, as did his team. Peter's brother, 'Snozz', quipped, 'We wouldn't know how to throw a game anyway,' a wry reference to Chelsea's serial disorganisation during this period.

While such allegations were shocking, it was not as if British football had been free of such scandals beforehand. For, in 1905, Alex Leake of Aston Villa accused Billy Meredith, then of Manchester City, of attempting to bribe him to 'throw' their final game. Attempting to distance himself from the scandal, Meredith clumsily or perhaps disingenuously professed his innocence and retaliated by exposing illegal payments made by his club to fellow players. City were fined heavily, Meredith's manager, Tom Maley, was suspended for life, while 17 City players, including Meredith, were fined individually and suspended for one year.

Just five years after the alleged bribery of Watford players in 1958, a greater scandal shook English football. At the start of the 1963/64 season, a journalist with the *The People* accused two virtually unknown players of wrongdoing. One of those accused, Ken Thomson, a Hartlepools United full-back, admitted taking £200 in order to help his side lose. Thomson's 'defence' was that his team 'would have lost anyway'. It was the first rockfall in a major landslide.

The People then went on to identify Jimmy Gauld, a Charlton forward, as the promoter of a much larger betting scandal, the full details of which did not emerge until April 1964. This was when David Layne, Peter Swan and Tony Kay, three high-profile First Division players, were accused of participating in a betting syndicate seeking to 'fix' the results of several games. One of these was Sheffield Wednesday's match at Ipswich, in December 1962, in which Layne, Swan and Kay took part. While all three denied acting with any fraudulent intention, each admitted to placing £50 fixed-odds bets which would have paid out handsomely had York beaten Oldham,

Lincoln beaten Brentford and Ipswich beaten Wednesday. But both Oldham and Brentford won, so that the £100 each player received was probably no more than their weekly wage. Swan and Kay were England international players. By 60s standards, all three were well paid given that the maximum wage had been abolished in 1961. Soon after the game, Kay moved to Football League champions-elect Everton for £60,000, a £30 million transfer in today's values.

Swan maintained in his biography, *Setting the Record Straight*, that Ipswich won the game legitimately. He denied betting on numerous lower-league games knowing that they were 'bent'. While various gamblers made thousands of pounds from this betting syndicate, the Wednesday trio gained relatively little and were jailed for four months and banned for life from any form of organised football. Ringleader Jimmy Gauld was jailed for four years with £5,000 costs. After a pardon was belatedly granted, Swan resumed his professional football career in 1972. But his best days were well behind him.

Future Brighton striker Willie Irvine said in his biography *Together Again* that when he was at Preston in 1968, he and his team-mates were offered a bribe to 'throw' a game. If true, the harsh punishments meted out to the 'Wednesday trio' did not provide the desired deterrent. Non-league games were not exempt either. A former Hastings United player told me that his previous manager once offered a bribe to his counterpart to 'throw' an important game. The bribe was supposedly accepted, and a weakened team selected as agreed. But the weakened side fought like dervishes and won. The frustrated manager demanded the return of his bribe. This was refused. His counterpart pointed out that he had kept to their agreement. Given that the bribe did not cover this aspect, he did not instruct his team to lose.

1958 My First Walk on the Wild Side
'At the Hop'

I MISSED my parents' passion for music. My aunt's only concession was to play *Two-Way Family Favourites* on the radio during the steaming Sunday lunchtimes. It seemed as if the BBC was determined to suppress rock 'n' roll with battalions of bland crooners, such as Perry Como, Dean Martin and Michael Holliday, or bury it beneath the bubbly banality of Alma Cogan, Patti Page or Rosemary Clooney. However, my aunt cut me unprecedented slack, allowing me to head off to the town's coffee bars where thumping juke boxes kept the faith. Here, I was intrigued by the coffee bars' hissing Gaggia espresso machines which dispensed frothy coffee into glass cups. There was something deliciously salacious about these haunts. Their cane furniture, low glass-topped tables, huge rubber plants and dark recesses hinted at a garden of unearthly delights. Feeling excluded on grounds of age, I positioned myself uncertainly in their open doorways. Here, I would gawp at those inside, the truculent, brilliantine quiffed, 'draped' young men with their narrowed trousers, and their bountifully petticoated girlfriends. I could also nod to the honking horns of the Upsetters or tap my feet to the panting insinuations of 'Be-Bop-a-Lula'. Sometimes, my presence irritated the surly inhabitants. Then, one of the gum-chewing fraternity might emerge and cuff me around the ears, telling me to 'push off, squirt'.

One day when visiting my cousin, she pulled me into her front room. 'Listen to THIS!' she insisted, putting a 45 single on to the record player. After a brief hiss and crackle, I was jolted into motion by a furious chopsticks assault. A doo-wop harmony followed with a succession of ascending scales. Then we cut to the real action. Has there ever been a more exultant, exuberant call to dance. Even a bloated bullock like me couldn't resist the urge to strut and sway. We played it repeatedly. Even 'Jailhouse Rock' couldn't compete. What bliss this was to be 'At the Hop'.

By then I had begun skipping school. If I had any spare cash, I tried to inveigle an adult cinema-goer into escorting me into an 'A' feature, preferably one with a sinister theme like *Night of the Hunter*. Otherwise I would make for a bolthole at the local mainline railway station. I was absorbed by the rocking, steam-hauled expresses that hurtled by with fleeting scents of scorched oil, tar and sulphur. I sometimes imagined joining them, seeing myself on a faraway Cornish beach of sweeping sands and booming breakers. On dark, winter evenings, the reflections of the locomotives' roaring fires flickered along the grimy station walls. My mum was then 80 miles away in a sprawling Victorian hospital suffused with a smell of disinfectant and heavy polish. I was never in doubt about my welcome, when a fellow inpatient pinched her nose whenever I passed. Predictably, I failed my 11-plus examination.

There was no solace in solitude. I craved affirmative company. My dad's cousin came to my aid. He was a burly, genial man who dispelled my moroseness with a quip and a relaxed smile. I envied his casual, confident command of life, riding knocks with cheery equanimity. I began to share his love of black American blues and jazz. But my strongest association is Ray Charles's breezy single, 'What I'd say'. Here, Charles conflated jazz, boogie woogie blues and gospel influences. In mimicking evangelical preachers' 'call and response', he secularised, even 'sexed up', the gospel tradition. Being oblivious of such controversial ramifications, I was just grateful to be lifted out of the rut and into the groove.

Brighton & Hove Albion
v Aston Villa

Football League Second Division, 22 August 1959

'Living Doll'

WHILE I was staying with relatives in Crawley, Dad unexpectedly arrived, offering to take me to a game at nearby Brighton. Almost a year had passed since our last visit to a football ground. As a permanent way labourer, though, he had to work on the railways at night and weekends. This was another scorching day in one of the hottest summers on record. We caught a Southern Electric train which was already full at arrival, compelling us to stand in a crowded corridor. Smouldering heat emanated from the button-clothed, horsehair seats, releasing the stale scent of perfume and tobacco. Even now, I can occasionally summon that sensation.

The humming train accelerated past the shrivelled, straw-strewn fields, already plundered by the locust-like combine harvesters. If this signalled the last days of summer, the tropical temperature did not. As the hazy outline of the South Downs came into view, my sense of anticipation sharpened. The Goldstone Ground, the home of Brighton and Hove Albion, lay beyond.

After promotion in 1958, Billy Lane strengthened his squad by bringing in bustling six-foot, 13 stone John Shepherd, a centre-forward from Millwall, for £2,250. Despite being afflicted with polio in 1951, and facing the prospect of never walking again, Shepherd recovered remarkably. In 1959 this disease took the life of Birmingham and England full-back Jeff Hall, prompting a national vaccination programme. Eighteen months after his scare, Shepherd scored four times at Leyton Orient in his first away game for Millwall. He completed the 1952/53 season as the Lions' top gun, having scored 21 goals in 22 appearances. Shepherd scored 82 goals during his Millwall career, placing him 11th in Millwall's all-time leading goalscorers. He wasn't slow to make an impact at the Goldstone, either.

Billy Lane also splashed out on a pair of promising young Arsenal forwards, inside-right Ronnie Clayton and left-winger Freddie Jones. While Jones played regularly under Lane, Clayton failed to meet his potential and moved on to Hastings United in the summer of 1960. Lane bolstered his midfield, too, by capturing Workington wing-half Jack Bertolini. But Brighton struggled at first.

After their first four games, Brighton were bottom with a solitary point, taken from a creditable 2-2 home draw with Charlton. Their goal average was awful with only two goals scored and 19 conceded. Their opening game at Ayresome Park was a traumatic affair as Brighton were thrashed 9-0. Middlesbrough centre-forward Brian Clough scored five times. At the final whistle, Brighton wing-half Glen Wilson asked the referee to have a feel of the ball, explaining, 'I didn't get a touch in the game.'

Billy Lane reacted to the poor start by signing Manchester City full-back Roy Little for £4,850 in October. Little had been an FA Cup winner with City in 1956. Arsenal winger Mike Tiddy also joined in the same month, followed by Tommy Dixon, Reading's leading goalscorer, who had maintained a record of scoring in every other game while at West Ham and

Elm Park. Creative, Scottish inside-forward Ian McNeill also signed from Leicester City for £7,000 in March 1959.

Gradually the tide turned. Leading striker John Shepherd scored 18 goals in 36 league appearances, complemented by Dixon with ten in 30 games. Young Thorne chipped in with ten, too, in just 15 outings. Brighton's final place of 12th was satisfactory, bearing in mind that Middlesbrough had hammered them twice, with Clough scoring eight of the 16 goals Brighton conceded.

Thorne rated the 3-0 Yuletide victory over promotion-bound Fulham as one of Brighton's best results of the season. The Fulham side contained four internationals: the immaculate playmaker Johnny Haynes, left-back Jim Langley, a former Brighton player, fast, raiding Scottish winger Graham Leggat, and utility player Roy Bentley. A record 36,747 crowd squeezed into the Goldstone Ground to see Tommy Dixon score two and Adrian Thorne, one, in a prestigious victory. As a winger or an inside-forward, Thorne scored 44 goals in 84 appearances for Brighton before his surprising transfer to Plymouth in 1961 for only £8,000.

The Brighton fans were pleased with their side's first season in the second tier. Albion's average attendance had risen from around 16,500 during the 1957/58 season to approximately 22,400, a rise of 36 per cent. Brighton was not a wealthy club, though. When attempting to strengthen his side, Lane had to look out for bargains among established players at the end of their careers such as Tiddy and Little, promising young talent such as Jones, or proven lower-division performers hoping to better themselves, such as Bertolini.

In preparing for the 1959/60 season, Lane believed he needed greater attacking potency. Dixon's customary scoring ratio had slipped to one in three, and at the age of 30, his best days were probably past. Lane, therefore, persuaded his board of directors to part with £15,000 to sign Newcastle's 24-year-old reserve centre-forward Bill Curry. Curry had been capped for the England under-23 side. This was a substantial investment considering the high cost of reconstruction of the Goldstone Ground's West Stand. But with Curry, Lane discovered gold. It was incredible that Newcastle chose to shed a striker with 21 First Division goals in just 33 appearances. But Curry had the fast and prolific Len White ahead of him.

Brighton began the new season, on 22 August 1959, with another daunting challenge, a home fixture against newly relegated Aston Villa. Villa had won the FA Cup only two years before, denying Manchester United the first 'Double' of the 20th century. They were managed by the tactically astute Joe Mercer, a former Everton, Arsenal and England wing-half.

Mercer had taken charge of Villa just before Christmas 1958. He was one of the 'new-style' managers – a coach, capable of improving the players in his charge. Like England boss Walter Winterbottom, Mercer preached the coaching gospel, which few of his contemporaries emulated. His managerial career had begun inauspiciously at Sheffield United. The Blades were relegated in 1956, at the end of his first season in charge, but when he left Sheffield the Blades were no longer in debt and poised for a return to the First Division, which they achieved in 1961. At Villa, Mercer could not avert relegation in 1959, but restored their top-flight status after only one full season in charge. Despite suffering a stroke in 1964, he and Malcolm Allison then set about successfully transforming the fortunes of languishing Manchester City, achieving both domestic and European silverware. As a player and manager, Mercer was a winner.

Mercer had turned down the top job at more prosperous Highbury, electing to take on what some saw as a poisoned chalice at Aston Villa. Mercer felt he still needed to prove himself as a good manager and he thought Villa would give him the necessary scope to achieve this. His initial impression of Villa Park was that, 'the place was morbid and lifeless, and the club choked by tradition'. Mercer made the telling observation, 'Tradition can be a wonderful friend but a dangerous enemy.'

Mercer only took the job with the proviso that he would be given a free hand in team matters. Although Villa were struggling when he arrived, he was cheered by the players' positive responses to him. He found no defeatism and was reassured by the fans' continued loyalty. By Easter 1959 Mercer thought he had turned around their fortunes. They had reached the FA Cup semi-final and were five points clear of the relegation places. Alas, Villa failed on both counts. Mercer attributed their failure to the effort expended in the cup, believing this quickened the retirement of his captain, Peter Aldis. Aldis left to join Southern League Hinckley Athletic, with whom he masterminded a memorable victory at promotion rivals Hastings in March 1963.

Mercer knew that success in football is founded upon a sound defence. He had showcased this at Sheffield United, where he introduced 'catenaccio' to the Football League. At Villa Park he tightened his side's defence immediately, but found that in so doing the goals dried up at the other end. But Mercer believed his side could avoid the drop even up to the 88th minute of Villa's last game, whereupon West Bromwich equalised, sending Mercer's side down by a point.

Mercer insisted that the foundations for Villa's return were laid in the dressing room after the West Bromwich game. Everyone was there. It was only the second time in their 85-year history that Villa had slipped into the Second Division but there was no recrimination from the directors. He bought a few players: Jimmy MacEwan, a right-winger from Raith, Bobby Thompson from Wolves at inside-right and Jimmy Adam from Luton Town, who played in four different positions. Although granted £25,000 by his directors for team strengthening, Mercer chose to spend this sum on creating a new training ground. He was convinced that Villa's young players would not have made the progress they did without the ground.

Mercer devoted long hours to 'administrative work'. This was generally required of British managers of this period. He was always at the office at nine and often did not return home until past midnight. However, he refused to be office-bound, spending two hours every morning with his players. It was during these sessions that he helped improve the ability of his barnstorming centre-forward Gerry Hitchens. Mercer recognised that Hitchens could kick a ball perfectly but would then freeze, giving the defenders time to get in a tackle. He also came back square to the ball instead of half-turning to see the opposition coming in. Although fast and energetic, Hitchens had a habit of bringing the ball back to his right foot, giving the defence time to recover. Hitchens worked hard on strengthening his left foot, too, so he could cross first time. Hitchens was already a prolific goalscorer, but Mercer noted that he tended to hammer the ball at any given opportunity. By slowing his striking motion, Hitchens achieved better accuracy, but it took hours of practice with Mercer to gain automatic command of these various skills. Although absent for the Brighton game, Hitchens became Villa's leading scorer during this season with 23 league goals. Fame and fortune awaited him as an England and Serie A striker.

Upon arrival at Hove station there was an almighty crush. Easing ourselves out of the train, we were pushed up the footbridge steps by the force of the multitude behind. We then shuffled slowly over the bridge that spanned both platforms and the adjacent sidings. The queue for the Goldstone entrances started almost upon reaching the other side. While trapped in this churn, Dad reached out to a badge seller, buying me one of Peter McParland, Villa's forceful, free-scoring left-winger. It was his reckless charge which deprived Manchester United of their goalkeeper, Ray Wood, for most of the 1957 FA Cup Final. Wood sustained a broken cheekbone and concussion, but, as was the way back then, he returned heroically to play as a wobbly right-winger, frequently dabbing his nose with smelling salts. With the war still fresh in our memories, health and safety considerations were less pressing then. To add insult to inflicted injury, McParland then smashed in two second-half goals – a bullet header and an unstoppable drive – past deputy keeper Jackie Blanchflower, to win the FA Cup for Villa. In Sweden, McParland's heroics were without controversy. His two goals in the play-off with Czechoslovakia enabled Northern Ireland to qualify for the quarter-finals.

Drenched with sweat on account of the searing sun and the compressed crowd, my legs buckled and my head swam. The stand roofs seemed to oscillate in the humid heat. Propped up by Dad, we eventually pushed through the ratcheting turnstiles and made for a less-crushed spot at the highest part of the East terrace. 31,484 people eventually crammed into the ground. The terraces shook with the pounding of so many feet as the home supporters greeted their heroes, dressed neatly in blue-and-white striped shirts and long white shorts. Their white socks had twin blue hoops on the folds. They looked the part.

For this game, Mercer had to make several changes. He replaced the injured Hitchens with former England international Jackie Sewell, who had played at Wembley against the Magical Magyars in 1953. Former Burnley left-back Doug Winton was drafted as temporary cover, pending John Neal's recruitment from Swindon. Young Terry Morrall deputised for experienced Jimmy Dugdale at centre-half. Mercer moved Jimmy MacEwan to inside-right, allowing Jimmy Adam to take the right-wing slot. If Villa were a makeshift team, they did not play like one.

Brighton were under the cosh from kick-off and went a goal down before half-time, MacEwan being the goalscorer. But urged on by their raucous supporters, Brighton struck back through John Shepherd, who had put his brawn to good use against the novice Villa centre-half. But despite withstanding increasing pressure, Villa won the game through veteran Jackie Sewell. It was his last goal for the club before leaving for relegation-bound, Second Division Hull City.

Brighton's scorer John Shepherd left, too, in mid-season, after losing his centre-forward position to Curry. Gillingham would be his last Football League club. Although he played 53 times for the Gills, scoring 22 goals, he regretted leaving Brighton, believing he should have stayed and fought for his place. After departing Priestfield Stadium in the summer of 1962 to play semi-professional football at nearby Ashford and then at Margate, recurring injuries prompted him to pursue a career in coaching and management. He subsequently became a very successful player/manager at languishing Southwick in Division Two of the Sussex County League, guiding them to the Division One title and the Sussex Senior Cup. He then resumed employment at the Goldstone Ground as a scout and youth coach, where he founded the club's first-ever youth team in 1976, in collaboration with Alan Mullery and Mick Fogden. Shepherd spent almost 30 years with Brighton as a player and coach, under Alan Mullery, Brian Clough and Jimmy Melia.

What I remember best about this game was McParland's pace and power. He was so dominant, heading the ball with venomous power while possessing an explosive shot in either foot. Each loose ball was contested hungrily, no tackle shirked. Although happy to run at his full-back he was not content to hug the touchline. Sometimes he assumed the role of a centre-forward, creating mayhem in the box with his aerial strength. There, he would jostle aggressively for space, levering himself above the mix to produce whiplash headers. I was surprised to find that McParland was marginally less than six feet tall, weighing just over 12 stones. He seemed larger than that, but this was the size of the man's performance. He would complete the 1959/60 season with 22 league goals, just behind Hitchens.

Despite losing their opening game, Brighton managed to maintain a mid-table position, albeit two places below their 1958/59 ranking. Although it took Curry a few games to find his feet, he demonstrated quickly that he was the 'real deal'. By April 1960, he had scored 26 goals, including three hat-tricks in 40 league games. His £15,000 fee seemed a snip.

A Brighton *Evening Argus* reporter recalled, 'Bill Curry had that rare gift of hovering in the air. He seemed to do so while making up his mind whether to direct the ball either into the back of the net or to the feet of a better-placed colleague. This ability he shared with the great headers of the game, although the nearest Curry came to international level was one appearance for England under-23s while a Newcastle player. Ask any Albion fan today who saw Curry what they remember best about him, and they will confirm that not only was his aerial power extraordinary but his pace and bravery for a player of no more than 5ft 10in was something worth going a long way to see. Those spring-heeled leaps were all about matchless timing. Bill scorned any notion of lurking in the box and poaching chances created by others. He mixed it with the toughest of the tough and could kick with the best. Off the park he was a perfect gentleman, and when Billy Lane saw him score a hat-trick at Fratton Park during the previous season, his eyes lit up on learning afterwards that the man he wanted had an exemplary track record on and off the pitch.'

Adrian Thorne added, 'Bill Curry was, perhaps, the finest header of the ball I played with. He would position for crosses and lay the ball back and down to feet. At other times he was deadly in front of goal and could out-jump any defender. Bill possessed a very rare skill indeed. We combined well on four occasions during the 1959/60 season. For example, in the 5-4 victory at Bristol Rovers, Bill got two goals and I got one. We each scored when Derby went down 2-0 at the Goldstone. And in the memorable FA Cup fourth-round second replay, against Rotherham at Highbury, Bill got a hat-trick while I scored two in a 6-0 win in front of a 33,000 crowd. Bill and I scored a brace apiece at promotion-chasing Cardiff, too, where Albion won 4-1.'

After the game, Dad and I walked down to the sea. The sea scintillated in the evening sunlight. Trolley buses hummed around Old Steine, their rooftop arms clicking and clacking at the joints in the overhead cables. Dad told me that he and Mum had decided to get back together. I did not know what to say. Dad bought me candyfloss at the Palace Pier, where even the vicious rat-a-tat-tat of the tail-gunner video game, a relic from a wartime training exercise, failed to drown the screaming from the perilous helter-skelter. Here, terrified punters were shot out over the sea in their lurching descent. I wondered what the future might bring.

Hastings United v Wisbech Town

Southern League Premier Division,
22 August 1960

'Apache'

THIS WAS the start of our motorway age, but what I saw at the Pilot Field on 22 August harked back to post-war austerity. The town's tourist strapline read 'Popular with visitors since 1066'. It was apposite, for several of those taking part had their heydays in the late 40s and 50s. Hastings's 'Dad's Army' was represented by ex-Spurs star Len Duquemin and former Northern Ireland World Cup goalkeeper, Norman Uprichard. Meanwhile the Fenland town of Wisbech included two ex-England internationals, Jessie Pye and Billy Elliott, plus veteran goalkeeper Ken Nethercott, a hero in Norwich's stellar FA Cup run of 1958/59.

Len Duquemin, the 1959 Southern League 'Player of the Year', was introduced as this season's captain. He had spent 11 seasons with Spurs before joining Bedford Town in 1958. Here, he scored 76 goals in two seasons, helping his team to win the Southern League championship in 1959. Len was described as 'a very consistent player who trains hard at Tottenham where he is still considered one of the "family".' Len had apparently 'opened a tobacco and confectionery business quite near the Tottenham ground'. In Len's obituary, written for the *Independent* in April 2003, Ivan Ponting described him thus: 'The Guernsey-born marksman, a ceaselessly competitive study in perpetual motion on the pitch, was a quiet, gentle, engagingly unassuming fellow away from the action, and it was not difficult to imagine him moving tranquilly among the monks as he tended their garden during the German occupation of the Channel Islands in the Second World War. Indeed, of his two nicknames, "Reliable Len" and "The Duke", the first fitted his character far more neatly, offering due recognition of his unobtrusive but incalculably valuable service to one of the outstanding sides of the era, while the second was no more than a glib abbreviation of his surname.

'Duquemin scored 134 goals in 308 senior games for Spurs, his only Football League club. Despite his lack of extravagant natural ability, he was considered a key man by both manager and teammates as he helped to lift the Second Division title in 1949/50, then the First Division crown in the following campaign. Arthur Rowe's team were renowned for their flowing push-and-run style, which involved slick interchanges of short, accurate passes as they swept from one end of the pitch to the other. It was a fresh, swashbuckling approach which lit up the post-war soccer scene and won lavish plaudits for the ball-playing likes of the inside-forwards Eddie Baily and Les Bennett, the wing-half and skipper Ronnie Burgess, the wingers Les Medley and Sonny Walters, and a full-back named Alf Ramsey, who one day would lead England to World Cup glory. But there was a need, too, for players who would run ceaselessly when they were not in possession, providing extra passing options for their artistic colleagues; they didn't always get the ball and rarely took the eye, but without them the system would have foundered. One such was the wing-half Billy Nicholson, destined to become the most successful manager in Spurs' history, and another was Duquemin, whose honest sweat was an important lubricant to the smooth running of Rowe's captivating machine.

'Duquemin was tenacious. At Spurs he successfully saw off the challenges of Dave Dunmore from York, and Alfie Stokes, before succumbing to Bobby Smith's greater youth and potency in 1958. Typically, it was his goal at Sheffield Wednesday which secured the First Division title for Spurs in 1951. As an industrious battler for the cause, Bill Nicholson recognised in Len a kindred spirit. They remained close friends long beyond their playing days.'

But when Len joined Hastings United, he was 36 years old. He seemed middle-aged. People of his generation lived harder lives, impeded by poorer nutritional standards and less advanced health care. But whether muscular or wiry, many men of Len's age were tough, no-nonsense individuals. They appeared suited to the military wear many of them wore at work – perhaps a slanted army beret or a khaki tunic gathered above their waist. But age did weary them. Today, a man looking like Len did in 1960 would pass for someone 20 or 30 years older. And it wasn't all about appearances, either. Remembering Arthur Rowe's mantra, Len still tried to 'make it simple' but could no longer 'make it quick'. At Hastings, the griping brigade were soon on his case. 'Duquemin's too slow,' they muttered. 'He holds up the whole forward line.' If a striker today bagged 28 goals in a season, as Len did for Hastings in 1960/61, they would expect resounding applause. Churlish Hastings supporters worked to a meaner standard.

Opposing Len was another star centre-forward of yore: 40-year-old former Treeton collier Jesse Pye. Pye began his football career in 1938 when he signed for Sheffield United. With the outbreak of hostilities, he joined the army, serving in North Africa and Italy. After being demobbed, he signed first for Notts County and then Wolves, whom he represented with distinction, scoring twice in their 1949 FA Cup Final victory over Leicester City. He played for England in a 'Victory International' and was then capped against the Republic of Ireland in 1949. It became England's first home defeat against a 'foreign' side. Pye was never re-selected. However, he scored

95 goals in 209 games for Wolves before moving on to Luton, in 1952, where he helped a young Gordon Turner hone his predatory skills, and thence to Derby, where he completed his Football League career. In 1957 Pye moved to Wisbech, becoming the landlord of the Mermaid Inn in the Market Place before opening a sweet shop. In 1960, he became player-manager at Fenland Park.

Also facing Len was the feisty, combative former Bradford, Burnley, Sunderland and England left-winger Billy Elliott, then in his 35th year. Elliott is probably the only Football League player to be dismissed – a very unusual event in the 50s – for 'a look of intent', as if his look could kill. His aggressive competitiveness on the field of play was legendary. During the 1951 Christmas Day clash between Burnley and Preston, that icon of sportsmanship Tom Finney had to move his ultra-tough right-back Willie Cunningham to the opposite flank in order to restore festive peace and goodwill. In writing Billy's obituary for the *Independent* in 2008, Ivan Ponting described him as follows: 'In action [Billy] was a study in high-velocity pugnacity laced with deceptively subtle skills. His attacking specialty was racing beyond his marker to reach the byline, then driving a low cross into the penalty area, often through a tangled forest of legs, for conversion by lurking marksmen.' Elliott played just four times for England. He was unfortunate that Tom Finney was ahead of him.

The two goalkeepers on show in this game had pedigree, too. Hastings had Norman Uprichard, a member of Northern Ireland's 1958 World Cup squad, and according to one long-standing Pompey supporter he was 'the best goalkeeper to represent Portsmouth, better, even, than Alan Knight or David James, at least when sober.' The Wisbech keeper Ken Nethercott was an heroic member of Archie Macaulay's Norwich side that reached the semi-finals of the 1958/59 FA Cup competition.

After our family reunited in Hastings in the spring of 1960, I decided I would resume my interest in Hastings United.

Although my dedication to football remained unassailable, I surprised myself how quickly I divested myself of other associations with the past three years. I gave away most of my favourite books, which I had tended to carry around in a suitcase, I hung up my toy guns for good, I changed my forename, using my second name instead of my first, and I began to lose weight. I rediscovered the knack of making friends and came to appreciate that the 60s offered technicolour, whereas the 50s remained shrouded in monochrome.

On 22 August I queued in the town centre for the football bus beneath the wheeling, plaintive gulls. The shop canopies gave welcome relief from the scorching sun. Once seated inside the Maidstone & District bus, the temperature became overwhelming. Even with every top window slid well back, we had to mop our streaming faces continually, almost gagging with the intensity of the heat. Slowly, the bus climbed out of town, its engine growling and its interior fittings vibrating alarmingly. The gearbox rebelled on the sharp slopes, crunching and grinding, before a lower gear was conceded. Frequently the bus paused as if waiting for a second wind, before juddering forward with arthritic ire. The stench of mucky oil and petrol swept through the upper deck, mingling with the sour smell of tobacco, producing a dizzying sensation. Eventually, we found enough height to gaze back across the town's rooftops towards the gleaming Pevensey Bay and the indistinct silhouette of Beachy Head. It was hardly the weather for football.

A sizeable crowd had gathered, later confirmed to be 3,749, respectable by modern League Two standards. Many supporters were basking on the Eastern flank grass bank as if this was a popular picnicking spot. Most of them were forced to shield their eyes from the burning sun as they surveyed the verdant pitch and the distant sea beyond. Thankfully, a refreshing onshore breeze cooled us, ruffling the flag bearing the town's ancient crest and causing the music from the crackling tannoy to waver in volume. It was my introduction to 'Ladies of Calcutta', a bright brassy tune that was played at all home games before the Mersey beat infiltrated the PA box in 1963, forcing its incumbent to concede that the 60s had arrived. When the teams took the field, though, the parochial rallying cry of 'Sussex by the Sea' was cranked up, just as it was when I first came to the Pilot Field with Dad six years before.

In 1960, many British teams were still adopting the WM formation, featuring a back three, comprising two full-backs and a centre-half; two wing-halves, one attack-minded, the other more defensive; two inside-forwards, one an auxiliary striker, the other a deep-lying, playmaker, combining with the attacking wing-half; and two wingers and a spearhead centre-forward. That was the anachronistic theory. Hastings's interpretation of this system was the Wimp–Marshmallow kind. On this parched afternoon they were swamped. Billy Elliott had obviously lost some of his former pace, but he was far too quick for Hastings's lumbering, disorganised defenders. His daunting presence remains. In a flickering, over-exposed snatch of film stored in my memory, there he is, grim-faced and fiercely focussed, accelerating along the left flank in the blinding glare of the sun, fizzing one low centre after another across hapless Hastings's box. He seemed unstoppable.

The Hastings & St Leonards Observer reported, 'After just 90 seconds, Wisbech were ahead. Centre-forward Jessie Pye rifled home a free kick with such venom that the ball cannoned off the board behind the goal and back into play before anyone realised what had happened.' Almost from the restart, Wisbech's left-winger, Billy Elliott, crossed for Pye to nimbly side-step several inadequate challenges before flicking in his second. And with only 15 minutes gone, Elliott was once again the provider as Pye completed his hat-trick with a vicious volley.' Hastings's keeper, Norman Uprichard, could only admire the power of Pye's finishing. Capitalising on Elliott's low raking crosses, there was no need of Pye in the sky. The Treeton collier was advanced in age but retained the predatory instincts of his youth.

Hastings then retaliated. Right-winger Micky Bull pulled a goal back seven minutes later and then Len Duquemin lashed home a second. But even before the half-hour mark, Wisbech had restored their two-goal advantage. This was like a primary school game. After Ronnie Clayton, the ex-Brighton forward, had fluffed a second-half penalty, Wisbech added a fifth, crushing this newly assembled Hastings side with disdain. Heaven knows whether Uprichard was sober or not. It hardly mattered. Even as inexperienced as I was, I could see how little protection he was given. Just two weeks later, he sustained a cartilage injury which ruled him out until the season was almost over.

That sunny day in a generally disappointing summer was soon eclipsed by a drenched autumn, as wave after wave of Atlantic fronts flooded the British Isles. 'Apache's' twanging Hawaiian chords became the soundtrack for those damp, dull days. Before each game I would await the football bus in a town-centre café morosely looking out at the spattering rain through condensation-beaded windows. The stale air inside was overwhelmed by the odour of sweaty plastic macs, stewed tea and chips. Hastings in the wet autumn of 1960 was like an enactment of a Giles cartoon – a grey, wet, choppy Channel resort inhabited by demonic grannies, anarchic kids and buffeted parents.

As testament to the huge volume of rain that fell during those autumn months, steam trains were restored on the electrified routes through Lewes where the Ouse flood waters reached platform level. And as if Hastings United's cavalry was not slow enough, the Agincourt conditions of autumn and winter reduced it to a halt. In game after game, Hastings were anything but United, slumping off the field at the final whistle with mud-stained kit and downcast expressions, to the derision of a dwindling crowd. It was pointless that Len Duquemin could still score goals with apparent ease because many more were conceded at the other end. I learnt to feed off the leanest of pickings.

1960 'Great Balls of Fire'

'Cathy's Clown'

IN MAY 1960 I was selected to play for my school against a posh lot at their plush ground. The Everly Brothers' 'Cathy's Clown' was on repeat inside my head. Don and Phil needed no blandishments. I could have done with some, though. Here I was, an imposter. I was no sportsman. I was just a fat clown. Why should these cross-legged children look at me, let alone watch me? The manicured pitch and lush, leafy ground made me feel even more preposterous. I looked on nervously as a blond boy from the opposing school tossed a shiny, red cricket ball from hand to hand as he marked out an absurdly long run. Before our opening batsmen had reached the crease, he charged in at full tilt and, in a blur of wheeling arms, took out the unguarded middle stump. 'Just practising,' he chirped. Whacking a tennis ball around the playground was fun, but this was a terrifying spectacle. Our ripped, stained pads and threadbare batting gloves looked hopelessly inadequate, and so were we.

By the time it was my turn to slouch to the crease, most of our team were out, and we had yet to reach double figures. My teacher at square leg reminded me to ask for a guard. I thought of opting for square leg, behind him. At the inevitable demolition of my stumps I was confronted by the blond boy's malicious glee. 'Eight for two,' he gloated. 'Just two more to get.'

As I trudged back to our demoralised team, my wobbling weight drew the customary catcalls. Don Everly's stinging words compounded my shame. The song's grave drumbeat suggested that Don was about to face a firing squad. I thought I was, too.

Not long after my dismal debut, our dog found a ragged cricket ball. I eagerly drew it from his disappointed jaws and stuffed it into my pocket, vowing to turn myself into a fast bowler. Over the next 12 months I practised with feverish compulsion, aiming at stumps I chalked on a nearby garage door, annoying the neighbours with the incessant metallic reverberations. But nothing would deter my quest.

My second debut came two years later when I first represented my senior school as an opening bowler. The game was played on a clifftop blurred by low cloud and muslin shrouds of drizzle. But the heavily overcast conditions did not impair the startling shine on the new ball I was presented with. Not being Waqar Younis, the ragged specimen I used in practice had no chance of swinging, but this beauty hooped around like a boomerang. While our opponents struggled to lay their bats on any of my deliveries, I had less difficulty in locating their stumps. My mind went back to the humiliation I had endured two years before. As each disconsolate batsman returned to the shack-like pavilion, I mentally stapled a mask of that gloating blond boy upon their downcast faces. For several days after, my life hovered on a bloated cushion of hubris. I fantasised about playing for England on tropical islands, edged by lapping, cerulean waters of cut-glass clarity, with palm fronds swishing gently in the coconut-scented sea breezes. And then a week later I was taken apart by a burly youth who proved that style was no match for substance as each of my opening deliveries whistled to the fence. I quietly slid my feet back into the comfy slippers of modest expectation.

Hastings United's squad 1948/49. Player/manager George Skinner is in a pale winter coat. Bernard Moore on his left scored 138 goals in 121 games. (photo by kind permission of Roger Sinden)

Hastings United's squad during the mid-50s. Manager, Jack Tresadern is at the back in a flat cap. (photo by kind permission of the **Hastings & St Leonards Observer***)*

West Ham, Burnley, Northampton and England left-half, Jack Tresadern, in his 'Irons' playing days. As a player and manager his shrewd tactical awareness often put him ahead of his peers.

The U's beat Guildford City 1-0 at the Pilot Field, earning a second round home FA Cup tie with Third Division South Swindon Town. (by kind permission of the Hastings & St Leonards Observer*)*

'Who killed Cock Robin?' Hastings United thrashed Swindon Town 4-1 before a 9,917 crowd, drawing the plaudits of the national press. (by kind permission of the Hastings & St Leonards Observer*)*

Tresadern's squad limber up for their next FA Cup opponents, table topping Third Division South Norwich City. A record Pilot Field crowd of 12,527 watched a thrilling, switchback 3-3 draw.

SEASON 1954-5

SHEFFIELD WEDNESDAY
FOOTBALL CLUB

FOOTBALL ASSOCIATION CUP—THIRD ROUND

On Saturday, 8th January, 1955, Kick-off 2.15 p.m.

v. Hastings United

OFFICIAL PROGRAMME 3ᵈ

The greatest day in Hastings United's life which ended in a cruel, undeserved 1-2 defeat.

SHEFFIELD WEDNESDAY
Blue and White Striped Shirts, Black Knickers

Dave McINTOSH

Tony CONWELL   Norman CURTIS

Eddie GANNON   Don McEVOY (Captain)   Mick TURLEY

Albert QUIXALL   Jim McANEARNEY

Jackie MARRIOTT   Jack SHAW   Ron GREENSMITH

Referee :
T. L. WOOD,
(Bury).

Linesmen :
J. BARRADELL, Barrow-on-Soar
(Red Flag) :
E. T. ROBERTS, Liverpool
(Yellow Flag).

one game last season. He had valuable League experience with Luton Town and previously had a spell with Merthyr Tydfil, though he was a centre-forward in those days. But it is nothing unusual for a back to have been a centre-forward and vice-versa.

George Peacock, the right half-back, graduated at Westbourne and has been with Hastings about 18 months. He's keen as mustard, with an attacking role his favourite policy. He can play very effectively as an inside-forward if necessary and knows the way to goal.

Bill Griffiths, the centre half-back, has played here before, for he used to be in the defence of Bury and built up a sound reputation. He has been with the southern club two and a half seasons. Griffiths has made something like 70 consecutive appearances.

Dennis Hillman, the outside-right, is a part timer and on the strength for some two seasons. He picked up good experience with Colchester United and Southend United, Southern Section members.

His partner, Alan Burgess, is the only local-born product in the team and was obtained from Eastbourne last season. A fighter, he has a good shot with either foot. Syd. Asher, centre-forward, has had service with Portsmouth and this is his third season with Hastings. Last season he scored 19 goals and season before got 33.

Albert Parks, inside-left, developed with Glenavon and Notts. County and is a shrewd schemer; also a hard worker both in attack and defence. He will find former Nottingham colleagues here in Jackie Sewell and Eddie Gannon. In his third season with the United.

Maurice Robinson, the ex-Doncaster Rovers' winger, is at outside-left.

In the event of to-day's game finishing in a draw, the re-play will take place at Hastings on Wednesday, 12th January. Kick-off 2.0 p.m.

Dick Girling, formerly with Crystal Palace, Brentford and Bournemouth, has been with Hastings the same period of time as Parks.

Maurice ROBINSON   Syd. ASHER   Dennis HILLMAN

Albert PARKS   Alan BURGESS

Dickie GIRLING   BILL GRIFFITHS (Captain)   George PEACOCK

Derek CHADWICK   John CRAPPER

Jack BALL

HASTINGS UNITED
Claret and Blue Shirts, White Knickers.

A south-west view of the Pilot Field, Hastings during the late 50s with the former speedway floodlights still in place. (photo by kind permission of the Hastings & St Leonards Observer)

Adrian Thorne (on the right) with ex-Arsenal winger, Mike Tiddy. Twenty-year-old Thorne scored five goals against Watford in the final game of the 1957/58 season, taking Brighton up to the Second Division.

Miraculously John Shepherd survived polio, becoming top goalscorer at Millwall and Brighton. Here he is attacking the Sunderland goal in 1958. His 18 goals in 36 league games helped Albion stay up. (photo: Brighton & Hove Albion)

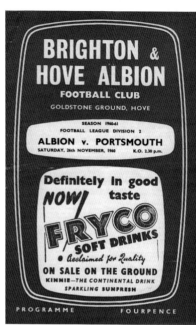

Brighton began the 1960/61
season in shaky shape but a
late surge of victories preserved
their Second Division status.
On 26 November they drew
2-2 with relegation-bound
Portsmouth.

Extract from the programme for the
Albion's fourth round FA Cup tie on
28 January 1961 with the current
Football League champions, Burnley.
An exciting 'nip and tuck' contest ended
in a 3-3 draw. Albion players from left:
Windross, Nicholas & Laverick.

Windross on the
attack during the
Albion's 0-0 home
draw with Swansea
on 25 March 1961.
(photo: Brighton
& Hove Albion)

Guernsey-born Len Duquemin scoring for Spurs at White Hart Lane in the early 50s. Sadly, his 28 goals for Hastings United during the 1960/61 season did not prevent relegation.

Richard Langridge (left) and Denis Foreman opening the batting for Sussex at Hove in the early 60s. South African Foreman also played football for the Albion and briefly for Hastings United in 1962.

In 1961, Wes Hall inspired me to become a competent pace bowler.

George Curtis, a skilful player and brilliant coach but a disappointing manager of the Albion in the early 60s. Largely under his watch, Albion fell from the second division to the fourth.

[Left] 'Renaissance man' Ted Ballard took Hastings United from zeroes to heroes in the 1962/63 season. Despite becoming one of the best non-league clubs in the country in 1964, swingeing cuts sent the U's back to the lower division, prompting Ballard's resignation. Disillusioned, he left football for good. [Right] Jimmy Hernon, a highly accomplished player with Bolton and a respected coach at Hastings United. Both Ballard and Hernon are shown at the Pilot Field in late 50s Hastings United kit.

The Goldstone during the arctic winter of 1962/63. Brighton made valiant efforts to beat the freeze, even chartering a tarmacadam spreader to melt the ice, which

unfortunately waterlogged the pitch! The 'big freeze' left many clubs very short of revenue. Hastings did not play for over two months. (photo: Brighton & Hove Albion)

[Left] Sussex CCC were the first winners of the one-day Gillette Cup in 1963. Back row from left: Lenham, Snow, Bell, Bates, A. Buss, Cooper, Langridge. Front: Suttle, Parks, Dexter, Oakman, Thomson.

Hall [right] and Charlie Griffith [below] produced 'pace like fire', helping 'the Windies' to win consecutive Test series in England, in 1963 and 1966. This formidable opening pair shared 80 wickets in these two series, at a combined average cost of 26 runs per wicket. And yet lowly Sussex thrashed the 'invincible' West Indies at Hove in June 1966, a remarkable feat described in this book.

Brighton & Hove Albion v Burnley

FA Cup Fourth Round, 28 January 1961

'It's Now or Never'

IN HIS programme notes for the Burnley game, Brighton's generally genial manager, Billy Lane, inferred that he was under strain. He wrote, 'I am not "flannelling" when I state that, here at the Goldstone, we have the most loyal and understanding supporters of any club. I, as well as many other managers, know that when things are not going too well, they are recipients of many letters of abuse etc. Not so with our supporters. In fact, I have received many letters of encouragement. It certainly makes my job far easier in times when everything appears to be adverse. Well, supporters, here's a big "thank you" from the players and me for your loyalty.'

After an extended period of stability under the chairmanship of the kindly Major Carlo Campbell, the club became beset with boardroom squabbles. These intensified during the autumn of 1960, souring the relationship between the board and their manager. New chairman Alec Whitcher was under pressure. A takeover bid had been lodged by Reggie Coleman-Cohen of the Alliance Building Society. Although the bid was blocked many supporters were unhappy, believing a vital investment opportunity had been missed. With his health failing, Whitcher bowed to growing pressure and resigned, taking the honorary position of vice president instead. Gerald Paling succeeded him as chairman, but the sour atmosphere remained.

Alec Whitcher was a very different personality to Campbell. Campbell had treated Lane like a son, protecting him from censure during the tough times. The often grumpy Whitcher was more demanding. He was particularly critical of Lane's dealings in the transfer market, which had cost £30,000 plus without conspicuously improving the squad. He also reprimanded Lane for smiling after a home defeat. Lane disliked this fractious mood, deciding that this season would be his last here.

John Vinicombe of the Brighton *Evening Argus* recalled, 'the Goldstone dressing room in the late 50s comprised two camps: those who got on with the manager and those who did not. Whatever the rights and wrongs of his ten-year reign, there can be no argument about Albion's success in that period. Not only did Billy achieve the distinction of being the club's only Football League manager to gain promotion, but there were enough near misses before winning the Third Division title in 1957/58 to give the public splendid value for money.'

The sombre mood behind the scenes at Brighton was not helped by the team's poor start to the 1960/61 season. Heavy defeats were suffered at Derby (1-4), Alf Ramsey's Ipswich (0-4), and Southampton (2-4), and at home to Ipswich (2-4) and Charlton (3-5). After a home loss to Stoke City at the end of October, Brighton had just three victories and three draws in their opening 15 games (three points for a win was not introduced until 1981). This meagre haul left Brighton in bottom place, a point behind Luton Town, who were in free fall. A welcome 3-0 victory, though, at relegation rivals Swansea on 5 November lifted Lane's mood. In his programme notes for the Luton game, on 12 November, he wrote, 'It was a great win at Swansea, with a brace of goals from Bertolini and one from Thorne, that took us off the foot of the table. Despite being on the receiving end in the first ten minutes and the last quarter of an hour, the lads played with great spirit, but were prone to fall back in defence, despite being in front. Attack is always the best means of defence.' With Brighton fortified by new signing Tony Nicholas, they beat Luton 1-0.

Given Brighton's shaky start to the 1960/61 season, it seemed strange that Lane agreed to Bill Curry's transfer to Derby. Curry had played in each of the opening nine league games, scoring three times. Looking at his overall scoring record at Brighton, he had found the net 26 times in 49 league appearances, a ratio slightly better than one in two. With the club placed precariously in the table, it appeared odd that he should be allowed to leave, particularly to Derby County, who were then fellow strugglers. It made even less sense that he should leave for a £12,000 transfer fee, around £3,000 less than what Brighton had paid for him a year before. This looked like very poor business.

In his programme notes for the Scunthorpe game on 27 December 1960, Lane expressed his delight at Brighton's recent home victory over Derby, a game in which his team turned around a two-goal deficit to win 3-2. Bill Curry had opened the scoring for Derby. Lane commented, 'Bill Curry, I thought, played far better for Derby than he did whilst on the Albion's books and I congratulate him on his play. Our centre-half, Roy Jennings had many tussles with Bill, with honours even. Late in the game a tackle on Bill Curry by Bobby McNicol was rather robust, but Bobby was the first to admit his fault. A great sport is Bobby.' The normally courteous Lane was clearly triumphant. But was *Schadenfreude* really to his taste? If it was, an ensuing FA Cup third-round victory over Derby must have felt like a delightful binge.

Lane seemed reluctant to hang on to players who were unhappy at his club. This applied to Adrian Thorne, too, after the young marksman became dissatisfied with his limited first-team opportunities. Lane released Thorne to join Plymouth in the summer of 1961 for a modest fee of £8,000. Thorne scored 38 goals for Brighton in 76 appearances, a similar strike rate to Curry. Thorne completed the 1960/61 season as the club's leading goalscorer with 14 goals in all competitions. It was difficult to understand Lane's reluctance to use him more.

In November 1960 Billy Lane replaced Curry with Chelsea's inside-forward, Tony Nicholas. Nicholas had fallen out with Ted Drake, the Chelsea manager. Despite making his debut for Chelsea's First Division side at the age of 18 years, his career had stalled at Stamford Bridge. Goaded by Drake's criticisms, after Chelsea's January defeat in the Burnley snow, the outspoken Nicholas kicked a hole in the manager's office door. Nicholas explained, 'Eventually I accepted the chance to join Brighton just to get away from Ted, but two weeks later he got the sack and after I went, Tommy Docherty was appointed. I think that would have suited me as he liked a runner.' However, Nicholas, a former England youth international, had no qualms about joining Brighton. He liked Billy Lane, whom he described as a 'gentleman', and enjoyed life in the town. The deal cost Brighton £15,000, around £15m today.

Lane also added Middlesbrough's reserve centre-forward, Dennis Windross, to his squad. Despite scoring 43 goals for Middlesbrough's reserves during the 1959/60 season, the stocky Windross scored only two goals for Brighton in 18 league appearances. Brighton fans became exasperated with his lack of composure in front of goal. Despondent at his lack of success, and homesick for his native North East, Windross was transferred to Fourth Division Darlington in the summer of 1961. It was a straight swap involving 'Darlo' forward Bobby Baxter. Baxter later became an effective left-back at the Goldstone Ground, winning a Fourth Division championship medal in 1965. As for Windross, even at lowly Darlington he found goals hard to find. He subsequently moved on to Doncaster, where he became a competent left-half.

During the summer of 1960, Lane splashed out another £15,000 fee on Everton inside- or outside-left Bobby Laverick. The fast and powerful Laverick proved frustratingly inconsistent, though. Nevertheless, he chipped in with ten league goals in 31 appearances for Brighton in 1960/61, sharing second spot in the club's goalscoring charts with Adrian Thorne. Only the enthusiastic Tony Nicholas, a quick, mobile forward with a strong shot, proved an immediate success, although he was employed more as an inside-forward than a forceful leader of the line in the Curry mould. He ended the season as top scorer with 13 goals in 27 games, netting all four in the vital end-of-season victories against Huddersfield (2-1) and Stoke (2-0), which ultimately secured Brighton's safety.

Other additions included Republic of Ireland international full-back Joe Carolan, at a cost of £10,000. He replaced the veteran Roy Little. Carolan was a composed defender, previously with Manchester United. He joined Brighton in December 1960 having played 66 senior games in Matt Busby's post-Munich side. He had become surplus to requirements at Old Trafford, after Irish colleague Noel Cantwell joined the club. Before the season was out, Brighton signed midfield enforcer Stan Crowther who had played for Villa, Manchester United and Chelsea. But Crowther no longer had any appetite for the game. His contract was cancelled after allegedly refusing to play for Brighton's third team. Crowther had previously been an England under-23 international, an FA Cup winner with Villa in 1957, and an FA Cup finalist with Manchester United in 1958, having received a special, 'Munich-related' dispensation to play for Villa and United in the same competition. At Brighton he made less than a handful of appearances. In an interview conducted in 1975, Crowther reflected bitterly, 'Football for me was wasted years. If I had my time again it would be the last occupation I would choose.' What a sad waste of talent. But given the pressures placed on him at Manchester United, his disaffection might have reflected depression. Few knew or cared about depression in those times, particularly among those caught up in war.

Leading up to the Burnley FA Cup tie, Brighton had enjoyed a six-match unbeaten run, which had lifted them into the relative comfort of mid-table. During this purple patch, Brighton had beaten a strong Liverpool side 3-1 at the Goldstone. Future World Cup star Roger Hunt played up front for the Reds.

In May 1960 Burnley had become First Division champions for the second time in their history. Just prior to the Brighton FA Cup tie, they had beaten a strong Hamburg side, featuring West German World Cup international Uwe Seeler, 3-1. This was in the first leg of the European Cup quarter-final. Burnley had surprisingly eliminated the 1959 finalists, Reims, in the previous round. They had superb footballers in all positions, eight of whom were, or would soon become, full internationals. There was strapping Scot, Adam Blacklaw in goal, a magnificent shot-stopper, supported by a pair of cultured yet uncompromising full backs, John Angus and Alex Elder, plus a defensive midfield trio comprising Jimmy Adamson, a sublime footballer, rugged man-marker, Walter Joyce and combative wing- or centre-half, Brian Miller. Up front were tearaway wingers, John Connelly, with a sharp eye for goal, and Brian Pilkington, flanking a roaming centre-forward, Ray Pointer, and 'hunter/gatherer' inside-left, Jimmy Robson. Pulling the strings was genius playmaker, Jimmy McIlroy. They also had an abundance of young talent in reserve.

The club owed much to its extensive scouting network and the innovative coaching under former manager and club captain Alan Brown. He introduced a bewildering array of set-piece routines. However, it was Harry Potts who guided Burnley to the Football League title in 1960, having built upon Brown's sound foundations. Potts brought massive enthusiasm and geniality to the party. The club's business interests were handled by bullish yet wily chairman Bob Lord. Alan Ridgill of the *Sunday Pictorial* described Burnley thus: 'Here was the almost perfect soccer machine – as smooth running as a Rolls-Royce, packing the punch of a centurion tank.'

And yet, this was a small-town club, the smallest ever to win England's top-flight title. Burnley's population in 1961, at 80,000, was not much larger than that of Hastings, and a third of the size of Brighton and Hove with its 246,000 residents. Even allowing for Burnley's satellite towns of Nelson, Colne and Padiham, its potential support was around 100,000 less than that available to the Albion. Moreover, Burnley had spent much less in assembling its First Division title-winning side (£13,000) than Brighton had in creating a mid-table Second Division team (over £30,000). This contest, though, was billed as one between the 'giants' of Burnley and the 'minnows' of Brighton, based upon their respective Football League positions.

28 January was a wild, wet day. The train seemed to pick its way between the sodden, slushy, marshes and the grey, grubby, foam-flecked sea. Shrouds of rain were driven back and forth on a gusting wind. Dad and I were already saturated in our walk to the station, leaving our rainwear to steam inside the warm carriage. A further soaking awaited us on the open Goldstone terraces. Fortunately, the rain became patchier soon after our arrival. The glistening pitch was already pitted with small pools of water, particularly in the grassless goalmouths, where the groundsmen set about their forking and sanding duties industriously. As they moved in our direction, each prod of their forks emitted a hiss of complaint. Despite the awful weather, a large crowd of 28,672 piled in, many, like us, occupying the exposed Eastern terrace. Our discomfort was soon forgotten, though, as the game got underway. The match was a corker, in the best tradition of FA Cup ties.

It was expected that these boggy conditions would sap Burnley's pace and yet the ploughed field on which they had beaten Hamburg did not incapacitate them. The Clarets started strongly with fast-raiding wingers Connelly and Pilkington making early inroads and quick, mobile centre-forward Ray Pointer pulling Brighton centre-half Roy Jennings around. But it was their powerful left-half, Brian Miller, who struck the first blow after 25 minutes when he beat young Brighton keeper Charlie Baker with a thumped drive.

As the game progressed the pitch churned up, enabling Brighton to compete more equally. They began to stall Burnley's free-flowing moves and attack with greater menace. With just two minutes of the first half remaining, Brighton wing-half Jack Bertolini found enough space to equalise. The roar was incandescent.

Lifted by their success, Brighton began the second half boldly, but their momentum was upset when Joe Carolan headed into his own net seven minutes after the restart. Undaunted, right-back Bob McNicol seized his moment. Summoning his considerable strength, he embarked upon a lone assault on the Clarets' goal. Ploughing through the mud, determinedly brushing aside all attempts at dispossessing him, the ball seemingly glued to his feet, he suddenly let fly from 35 yards. McNicol had never scored for Brighton before, but here he made perfect contact. The ball flashed past a knot of Burnley defenders, across our line of vision, and past Blacklaw's frantic dive. The Burnley keeper didn't have a prayer, the ball ripping into the net at incalculable speed. There was a split-second delay before realisation took hold. Then the whole stadium erupted as one. Surely, this was the best goal ever seen at the Goldstone Ground.

With an hour gone, Brighton were back on terms. Hope had turned to belief. Driven on by the excited crowd, the Albion pushed forward resolutely. With 24 minutes left, much-maligned Dennis Windross unexpectedly redeemed himself, slipping the ball past Blacklaw, to put Albion 3-2 up. Having been derided, by some, as the centre-forward who 'couldn't hit a cow's arse with a banjo', this was sweet vindication. Even Billy Lane had conceded that, 'Dennis has taken a little time to settle down.' The guttural roar that accompanied his goal bestowed instant forgiveness. Burnley were not beaten yet, though. Their success was founded upon millstone grit as well as flair. They counter-attacked immediately.

Many years later, Burnley legend Jimmy McIlroy told me that his team-mate, Jimmy Robson, was greatly under-rated, despite scoring 100 goals for Burnley in 242 senior appearances. McIlroy said, 'Jimmy rarely scored from distance. Most of his goals were nod- or tap-ins, but his anticipation was uncanny.' When I put this to Robson, he replied modestly, with a soft Durham lilt, 'It was easier scoring then. There was a lot more space compared with today, but I still had to time my moves.' Strikers are often extroverts. Jimmy Robson is not. With the Brighton defenders slipping and sliding in the oozing mud, Burnley's shy assassin sneaked into position to poke in a 73rd-minute equaliser. Although both teams continued to slug it out, toe to toe, with close calls at either end, the deadlock could not be broken. Brighton's chance had passed. Despite putting up a brave fight, they lost the replay 0-2 at Turf Moor.

Although Brighton slid into relegation trouble once more during February and March 1961, a pair of victories over Plymouth during the Easter weekend righted the ship. And following home wins over Lincoln and Huddersfield, and an away victory at Stoke, Brighton secured their Second Division status for a further year.

In his programme notes for the critical home game with ailing Lincoln, Billy Lane reflected upon the twin victories over Plymouth. He wrote, 'On Good Friday a good second half won us the day at home against Plymouth, Tony Nicholas and Bobby Laverick obtaining the vital goals. It was fitting that Tony scored, as his tenacity at centre-forward was perhaps instrumental in infusing the other players with that urgency in their play. Despite the 0-4 setback at downward-bound Portsmouth on Easter Saturday, there was a little "get together" before the return game at Plymouth, resulting in each player doing everything that was expected of them. It was a real team spirit which won us the day and I know the players would like me to mention the play of Tony Nicholas and his persistence which enabled Adrian Thorne to score our second goal. Three times Tony was dispossessed in the penalty area, but he fought back on each occasion. Eventually Adrian had the chance to score through Tony's "never-give-up" spirit, when the ball ran loose. The first goal was a header from Adrian Thorne from a perfect centre from Michael Tiddy. Although Plymouth missed a couple of chances, we were definitely the better side.'

With Billy Lane resigning at the end of this season, troubled times lay ahead for his former club. Lane moved to Southern League Gravesend & Northfleet, guiding them on their inspirational FA Cup run in 1962/63, during which they defeated Football League sides Exeter City and Carlisle United before being beaten by Sunderland after a replay at a snowy Roker Park.

The 1960/61 season saw the abolition of the maximum wage in English professional football. Led adroitly by Fulham's 32-year-old inside-forward, Jimmy Hill, the 2,700-strong Professional Football Association (PFA) successfully challenged the feudal power of the clubs. The crisis came to a head in November 1960. The Football League tried to head off the mounting dispute by proposing that the clubs raise the maximum wage from £20 to £30 per week and offer players longer contracts. But this was widely rejected by PFA members. Before 1961 each player was on a one-year deal only. This afforded them and their families very little security. England star Tom Finney remembered, 'The retained players were called in one by one and it would be something along the lines of "Well, you've had a good season and we're offering you the same terms as last season, sign here" and he would sign a blank form and they would fill in the terms later.' The clubs held the whip hand, also holding the players' registrations for as long as they saw fit. This practice prevented a player transferring to a club of his choice when his contract ended if he did not have his previous club's approval. This was what happened to George Eastham until a High Court judge ruled that this practice represented an unlawful restraint of trade.

Billy Lane was very concerned at the prospect of a players' strike. He wrote in the Liverpool match programme on 14 January, 'Much has been said and written of the threatened strike of League players. I sincerely hope, not only for their sake, but of the footballing public, in general, that they do not take the drastic action they threaten. I have always advocated that players have better terms providing the cash to cover increased wages etc. comes through the turnstile. There are, in my opinion, 60 per cent of League clubs at the present time running at a loss, and I should say would welcome a break and so ease their losses. There is a great difference when a £10 per week and a £25 per week man goes on strike. I quote £25 as this is the approximate wage Albion first-team players receive during the season. Now that the maximum wage may be abolished, the Albion can no longer pay the maximum wage to first-team players. This has been the practice here during the past ten years.'

A £25 weekly wage in 1961 equates to one of £566 today, in other words roughly equivalent to the current average national wage, but only if hyper-inflated top professional footballers and financiers are excluded. Based on that comparison, Brighton's top wages were hardly generous. Yet Billy Lane was in favour of keeping a tight lid on wage increases, fearing for the future sustainability of his club. But with power progressively shifting away from the clubs to the players, after the PFA's actions, there was little chance that his objections would halt this trend.

Hastings United v
Brighton & Hove Albion

Sussex Professional Cup (Second Leg),
1 May 1961
'Blue Moon'

HASTINGS UNITED had approached the 1960/61 Premier Southern League season with great optimism. Chairman Dennis Schofield wrote in the programme for the opening home game against Wisbech: 'We feel our manager Tim Kelly has done a good job in his choice of players and if the team plays as well as they should do from their reputations, then we shall all be happy. We would impress upon you that all the directors are behind the manager in his efforts to produce an entertaining and successful team and if we can count on your continued support, we shall continue to invest in good new players as and when required.'

Tim Kelly was a charismatic Irishman who had led Bedford to the 1958/59 Southern League title after a play-off with Hereford United and guided them to victory over Norwich City at Carrow Road in an FA Cup tie. Kelly had also been a coach at Luton Town. In transferring from Bedford Town, he brought with him the inaugural 'Southern League Player of the Year' Len Duquemin, a prolific goalscorer at Bedford and formerly at Spurs. Ex-Hastings right-winger Micky Bull joined Kelly in his move to Sussex.

Hastings United had completed the previous season in 14th position and managed a decent FA Cup run, which ended with a 1-2 home defeat by Notts County. Despite Hastings performing satisfactorily in the 1959/60 season, Kelly made wholesale changes, bringing in many players with Football League experience. Some were young and swift, such as former Brighton and Arsenal inside-right Ronnie Clayton, and Palace's Welsh winger Billy Rees, but others were in the twilight of the careers, like Duquemin, full-back Jack Harrop from Watford, and ex-Brentford centre-half Bill Livingstone. Only experienced defender Hendry McGuiness and inside-forward Hugh Stinson remained from the 1959/60 Hastings side and they were two of the better performers in the dire season that followed.

By 1 October, when the autumn rains had set in, Hastings were in the relegation zone with just one Southern League victory in nine games. In his programme notes, Kelly regularly castigated his side for conceding 'silly goals' while cursing their luck in games they should have won. As the pitches became heavier, he became increasingly exasperated that his players failed to recognise that a dribbling, short-passing game in such cloying conditions was futile, pointing out that a more direct, 'steamroller' style of play was called for. It seemed as if the Hastings players could not divest themselves of Kelly's original instruction to play in an entertaining, quick, inter-passing way. Only a 7-0 thrashing of Tonbridge in the Southern League Cup and a promising FA Cup run gave any cause for cheer, although upwardly mobile Northampton brought their FA Cup dreams to an abrupt end in early November. By 17 December Hastings had still won only once in the Southern League, an insipid home victory over lowly Cheltenham.

Kelly was also troubled by a proposal made by 12 Midland clubs to leave the Southern League on account of the ruinous long-distance travelling requirements. Kelly reported that a spokesman for five of these clubs suggested that they would be happy to remain with the Southern League if it reverted to geographical divisions. While most clubs eventually voted in favour of maintaining the status quo, a similar secessionist proposal was put forward by a consortium of Kent and Sussex clubs during the mid-60s. The reality was that Southern League football was haemorrhaging fans faster than the Football League clubs, which had also experienced a substantial decline in attendances. During the late 50s, the bigger Southern League clubs such as Bath City, Hereford United, Chelmsford City, Cambridge City and United, Oxford United and Yeovil regularly drew gates of over 3,000. As the 60s progressed, many Southern League clubs drew less than 1,000 fans to their league games.

On 11 March Hastings United were bottom of the Southern League Premier Division, ten points below the safety margin. Home gates had dropped alarmingly, compelling chairman Dennis Schofield to announce before the Boston game, 'Owing to the present critical state of our finances we have decided to launch a SURVIVAL FUND appeal in order to settle some of our pressing and accumulating debts. We are asking all who can afford to and wish to help the club in its present difficulties to contribute towards this end and at half-time today we are going to make a collection.

'We would be glad of volunteers who would be willing to take the sheet round at half-time and hope that the support forthcoming will help us on our way. During the next few weeks we shall be distributing leaflets giving you a detailed list of our overhead expenses together with wages which will show you that our weekly income is insufficient to cover our contracted expenses. We would like to point out that every endeavour is being made to find ways of economising, some of which are already put into practice.

'We would like to thank those regular supporters who are following us through thick and thin, who come to see us, first team or reserves, fine weather or bad. We hope by managing to get through this season we will be able to budget so that in future we will keep within our income. The first team is playing well presently, and after a good game against Romford (2-0) there was an encouraging display at Weymouth, which with a little luck might have resulted in victory (1-2).'

Kelly once again cursed his side's ill fortune after their 4-1 defeat at Bedford, his former club. And despite achieving a creditable 1-0 victory over Dartford on the Pilot Field's hard, bare and uneven surface, calamity struck on a sunny Good Friday when Tonbridge came, saw and plundered (1-5). The die was almost cast. Although Hastings won 1-0 against a coach-lagged Hereford side, on the following day this did little to assuage fears of the drop. On a wet Easter Monday, they once again relinquished an early lead, in drawing 1-1 at Tonbridge. During this testing season Hastings were incapable of winning even one league game away from home.

For the final home game against Worcester City, Kelly wrote in his programme notes, 'This has been a very trying and exasperating season for us, which has seen us take the drop from the Premier Division. After a clear-out from last season, we were hoping for better things, but unfortunately even the best of intentions has a habit of coming unstuck. I honestly think that we are rather unlucky to be relegated. Many of the games lost could have quite easily been won. True, some of our players did not play up to expectations but nevertheless they were always trying to play entertaining football. However, you are not awarded any points for moral victories. All we can do now is make a big effort next season to win our way back to the Premier Division.'

Hastings's record was played 42, won eight, drew nine and lost 25, goals for 60, against 99, points 25. A better second half of the season enabled them to leap-frog Wisbech, who had thrashed 'Kelly's heroes' in the opening game and won the return match at Fenland Park (2-3). They also overtook Boston United who, despite taking three points off Hastings, came bottom with 20 points, having conceded 123 goals. Hastings completed their season 12 points from safety. Despite Kelly's entreaties, Hastings were deservedly relegated.

Ironically their best performances were in the two-leg final of the Sussex Professional Cup against a much stronger Brighton & Hove Albion side. The first leg was played at the Goldstone Ground on 24 April. Kelly wrote in his programme notes for the return leg, 'Brighton have many talented players. They certainly served up some grand stuff last week, especially during the first half, in which they took a 2-0 lead. After the interval, our lads really got going with great moves which resulted in Micky Bull and Hugh Stinson neutralising Brighton's advantage. Both teams tried hard for the winning goal, and although there were some narrow escapes at either end, there was no further score. It was an entertaining game which resulted in a deserved draw. If tonight's game is as good, you will have no cause for complaint.'

On a grey evening at the Pilot Field, Billy Lane again put out a strong side: Carter; McNicol and Carolan; Bertolini, Jennings, and Burtenshaw; Tiddy, McNeill, Nicholas, Foreman, and Laverick. While my grasp of the game's details is limited after the elapse of almost 60 years, several outstanding features remain. Brighton dominated possession, taking the lead twice, but were pegged back on each occasion by Clayton and Stinson, showing unfamiliar composure and precision in front of goal. Brighton's left-winger, Laverick, was robust and direct, although wasteful, while on the other wing Tiddy was neat and tricky, producing a series of testing crosses. Nicholas darted here, there and everywhere, unsettling the Hastings defenders. However, it was Roy Jennings who impressed me most. He was so commanding, at the back and up front. I had yet to see Spurs' Maurice Norman play. I understood that he was one of the first attacking centre-halves. Here, Jennings emulated him impressively. He was a constant menace in the Hastings box, and, if I remember correctly, he headed one of Brighton's goals, pugnaciously winning an aerial challenge. Up front, the U's fleet-footed left-winger, Billy Rees, gave McNicol a torrid evening. Had Hastings shown this resilience and defensive rigour in their league games, they might have escaped the drop. But I felt unable to indulge such facile fantasies for long. Next season what I saw was solely for pious flagellants.

Sussex CCC v Lancashire CCC

Central Cricket Ground, 8 July 1961

'Runaway'

MY INTEREST in cricket was first stirred when our family lived in Netherfield, near Battle, in the early 50s. I can recall lying in the long grass on the edge of the village's recreation ground, watching Dad bat in the hum of a hot summer day. He was such a strong man on account of his daily wrestling with the notoriously stiff gear levels on the gypsum mines' giant bulldozer. I was captivated by his power as he brutally despatched the ball over the swings and into the melting road and then clobbered it on to the village hall roof where it clattered against the slates. I remember, too, Dad waking me early so I could hear bulletins of Frank Tyson's feats 'down under' before he set off for work in the crumpling snow. With the landing oil heater providing necessary protection against frozen pipes, my bleary, early memories of Frank are forever associated with the pungency of paraffin.

My intoxication with fast bowlers began when dad took me to a cinematic showing of the 'History of the Ashes', soon after our family came together again in the spring of 1960. Here, I saw Harold Larwood, one of dad's heroes, bustling in, short, sturdy and grim-faced. With a smooth rotation of his right arm, he released balls of fire that left many Aussie batsmen recoiling with pain. This was 'Bodyline' apparently.

I was equally intrigued by images of Frank Tyson in his pomp. Remembering my early impression of him as a hairy, untamed beast, it was difficult reconciling this image with what I saw on film. For here was a balding, apparently elderly man creating constant mayhem. He didn't appear to be particularly muscular either. But none of the Australian batsmen seemed to hang around while he was strutting his stuff. He began his approach with a curious foot-pawing gesture as if mimicking an enraged bull.

Despite his leanness, he exuded wiry strength. Leaning forward into ever-lengthening strides, there was a sense of mounting elasticity, and power. His bowling action was a crescendo of force. Upon reaching the point of delivery, his head and body suddenly rose; he clawed for height before releasing the ball with ballistic fury, his left leg taking the shuddering impact of his follow-through, as he was flung far forward by the mighty effort expended.

Thanks to BBC TV coverage of the 1961 Ashes series in England, I discovered new fast-bowling heroes: Fred Trueman and Brian Statham. Trueman had a blacksmith's muscular physique – beefy shoulders, hefty thighs and calves – and a scowling expression beneath an unruly mop of jet-black hair. He spat volleys of salty wit, too. When reproached by his Yorkshire team-mates for his feeble dismissal by a Frank Tyson 'Exocet', Trueman reputedly retorted, 'Aye, I slipped in that pile of sh*t you lot left behind.' Like Harold Larwood and Aussie Ray Lindwall, whom I also saw on film, Trueman's action was not an erratic explosion of pugilistic strength. It was finely tuned, classical even. His curving, bounding, shirt-flapping, slightly pigeon-toed run of gathering speed was completed with a sideways twist, a thrusting aloft of his guiding left arm, a cocking of the right, and a giant stride forward, before a cartwheeling motion catapulted a ball of singeing pace at the batsman.

Brian Statham was reputedly as fast as his partner, Trueman, but had a contrasting, measured, seemingly reserved manner. He had a straight, relaxed, loping approach to the wicket, leaning forward into lengthening strides, the ball cradled in both hands. Smoothly accelerating towards the crease, he skipped at the point of delivery, with a crossing of his ankles, twisting his lean torso sideways, flicking up his guiding left arm in the guise of a periscope, and, with a supple, whippy action, dispatching the ball with laser-like accuracy and penetrative pace at the batsman's off stump. He used to say, 'You miss, I hit.' This was no empty boast for he was renowned for his accuracy. The Trueman–Statham partnership seemed to be one of fire and ice.

Jeff Jones, father of 2005 Ashes hero Simon, also joined my galaxy of speed merchants after watching him bowl on a duvet surface at Hastings during the early 60s. His Glamorgan side had run up a colossal score thanks to centuries by Alan Jones (121) and Tony Lewis (151). Whereas the Glamorgan centurions had mastered the Sussex attack in carpet slippers, Jones managed to extract astonishing life from this dead track. He began each delivery with a curious devotional gesture. Cradling the ball in both hands, he brought it to his lips, raising his spread elbows as he did so, as if making an ostentatious show of prayer, before scampering off to the wicket, leaning slightly to his right, and releasing the ball with a whippy, low, slinging action. Poor Richard Langridge had spent a hot day wilting in the slips waiting vainly for a chance, gloomily ruminating upon the wicket's lack of pace and bounce. But no sooner had he arrived at the crease to open Sussex's reply, he had to contend with a sharp lifter from Jones which he could only fend to Gilbert Parkhouse at first slip, departing disconsolately for nought. With Jones hitting his straps, this match became a different ball game.

My first experience of county cricket came on 8 July 1961 when Sussex met Lancashire at the Central Cricket Ground, Hastings. On account of Ashes duties, Sussex were without their star batsman, 'Lord' Ted Dexter, and Lancashire were deprived of Brian Statham and opening batsman Geoff Pullar. But vaunted Bob Barber, already capped by England, led the Red Rose side, supported by a strong cluster of seam bowlers – the genuinely quick Colin Hilton, nippy Ken Higgs and persistent Peter Lever. The latter two would eventually play for England. Meanwhile, Sussex were able to field most of the side that had achieved fourth place in the previous County Cricket Championship season, including England wicketkeeper/batsman Jim Parks.

Barber won the toss and chose to bat under leaden skies. I later discovered that the burden of captaincy shackled his adventurous batting, while also restricting use of his often, sharp leg breaks. He certainly began his opening innings circumspectly, understandably so, since, during the pre-lunch session, there was enough in the wicket to interest Sussex's battery of seamers.

Barber had imperfect vision in his left eye, which he compensated for by learning to bat left-handed at an early age. He was right-handed in other respects. This adjustment brought his stronger eye into line. But he was not at his best on the less reliable wickets in England. Whereas, on the true surfaces in South Africa and Australia, he prospered, smashing a belligerent 185 in the Sydney Test in January 1966. He had an uncanny ability to hit the ball on the rise off the front foot, almost irrespective of where the ball pitched. Because he adopted an unusually high grip on the bat handle, he commanded maximum leverage when swinging through the line. How the Australian pace men and spinners suffered on that hot afternoon in 1966.

Opening medium-fast bowler Don Bates had been a wing-half in Brighton's promotion side of 1958. With injury curtailing his football career, he decided to concentrate on cricket, with immediate success. In the previous season he had taken 109 wickets, at a respectable average of 23 runs each, and during this 1961 season he improved on that return, maintaining a similar average. After an hour's play, he struck the first blow as Brian Booth snicked an out-swinger to Parks with the Lancashire score at 41.

At the eastern end of the ground, Ian Thomson toiled away with customary accuracy, racking up half a dozen maidens in his initial spell. Thomson had the appearance of a furrowed, heavy labourer. His trundling approach to the wicket suggested residual fatigue, as well it might, for in each of the previous eight seasons he had bowled over 1,000 overs, routinely taking 100 wickets or more. Upon reaching the crease, he completed his delivery with a cursory skip and a heavy stamp of his left boot. He was once described by a disgruntled Fred Trueman as a 'good, honest county bowler only'. This was said in response to Thomson's selection for the 1964/65 MCC tour of South Africa, in place of Trueman.

But the gutsy Thomson earned his unexpected England cap, which came just one year before his retirement. While his in-dippers and leg cutters were often destructive on the wet or dusty county pitches, these were rarely penetrative on the Union's flat tracks, although he produced a peach of a delivery, at Durban, to dismiss Eddie Barlow for two, spearing the new ball into the South African's pads before finding sufficient bite for it to clip the off stump. Thomson took only nine wickets in the series, at a weighty cost of 63 runs apiece, but his unrelenting accuracy, maintained over 248 Test overs, meant that he conceded little more than two runs per over. He provided essential support to off-spinners Allen and Titmus in restraining the South African stroke-makers, reducing the time available for the Springboks to save the series, having lost the first Test.

However, the most dangerous Sussex bowler in the pre-lunch period was temporary captain Don Smith, with his left-arm, medium-paced swingers. His bowling looked innocuous from the boundary, but three Lancashire batsmen lost their wickets to his curved balls. Having patiently blunted the Sussex opening attack for over an hour, Barber played a fatally expansive cover drive which Hastings goalkeeper Graham Cooper snaffled at cover. Barber left with an exasperated swipe of his bat, knowing that he had forfeited the opportunity to capitalise once conditions improved, as had been forecasted. Jack Bond then snicked another Smith out-swinger to Oakman at slip while Australian Ken Grieves perished with an injudicious swat that Bates gobbled up. Suddenly Lancashire were 71/4.

Just when it seemed that Lancashire might collapse completely before lunch, their relatively inexperienced late middle order made an unexpected revival. By lunchtime Bolton and Houlton had calmly taken their side's score to 124, and in the flatter afternoon session, in which the sun shone brightly, this pair added a further 104 runs before they were separated. Growing in confidence in the benign conditions, both batsmen played freely, being particularly harsh in their treatment of medium-paced Tony Buss from Brightling. Both youngsters appeared to be playing the innings of their lives. Gerald Houlton, who made 78 here, bettered that in a later innings at Folkestone, but achieved little, subsequently ending this season with a mediocre batting average of 25. The same could be said of Bolton. Here, he scored 92 before being dismissed by Tony Buss, but ended this season with a meagre batting average of 18. After this pair had departed, the Lancashire tail offered little resistance, allowing Thomson and Buss to improve their bowling averages. A total of 290 was probably about par.

This left Sussex with around 30 minutes' batting. Barber set an umbrella field to disconcert the Sussex openers, Oakman and Langridge. At 6ft 6in tall, Oakman appeared to stoop over a bat that seemed too small for him. Jaunty Colin Hilton ran in hard, straining to achieve top pace which, on a sympathetic pitch, was decidedly slippery. But with the docile Central Ground wicket drawing his sting, he presented little threat. Taking advantage of the gaping gaps in front of the wicket, Langridge serenely drove two of his deliveries to the long-on boundary. On the other hand, Ken Higgs troubled Oakman more. His economical approach to the wicket belied considerable thrust and nip, and given his accuracy and impressive command of cut and swerve he was a dangerous proposition. One of Higgs's deliveries struck Oakman on the front pad, causing the Lancastrian to bellow 'Ow wazeee!' Talk about, 'We speak with an accent exceedingly rare.' Oakman was troubled and shortly before the close Higgs induced him into playing an imprudent drive which resulted in him snicking the ball to wicketkeeper Geoff Clayton. Sussex closed on 20/1.

Although Sussex capitulated meekly on Monday, being dismissed for 177 with only Ken Suttle (67) resisting for long, Lancashire collapsed, too, in their second innings, with Bates, Thomson and Buss cleaning up. Oakman took five catches in the slips, matching his performance in Jim Laker's leg-trap during the Old Trafford Ashes Test of 1956. This left Sussex with an exciting run chase which they completed successfully, scoring at a rate of around three and a half runs per over, a veritable sprint by standards of the time. I managed to see the absorbing final overs having raced to the Central Cricket Ground once school ended. There was no admission charge after the tea interval in those days. While engrossed in this run chase, a smartly dressed man, with what I later discovered to be an MCC tie, struck up conversation with me. He had a plummy accent which distinguished him from my usual company, but seemed genial, so I happily talked with him.

Beside me was Jim Laker's autobiography *Over to Me*. Upon seeing this, his mood changed. He angrily denounced it as a 'terrible book'. Not understanding why Laker's book should have upset him, I replied that it had opened my eyes to the evil of apartheid. I referred to its stark description of a road traffic accident, involving Sussex's Alan Oakman, Laker and a black South African, during the 1956/57 MCC tour of South Africa. Oakman attempted to help the injured black man he had inadvertently struck, later visiting him in hospital and giving him money to help with his loss of wages. Whereas a white South African policeman treated the victim callously, bullying the black onlookers into confirming that the injured man was solely responsible for the accident. My companion seemed indifferent to this, insisting that Laker had no right to denigrate the Marylebone Cricket Club (MCC) which then ran English cricket, calling this 'bad form'. Exasperated by my unconcern, he stood up abruptly and walked away. I came to realise that if the Anglican church represented the Conservative party at prayer, the MCC represented it at play.

English first-class cricket reflected the class divisions that the war and social mobility had helped erode. Although in retreat, deference was still a point of honour for many in the ruling elite, much to the amusement of satirists such as Peter Cook. Towards the end of the *Lady Chatterley's Lover* obscenity trial, in 1960, the prosecuting counsel summed up by asking the jury, 'Is this a book you would wish your wife or servants to read?' The 60s had yet to show any inclination to swing.

In 1961 first-class cricketers were classified as either 'gentlemen' or 'players'. 'Gentlemen' were typically educated at a public school and Oxbridge, while the 'players', mostly of lower or lower middle-class origins, were principally educated at state schools. Up until the late 50s, 'gentlemen' were granted superior dressing rooms, posher hotels and first-class travel, while the players made do with less grand provisions. The 'gentlemen' were supposedly amateurs, while the 'players' were professionals.

One of Laker's gripes, which upset my MCC companion, was that he would have been better off as an amateur on the 1958/59 MCC tour of Australia. Laker reasoned that amateurs received better remuneration, from generous expense allowances, than professionals did from their modest wages. Although the 'gentleman'/'player' distinction disappeared in 1962, with the cessation of an annual cricket match between the two, vestiges of this division remained for 35 years after.

During the mid-60s, I was playing in an impromptu game of cricket on the Hastings Central Cricket Ground outfield during the lunch interval. It was something that had become commonplace elsewhere. A public address announcer interrupted our play, insisting that, 'There are ten reasons why it is not permissible to play on the outfield. The first is that the committee say so and the other nine do not matter.'

This message was broadcasted when the sustainability of English first-class cricket was seriously in question, when the game was in critical need of radical changes that would attract and retain the interest of future generations. Before I left Hastings, cricket was already receding in state schools. Yet it was often difficult for young cricketers to join local clubs, which tended to be dominated by cliquey, older players. The myopic stuffiness of this committee and the reactionary attitude of that MCC member have certainly stood my test of time.

My summer of 1961 became clouded by England's unaccountable Ashes defeat. But while ruminating upon what should have been, in September I discovered an inspirational winner. It happened as I was sprawled on the unseasonably green turf of Hastings Central Cricket Ground, watching an England XI take on a strong Commonwealth side. I became entranced by a West Indian fast bowler. His jaunty, loose-limbed stride emphasised supreme athleticism. His wide smile exuded self-belief. Time and again, he pounded in off a prodigiously long run that began just yards from my cupped chin. His dishevelled shirt became progressively darkened with sweat. A gold chain, encircling his neck, glinted in the late summer sun as he accelerated towards the crease. With a quivering, flailing action he completed his delivery. The ball was barely seen as it reared sharply past the batsman's tentative prod and thwacked into the up-stretched gloves of the leaping wicketkeeper. Only the cackling seagulls mocked. He was so confident of his power that he had no need to flaunt it. There were no histrionics, no aggressive posturing. His jocular manner emphasised his love of a life that granted him his mighty talent. I yearned to have his relaxed conviction, his rhythmic power and his compelling presence. I wanted to become Wes Hall.

Brighton & Hove Albion
v Leyton Orient
Football League Second Division, 7 April 1962
'Wonderful Land'

IN HIS programme notes for the Wisbech Town game of 9 September 1961, Hastings manager Tim Kelly wrote, 'We have made a disastrous start to the season, having lost all six matches played. The heaviest defeat came in the Southern League Cup at Folkestone, last Tuesday, when the home team struck top form and scored seven times without reply. Last Saturday we ought to have come away with a least a point from Gloucester, having made the better start and opened the scoring. However, much against the run of play, Gloucester took the lead from two quick breakaways. Although we equalised before half-time, and held our own in the second half, Gloucester got the goal that mattered.'

The futility of Kelly's words lay in the realisation that they might have been written by him at any point during the previous season. In fairness to the beleaguered man, necessary austerity measures had dealt him a duff hand. Only centre-half Ashen and injured goalie Agate were adequate replacements for the previous under-performing players who had been shed. Goalkeeper and Sussex county cricketer Graham

Cooper was one of few to be retained. Kelly wrote regretfully that this competent goalkeeper, 'had been forbidden to play football this season following his recent illness'. I wondered which medical professional had come to his aid, possibly a psychiatrist. Certainly, the town's 'scratch' players gave the Pilot Field a wide berth lest they were pressed into playing. The standard of football was awful and, unsurprisingly, so were the home gates, which averaged 750, 3,000 less than the attendance for the opening home game of the previous season.

Despite a brace of victories in successive home games, by New Year's Eve Hastings had played 21 league games, winning just two and drawing one – a profligate 4-4 draw with languishing Burton – and losing 18, goals for 18, goals against 72. I had become so devout in celebrating abject failure that I urged my birthday guests to join me at a freezing reserve fixture against Gravesend, a dismal 0-0 draw. A rabid game of Monopoly followed. Eventually, Dad decided my OCD needed a remedy and took me to see the surprise package of Second Division football, Leyton Orient. This was a team that was punching well above its weight, having narrowly evaded relegation during the previous season. Yet, with a similar team, Orient had transformed themselves into promotion candidates.

On 7 April 1962 Dad and I went to the Goldstone Ground to see how Brighton fared against these underdogs. Their clubs appeared to be heading in opposite directions, not that their respective balance sheets gave any clarification. Although hardly rich, Brighton had splashed out almost £50,000 on its squad, whereas Orient had spent only a third of that figure in placing itself on the cusp of top-flight football.

George Curtis had replaced Billy Lane as Brighton's manager in the summer of 1961. Curtis had previously been a nimble inside-forward with Arsenal before the war and with Southampton afterwards. He had been dubbed 'twinkle toes' at the Dell, not only by his appreciative fans, but also by his frustrated team-mates. Having spent the 1952/53 season with the French side Valenciennes, he completed his playing days as player/manager with Chelmsford City. Like Joe Mercer, George preached the coaching gospel. He gained his FA coaching qualifications at Lilleshall before accepting a coaching post at Sunderland in 1957. Here he worked under a fellow coaching enthusiast, the censorious but far-sighted Alan Brown, the architect of Burnley's rise. George Curtis seemed an ideal replacement for Lane.

Outspoken Tony Nicholas thought otherwise. Nicholas later told an *Evening Argus* reporter, 'I like to think that I had helped keep Brighton up in 1960/61. When George came, he only bought one player – Joe Caven from Airdrie. I reckon Brighton were done paying £15,000 for him. He came with a reputation of being a free-scoring centre-forward but didn't get one for us. The trouble was that we needed new players but there wasn't sufficient money. We needed two or three good 'uns. If we had had another two or three players of the right calibre, we could have done quite well instead of finishing bottom. George's idea was to make world beaters of people with little or no ability. [On the other hand, Orient boss Johnny Carey did very well with his limited hand.] There is a complete difference between managers and coaches and George was definitely a coach. When George took over, he told all the players, "any problems, don't see me, see Joe Wilson". George just didn't want to know. Once, when I went to see him for the refund of a taxi fare of 9/6d, he handed me a ten-shilling note. I started to walk out of the office when he called me back and asked for the change. He wasn't joking. Don't get me wrong, George was a charming chap, a gentleman and a good coach, but a dead loss as a manager. I think he knew it.'

Inside-forward Ian McNeill agreed, adding, 'George Curtis ruined the club. Yet he was the best coach I worked under. He kept saying he wanted youngsters in the team, but they weren't good enough. He'd coach one style during the week but, on a matchday, he would be calling for long balls over the heads and all the preparations went out of the window. Bob McNicol was a firm crowd favourite who had played in practically every game until Curtis brought in David Smith from Burnley. At training we'd form up in opposing sides and, after being left out, Bob really clattered into George. Next time, George made sure he had Bob in his team.'

George seemed a strange cove. His programme notes for the Blackburn FA Cup tie on 6 January 1962 included a quote from the medieval Persian poetry of Omar Khayyam, prefaced by his own impenetrable thoughts. Curtis wrote, 'We all appreciate some of the players' problems. Some appreciate them all. Our players, particularly the young ones, are paying the price of experience and circumstance by criticism. In the end it will reward them richly. Meantime, this quote might well encourage them: "The ball no question makes of ayes and noes, but right or left as strikes the player goes; and he that tossed thee down into the Field, he knows about it all, he knows."' Lurching from the obscure to the obvious, during his stint in Norwegian football, during the late 60s, Curtis once pointed at a leather football and solemnly told his Rosenborg players, 'This is a ball,' prompting his principal striker to comment, 'George, don't go too fast, now.'

Surprisingly, George explained his recent choice of tactics in his programme notes for the Orient game. He wrote, 'At Huddersfield it was agreed that right winger Mike Tiddy would play a flanking midfield game, not only to draw Ray Wilson [a World Cup winner in 1966] further from his goal line, but to present a vacant wing area behind him, into which either Nicholas or Caven might move, but to "ferret" for the ball should the wing-half be prepared to move into attack. Tony Nicholas's role, as a support man for Caven, proved not without successes, for two scoring chances were created, from which, unfortunately, Tony's shots were off target. This afternoon, for example, we might well anticipate the similar wanderings of Orient's Deeley and McDonald.' George Curtis had previously been a colleague of Alf Ramsey at Southampton. What Curtis appeared to be suggesting here was a facsimile of Ramsey's successful tactics at Ipswich, where his withdrawn wingers enticed the opposing full-backs to follow them, leaving unprotected gaps behind, where the prolific Ipswich strikers, Crawford and Phillips, could plunder. As England's manager Ramsey adapted this plan in creating his World Cup 'wingless wonders'.

Despite his tactical awareness, George presided over a sinking side. Having occupied a relatively comfortable mid-table position at New Year, the Albion had crashed to the bottom by 7 April. The programme for the Orient game advertised the Hollywood blockbuster *El Cid* at the Astoria. Brighton were surely in need of a rescuing knight.

Brighton's 1961/62 season had begun slowly. A 3-3 draw at Scunthorpe was followed by a 1-3 home defeat by misfiring Leeds, still awaiting Revie's restoration. Then, visiting Swansea escaped with a 2-2 draw, after Brighton blew a two-goal lead. A *Daily Mirror* reporter observed, 'Brighton need to attract 16,000 spectators before their players can draw any bonus money. This crowd was 216 short.'

September featured a worthy 3-2 win at the Valley and a creditable pair of victories over Stoke, but a disastrous 1-6 hammering at Southampton on 7 October gave notice of Brighton's defensive frailties. Newcastle United and Plymouth Argyle duly exploited these on Albion's travels, both inflicting 5-0 defeats, while Leyton Orient won 4-1 at Brisbane Road following more shambolic defending. Although a declining Middlesbrough were defeated 2-0 at the Goldstone at the end of October, Brighton did not manage to win again until relegation-troubled Bristol Rovers were beaten 1-0 home and away over the festive period. Thereafter, Brighton nose-dived in the wake of an emphatic 0-3 FA Cup defeat by visiting Blackburn on 6 January. Only one of the next ten league games was won, when Walsall were beaten 3-2 at the Goldstone on 24 March. The disappointed Brighton fans began to vote with their feet. The average home gate for the 1961/62 season was 2,500 down on the previous year, although only 1,000 fewer than the average 14,083 attendance at Orient.

7 April was a dull, passionless day. Even the chilly offshore wind could not disperse a grey mist that smudged the sea, sky and surrounding downs. It was hard to believe that only 15 months had elapsed since Dad and I had stepped out into the Hove rain, oblivious of our saturated clothing, eagerly anticipating a muddy scrap between the Albion and the current league champions. But here we were only too aware of the dank cold that shivered my youthful timbers.

Large groups of Orient fans had congregated on the Eastern terraces. They were chirpily expectant. I had yet to follow a successful side, so I was perplexed by their persistent carping. I had yet to discover that the more you have, the more you want. Orient began by attacking the Old Shoreham Road end.

The game jolted into a snarling dog fight on a rutted glue pot of a surface. It was hardly the place for flowing football. There was no composure, just frantic lunges, hopeful punts and hasty clearances with possession ping-ponging between the straining sides. While Brighton hunted as a compressed pack, the Orient players were better at spreading the play, allowing both McDonald and Deeley greater freedom to run at the home full-backs. Following one such break on the left, McDonald cut in and, with his favoured right foot, hammered the bobbling ball goalwards. Brighton keeper Charlie Baker could only parry the skimming shot, allowing inside-forward Ronnie Foster to poke home the rebound. In the remaining 15 minutes of the first half, Brighton upped the tempo, but their attacks lacked cohesion and were easily snuffed out by the redoubtable Orient defenders.

As the half-time scores were displayed on the coded metal plates, The Shadows' hit, 'Wonderful Land' was played on the public address. It seemed poignant rather than joyful – appropriate, perhaps, given the glum mood of the Brighton crowd.

The second half was more open. Brighton's inside-forward Ian McNeill managed to get the ball down and provide thoughtful and incisive service for his tearaway forwards,

Nicholas and Laverick. The Orient defence was subjected to greater pressure. But with Brighton pushing forward in search of an equaliser the O's forwards enjoyed more space. Little Terry McDonald revelled in this freedom. From afar he seemed young and vulnerable, as if he was an altar boy, dragooned into playing. Up closer, he looked tougher, though, more streetwise. There was no doubting his ability. Once in possession he was calm and assured, continually drawing Joe Carolan towards him, only to confound the Eire international with his quick feet, and darting pace, bypassing the Albion full-back on the inside and out and pumping a succession of dangerous crosses into the crowded Brighton box. Whereas McDonald was nimble and nifty, Deeley, on the right flank, was forceful and direct, frequently making a beeline for goal with a scurrying motion, using his surprising upper body strength to shrug off the challenges. With Orient failing to capitalise upon the excellent service from their two wingers, Brighton remained in the hunt until the end. But it was to no avail. The Albion were no better at converting their chances than the O's.

Orient deserved their narrow victory, although Brighton boss George Curtis thought otherwise. He remarked, 'There was sufficient collective effort for our lads to have bagged both points and it was disappointing, to say the least, how Leyton Orient scored the only goal of the match. Results at our end of the table certainly didn't help us. Anyway, we can only help ourselves. We MUST help ourselves in the six games still to play.' Despite George Curtis's desperate entreaties, Brighton were unable to rescue themselves. A disappointing 2-2 home draw with Charlton was followed by a 3-1 defeat at Preston. Just when hope had almost expired, the Albion won two games on the bounce – only their sixth and seventh of the season. On Good Friday they beat Norwich 2-1 before facing Plymouth on Easter Saturday.

My friend Roger King was at the Plymouth game. He remembers, 'I saw a number of Brighton games over the years, though none were really "amazing". This one was. The Albion were almost down. I went with my friend from Reading, who was supporting Plymouth. To his consternation, and that of a significant Plymouth contingent, Brighton fought back from a two-goal, second-half deficit to win 3-2, thereby scuppering Argyle's promotion hopes.' The Orient fans in the crowd were as delighted as their Albion counterparts who had dared to hope again. I recall a Sunderland supporter, yearning for a change of fortune for his relegation-haunted team, saying, 'Nothing hurts more than lingering hope.' Many of us have been there.

On Easter Monday, Albion's hopes expired, dampened first by the persistent rain and then by their team's poor defending. George Curtis's lads had reverted to type, losing 0-3 to rampant Norwich, intent upon avenging their Good Friday defeat. Although Brighton earned a point from their final fixture at Derby, it was irrelevant. One year after Billy Lane had left them, Brighton were back in Division Three.

Albion's 42 league goals represented one more than Barrie Thomas scored on his own in that season, firstly with Scunthorpe (31) and then with Newcastle (ten). Albion's sharpest shooters comprised: ex-Sunderland inside-forward John Goodchild, with ten; Laverick, also with ten; and Nicholas with nine. Centre-half Roy Jennings added four. No other Second Division side scored fewer goals than Brighton, while no others conceded more than Brighton's 86.

Tony Nicholas told a Brighton *Evening Argus* reporter, 'When I went to Brighton it was on a two-year contract. After the first year the maximum wage had been abolished and when that changed so did the contracts. The first-team players were on £20 a week. I thought I should get more, but the board turned me down in no uncertain fashion. "More money, Nicholas?" they chorused. "What a nerve. The players have taken the club down and you come in here asking for an increase. No. There isn't any." In the end I got £28 a week to play for Chelmsford City in the Southern League. There had to be something radically wrong for that situation to come about. After all, Brighton had been a Second Division club. Nobody at Brighton could say I didn't give 100 per cent and the crowd liked me. I thought, "Why should I be stuck at the same pay level as some that weren't so good?" Brighton inside-forward Ian McNeill agreed and I don't think we were the only ones.' With that, Brighton lost one of their best players of the early 60s. It seems incredible that one of the country's brightest prospects, just two years before, abandoned a still-promising Football League career at the young age of 24 years.

While the abolition of the maximum wage favoured the best players, it did less for the remaining professionals, whose clubs faced greater financial pressures. Brighton was a club divided, unlike Orient, at least during their improbable promotion surge. Brighton paid the price of that fragmentation as the club careered towards the Fourth Division.

Tonbridge v Hastings United

Southern League First Division, 17 November 1962

'Let's Dance'

NEW HASTINGS United manager Ted Ballard announced in April 1962, 'I promise you that next season we will be at least more like a football club and every endeavour will be made to give you the football you and the town deserve.'

The club's rash bid for glory in 1960/61 had saddled it with an unaffordable annual wage bill of almost £13,000 – around £300,000 in present values. As club chairman Dennis Schofield stated in March 1961, the average home gate of 1,600 was not enough to balance the books. Fifteen professional players were released at the end of this season, leaving a handful of amateurs, some of whom graduated to the Southern League side, such as Alan Selway. Although Kelly was granted permission to recruit a dozen more experienced players, these were largely 'cast-offs' prepared to play part-time for very low wages. Only centre-half John Ashen and ex-Chelsea keeper Ian Agate performed at the required standard.

The 1961/62 austerity drive worked, though, returning Hastings to solvency. Helped by a 53 per cent reduction in wages, the 1960/61 deficit of £1,763, worth about £37,000 today, was reversed. This was remarkable given that the 1961/62 average gate of 780 was 50 per cent down on the previous season. Because of these severe privations, the club was able to announce an annual profit of £1,480, around £31,000 in today's values. The cost, of course, was borne by the U's thrill-deprived faithful, insensate with lamentable defeat in that wretched season. United managed just five wins and four draws, against 29 losses. Surprisingly, the 46 goals they scored was not the lowest tally in this division. Trowbridge trumped them by one goal. But the 115 goals they conceded was undisputedly the highest.

In these more brutal times, a beleaguered football manager like Tim Kelly would have been sent packing long before he was but the *Hastings & St Leonards Observer* correspondent was more gracious, describing Kelly as 'A victim of the economy axe', suggesting also that he left Hastings with his 'reputation untarnished'. Kelly seemed a kind, courteous man, who readily applauded his opponents when outplayed, something that happened far too frequently. In two years in charge he achieved a win percentage of 16 per cent. For new manager Ted Ballard, the only way forward was up.

Ted Ballard, a former lower-division defender with Brentford, Southampton and Orient, was a shrewd cookie. He had made a good fist of managing neighbouring Ashford Town, a small Southern League club set in a railway community of 28,000 residents. His budget seemed to comprise twigs and twine and yet he consistently assembled competitive sides. Hastings must have seemed a more attractive proposition, though, with its much larger population of 68,000 – well over twice the size of Ashford and almost on a par with that of First Division heavyweights Burnley. Besides, Ted had completed his playing career at Hastings United.

Like the best of non-league managers, Ted had a sharp eye for the neglected and unrecognised talent that lurked beneath the Football League radar. According to his sons, Ken and Alan, Ted was constantly on the lookout for better players. He spent hours and hours watching midweek games all over the southern counties – league and non-league. As his Hastings captain Keith Tucker pointed out, 'Ted kept a careful note of all the players that caught his eye. He put their names in his little black book. He knew exactly what players he needed and who might best fit in. And once he fancied a player he wouldn't let go. He tried to get me at Charlton, but the manager wouldn't release me. Ironically, I was put on the transfer list shortly afterwards.

'Wigan came in for me, offering big money for those times. They had a rich director with a big coach business. So, I went north but Ted didn't give up. After he found that I had gone to Wigan, he phoned me at the end of my first season there, telling me what he was planning at Hastings and how much he wanted me to be his captain. Eventually he persuaded me to come back south, although I was offered league football – at Stockport – on better money. Ted was very persistent and very persuasive. Mind you, when I phoned Ted back to say I had decided to join him, I thought he'd be pleased but he just moaned: "Bloody hell, why are you phoning me now? I'm trying to get a piano out of the road." That was Ted all over.'

Keith, formerly with Charlton, was one of Ted's first recruits at Hastings. Keith said, 'Ted had a fantastic knowledge. He may have had his narky temper, but he was very methodical. He knew exactly what he wanted from his players. That 1962 team came from all over the place, but he was determined to get most of us living in the town, so we could train together and become a tight unit, which we were. Only two lived outside. Ted sorted out digs for us and a local builder gave us jobs. We settled in quickly. From the start Ted got us into good routines. It was really important to him that the full-backs developed a close understanding with their wingers. So, he had us working on that until it became instinctive. He believed the wingers needed to back us up in defence. He wanted us to attack but also keep things tight at the back. He had us practising the free-kick routines, too.

He was such a perfectionist. When big Joe White played up front, we'd try to find his head – Joe was such a brilliant header of the ball – but Ted didn't like "hoofball". He was happy for Joe to work the opposing defenders using his strong physique. But this was done to give the ball players, like Terry Marshall, more room to play in. Ted stressed that he wanted us to pass along the ground – "that's what the best teams do", he'd say.

'It was good fun playing under Ted, but he was strict, mind. He always spoke his mind and he trained us hard, very hard. He didn't go in for the long-distance runs so much as the sprints. We had this routine where a group of us would jog around the perimeter of the Pilot Field then the bloke at the back tried to sprint to the front while the others did their best to out-pace him. It was utterly knackering. Yet we did this over and over again. This was the sort of fitness that matches demand. Even during that dreadful winter of 1962/63 when we didn't play for two months, Ted had us training on the sands and at White Rock baths. We always kept up our standard of fitness.'

As Ken Ballard, Ted's son, confirmed, Ted was a good coach: 'Dad taught me how to defend, how to position myself. Like the best coaches he knew that a successful side must have a strong, well-organised defence. He used the swivel system to reduce the chances of his defenders being caught square. It was unusual in those days to find a manager, like Dad, who was prepared to give detailed instructions. I played under Dad's friend and former team-mate George Curtis at Stevenage. He was an FA coach. George was Brighton's manager when dad came to Hastings. George was such a nice man but never told us how he wanted us to play. Sid Bishop, the former Orient centre-half, was the same when he took over from Dad at Hastings in 1965.'

Alan Ballard illustrated how hard his Dad could be. He recalled a time at Ashford when a head injury to his centre-half John Harris forced Ted to withdraw him from the fray.

Alan said, 'John was dazed but Dad brought him round and had almost persuaded him to go back on when this female supporter came from behind the barrier to have a closer look at John. Shocked at how battered he was, she exclaimed, "Oh... My...God!", whereupon John took fright and refused to shift from the bench. Dad was absolutely livid.' With the privations and horrors of war still fresh in their memories, many men of Ted's generation worked to tougher standards.

Keith Tucker remembered Ted's desperation to win. He recalled, 'We were playing Ashford. It was shortly after Ted had started at Hastings and he was determined to put one over his former club. Anyway, we struggled to get the better of them despite bossing the play. At half-time we came in at 1-1. Ted went ballistic and started throwing hot cups of tea at us. One whistled just past Eddie Stone's ear, causing our left-half to complain, "Boss, there was no sugar in that." Things didn't get any better after half-time. So, by the end, Ted was really stoked up. So much so that he threw all of our wage packets into the bath. There we were scrambling around in the dirty water trying to find our money. Someone picked out one sopping packet, weighed it in his hand and shouted, "This one seems a bit heavier. It must be yours, Terry." Terry Marshall was our most highly paid player. Even when Ted got mad, we'd still end up having a laugh.'

Keith continued, 'Ted was such a ducker and diver, always on the lookout to spring an advantage. We were playing at Barry in that season. Knowing I had a Welsh background and could put on a convincing "Valleys" accent, Ted told me to impress the ref with my Taffy lingo when we tossed up. Ted didn't want the ref penalising us because we weren't Welsh. Anyway, we were struggling for a while, so I started to get mad, effing and blinding at the others, completely forgetting I was supposed to be Welsh. The referee races up to me and tells me that he's booking me not only for bad language but also for taking the p***. It was the only time I was ever booked in my career. Thanks Ted!

'Ted knew I was a tough tackler and good at reading the game. I wasn't that fast, but I had good positional sense. When Jeanne and I got married, Ted told my wife, "If he (pointing at me) gives you any trouble just slap a number seven on your back. He's got no pace, you know. He'll never catch you."

'Mind you, Ted could be tight. We'd handed over a bill to him from a café we'd stopped at on the way to a game. Ted studied the receipt before demanding to know "Who's had two cups of tea?" We couldn't believe it. He even took the 2d when it was reluctantly handed over!'

Ken Ballard added, 'Dad didn't take any prisoners. If he didn't think you were up to it, he'd tell you straight. I remember when we brought in these young trialists for a training session with Ashford's first team. It was obvious they weren't up to scratch and Dad instructed his trainer to tell the boys they were no longer required. Our trainer was softer than dad, though, and didn't like to tell the lads straight out. This incensed Dad. "OK, I'll do it myself then!" he snapped and marched into the changing room where the young lads were sharing a bath with the senior players. "You two," he says. "I won't be needing you anymore. A waste of soap and water!" Grimacing with embarrassment, the rest of us had to avert our eyes. Harsh, eh?'

Alan Ballard added, 'Dad got good people to work with him, too – assistants like Jock McGuire, the Scottish physio. I once had a foot injury and Jock spotted it straight away without me having to tell him. He was that good at his job.'

Keith agreed: 'Ted had Jimmy Hernon as his reserve-team coach, too. Jimmy had such amazing skills. He had been a real star in the 1940s and 50s. He played under Bill Shankly.' Keith was right. Hernon had real pedigree. So much so that Bolton forked out £16,000 for him just after the war. Here, Jimmy played alongside the likes of Nat Lofthouse. Hernon certainly left a lasting impression with former BBC football commentator Kenneth Wolstenholme. Ken once said of Hernon, 'With one deft drop of the shoulder and a quick shimmy, Jimmy could leave defenders in a heap on the floor. He charmed me.' Reflecting upon the paucity of talent around Hernon in one game, Wolstenholme added, 'He stood out like an expensive jewel at a jumble sale.' Jimmy was certainly appreciated at Hastings, where he helped Ted turn a club of 'no hopers' into one of the stronger non-league sides in the land – that was until Ted's relationship with the Hastings board soured in the summer of 1964. Jimmy Hernon fitted in well with this happy, ribbing team. With his wonderful self-deprecating humour, Jimmy once said, 'I started at the top and, with a lot of effort, gradually worked my way down.' There were no 'Fancy Dans' in Ted's team.

Southampton Football Club's summer tour of Brazil in 1948 had opened Ted's eyes to the possibilities of 'total football'. It was a trip he shared with future England boss Alf Ramsey and George Curtis. It was meant to be an English master class for the supposedly inferior Brazilians, but the roles of teacher and pupil were reversed very quickly. Shortly before his death in 2008, Ted told Aiden Hamilton, author of *An Entirely Different Game*, 'They [the Brazilians] were all footballers – each of their teams comprised 11 footballers which British sides never had then. You played in the position you were given. We had full-backs who were good kickers of the ball who couldn't beat a man to save their lives. And that was playing for England. It was an entirely different game. They paralysed us.' Ted and his colleagues found that even a reserve Brazilian goalkeeper could perform outstanding acrobatic ball skills. Having previously dismissed the calibre of Brazilian football as 'a load of rubbish', Ted had to munch through a lot of humble pie. As a manager, Ted looked to recruit the most skilful footballers he could find for all positions.

Ted's team of 1962 was founded upon two strong, experienced full-backs: Bill Cockburn, formerly of Burnley and Gillingham, and Keith Tucker; two tough-tackling but creative wing-halves – Alan 'Spider' Brown, whom Ted successfully converted from an ineffective centre-forward, and

Eddie Stone, once of Crystal Palace and Charlton. Stone had a ferocious shot, too. Ted had a bit of a headache about his centre-half. Having splashed out £1,500 – around £31,000 in today's values – on Southampton's experienced stopper John Page, he found that the overweight Page was not mobile enough for the job and replaced him quickly with the muscular ex-Tunbridge Wells and former Hastings pivot Gerry Boon.

Up front, Ted had an embarrassment of riches. Inside-forward Terry Marshall was his stellar close-season signing. Marshall had signed for Newcastle in December 1958, together with Wisbech Town colleague, goalkeeper Bryan Harvey. Charlie Mitten, the Newcastle boss and ex-Manchester United star, had shelled out £7,000 for Marshall, but, unlike Harvey, Terry did not make the grade, managing just five First Division appearances in three seasons. Those extravagantly talented inside-forwards, George Eastham and Ivor Allchurch, blocked his path. But as Ted Ballard found, Terry could disappear in a scrap. He wasn't very physical. And if his head went down, he couldn't do a thing right. In the pre-substitute years there were no hiding places for under-performers.

Marshall returned to Wisbech in 1961 but found it hard re-adjusting to non-league football, despite helping the 'Fenmen' to the Southern League First Division title in May 1962. But Ballard was alert to Marshall's huge potential and proceeded to build a fluent, predatory attack around his pace, neat touch and eye for goal.

For good measure, Ted recruited Marshall's Wisbech team-mate, the tricky, skilful outside-right Bela Olah, a former Hungarian youth international. Olah had played in Northampton Town's Fourth Division promotion-winning side in 1961 after escaping the Soviet repression of the Hungarian Revolution in 1956.

Ted's other 'ace' was Gordon Burden, a little left-winger with scorching pace and an enormous heart. Burden had played much of his football under Ballard at Ashford Town, having had a brief professional career at Doncaster Rovers.

In reserve, Ted had Alan Back, a former Charlton amateur, who would eventually blossom into one of the most dangerous right-wingers in Southern League football. Like Burden, Back had everything in his locker – speed, skill and devastating finishing power.

The centre-forward slot proved troublesome, though. Ted decided quickly that lanky Alan Brown, a former reserve forward at Brighton, was better employed as a half-back. He turned to ex-Orient, Ramsgate and Tunbridge Wells forward Dai Davies instead. The mobile Davies proved to be a good finisher, once putting three goals past Peter Taylor, Brian Clough's future sidekick, in a 7-1 victory at Burton, but Ted was not entirely satisfied. Eventually, former Hastings fisherman Joe White was chosen for the part. Like Boon, the burly Joe White had previously played for Hastings before Kelly's clearout. He made an early impact, scoring four times in an astonishing 8-1 drubbing of promotion rivals Dover at their Crabble ground.

The inside-left position was passed around also. During Hastings's September cricket festival of 1962, Ted went to the Central Cricket Ground to persuade South African Sussex county cricketer Denis Foreman to take on the role. Foreman had played 211 games for Brighton, scoring 63 goals, but his knees were beginning to trouble him, so his tenure was brief. Trainee accountant and former Orient and Romford inside-forward Clive Lloyd eventually assumed the mantle.

Finally, Ted began the season by selecting Ian Agate as his first-choice goalkeeper. Agate was one of just two players inherited from Ted's predecessor Tim Kelly. Agate had been an FA Youth Cup winner with Chelsea in 1958/59, playing alongside Jimmy Greaves. It was envisaged that the agile but error-prone Agate would play second fiddle to new signing Bob Charles, a former Southampton regular and England youth international. However, Ted decided that 16-stone Charles was overweight and selected Agate ahead of him. This turn of events prompted Charles to up sticks and head for Weymouth. But Ted wasn't entirely happy with Ian Agate. Ian mixed spectacular stops with sloppy mistakes. He was at fault for at least one of the goals in the promotion battle at Tonbridge in November. According to Keith Tucker, Ted questioned Ian after the game, "Are your eyes alright?" Ian seemed to lose the ball in the floodlights. So, Ted brought in Alf Bentley to replace him. Alf was a good keeper – brave and reliable. He'd played at Coventry and Gillingham. Not much got past him. And he made sure his defence was well-organised, too.'

Although Hastings made a slow start to the season, drawing three and losing one of their opening four league games, it was readily apparent that this was a much stronger side than the one before. After their FA Cup elimination by a snappy Maidstone United team, including future Manchester United and England star David Sadler, they thrashed injury-depleted Tunbridge Wells Rangers 8-0. I then witnessed my first Hastings away win at sunny Canterbury on 22 September, thanks to a composed finish from Marshall and a blistering, long-range shot from young wing-half Eddie Stone. Ballard said, 'We are now settling down into a formidable formation and a hard-working side.'

A 3-2 victory over Jackie Milburn's Yiewsley, their third on the bounce, followed a week later. This win enabled Hastings to shoot up to third spot. Having endured two seasons of abject humiliation, I was never without my oxygen mask.

The Yiewsley game gave me my first and last sighting of Jackie Milburn as a player. By then, the former Newcastle and England centre-forward was 38 years old. He was about to become Alf Ramsey's successor as manager of current league champions Ipswich Town, after Ramsey had accepted the England job. On an afternoon of shimmering warmth, Milburn provided possibly the last glimpse of his sublime skill and power. This came late in the first half after Hastings had taken a two-goal lead. Up until that point, Milburn was content to fan measured passes out to either wing as if conducting a leisurely coaching session. Carrying greater weight than in his prime, he jogged into the vacant spaces, awaiting an 'out ball' from his defenders. Undeterred by the quality of the pass, he was able to control the ball instantly, turning away from any challenge with a nonchalant shrug before feeding his more industrious colleagues.

With the half-time break beckoning, he decided upon a different approach. Receiving the ball in the centre circle and with his back to goal, he shaped to play a lateral pass to his right-winger, only to fool his marker by spinning on a sixpence. Immediately, the after-burners were flicked on and we saw a snatch of that explosive acceleration which had terrified defenders during the early 50s. Caught on their heels by Milburn's burst of speed, the Hastings markers were swiftly bypassed. The full-backs were forced to converge but before they could intercept Milburn's run, he let fly from around 20 yards. Making a perfect connection, the ball fizzed goal-wards. Keeper Agate hurled himself to his right but to no avail. The ball evaded his groping palms, flashing just past the apex of the post and crossbar before thwacking against the corrugated back wall of the covered terrace. Those fans who had stood in the path of Milburn's shot took rapid evasive action. Recovering from his sprawling dive, Agate blew out his cheeks in relief while his defenders looked at one another, less in accusation, more in respect of Milburn's power. Standing next to me a grizzled older man peeled back a smile. With a knowing flick of his balding head, he remarked in a strangely lilting accent, "WOR" Jackie, eh!'

Milburn's sudden elevation to top-flight management was not a success, though. Ramsey had not pruned his ageing Ipswich team. There was no youth policy and no effective scouting network. Milburn had to rebuild from scratch. He was forced to sell Crawford – his only regular goalscorer – to finance essential replacements. Crawford recalled, 'Jackie was a wonderful man, but as a manager he didn't have a clue. Whereas Alf knew what he wanted. He got the players to play in a certain way. If you didn't do what he wanted, you would not play.' Like Icarus, Ipswich burnt out.

By mid-November, Hastings were behind leaders Margate, only on goal average. Their next opponents were third-placed Tonbridge, then managed by 'happy' Harry Haslam, Tresadern's assistant at Hastings during the mid-50s. In his playing days, just after the war, Haslam had been a full-back with Rochdale, Oldham, Brighton and Orient. After Tresadern had left the Pilot Field, he followed him to Tonbridge, taking over as manager following Tresadern's death. Haslam had previous experience of football management with amateur side Eastbourne United.

At Tonbridge, Haslam recruited several players with substantial Football League experience. The side he selected for the Hastings game included Republic of Ireland international full-back Joe Carolan, formerly with Brighton; ex-Burnley, Leeds and Everton centre-forward Alan Shackleton; and black South African winger Gerry Francis, once with Leeds and York City. All three had played recently in the top flight. Like Ted Ballard, Haslam had a knack of finding misplaced gems. During the late 60s he discovered a highly promising teenage full-back named Malcolm Macdonald, although it was Bobby Robson, as Fulham's temporary manager, who converted the youngster into a powerful centre-forward.

Haslam was prepared to search far and wide for untapped talent. While he was manager of Sheffield United, during the late 70s, he capitalised upon the networks he formed in South America by bringing the gifted Argentinean midfielder Alex Sabella to Bramall Lane for a bargain fee of £160,000. The young playmaker oozed class. Haslam sold him to Leeds in 1980 for £400,000, around £40 million today. Haslam's Argentinean connections enabled Keith Burkinshaw to sign Ossie Ardiles and Ricky Villa for Spurs, after the 1978 World Cup. It was rumoured that Haslam had been offered 17-year-old Diego Maradona when pursuing Sabella but could not afford the £200,000 asking price. How near Sheffield had been to the 'hand of God'! Although Haslam's spell at Sheffield United ended unhappily, he had shown at Luton how well he could manage on a shoestring budget, guiding the cash-strapped 'Hatters' to Division One in 1974, and narrowly failing to keep them there a year later. Harry Haslam was a formidable opponent.

17 November 1962 was a grey, greasy, grimy day. Chris Montez's 'Let's Dance' was playing on repeat inside my head. It powered my strides to the station. It fired the throbbing diesel as it lurched around the wet, wooded curves to Tonbridge. It suppressed the anodyne music on the Angel Ground's PA. It became buried in the pulsating rhythms of the game I had travelled to watch. I need no photographic record. 'Let's Dance' illuminates this drizzle-shrouded day forever.

The game was a cracker, played in front of a condensed, excitable crowd of 2,000 plus. After 16 minutes Hastings were ahead. Centre-forward Dai Davies set up Terry Marshall, who shook off two Tonbridge defenders and slid the ball so coolly past Fred Crump, the advancing keeper. It was as if Terry had become Jimmy Greaves. Ken Ballard recalled, 'Terry had so much talent. But his head dropped when things weren't going well. Then, Dad used to yell at us, "For God's sake don't give him the ball!" But this was Marshall's tenth goal of the season. He was playing with self-assurance, showcasing the ability that had once attracted Charlie Mitten at Newcastle. Clustered on the stacked railway sleepers, the Tonbridge supporters were not disheartened. They poured encouragement into the ear of their quick, compact left-winger, Johnny Dennis. 'C'mon Johnny, you can roast this guy. He's useless,' gesticulating at Bill Cockburn, our craggy right-back. Actually, Bill was Johnny's master, adroitly anticipating the winger's crude push and run stratagem, whereas on the opposite flank Keith Tucker was having a tougher challenge containing the sinuous swerves and nimble footwork of Gerry Francis. But according to Ted Ballard, 'Keith played Francis beautifully' that afternoon. Just before half-time Tonbridge equalised. The goal was a gift. Ian

Agate misjudged Francis's swirling cross, spilling the ball at the feet of Alan Shackleton. Tall, wiry 'Shack' didn't spurn an opportunity as simple as this, promptly side-footing the ball into an empty net.

After the break I was treated to a 'master class' of left-wing play. If Johnny Dennis was the great pretender, Gordon Burden was the real deal. Gordon may have been small, but he was tough, skilful and exceedingly fast. Time after time he whizzed past Joe Carolan, his distinguished marker, as if Joe did not exist. Gordon was simply uncontainable. In the ensuing months I honoured this memory by drawing stubby left-wingers belting around the margins of my school exercise books.

Ken Ballard recalled, 'Dad knew what havoc Gordon could cause. His attacking tactics were quite simple, "Get the ball and give it to Gordon."' With 20 minutes left, Dai Davies did just that. Burden streaked along the left flank leaving a succession of dumbfounded defenders in his spattering wake. Anticipating Marshall's speed, he fired a fast, low, fizzing centre across the Tonbridge goalmouth. Marshall latched on to it in a flash, haring into position and rifling a ferocious first-time drive past the statuesque Crump. His skidding shot was so fierce that the ball rebounded from the board behind the goal and flashed back into play, fooling many into believing the post had been struck. But the referee put us right, immediately pointing towards the centre circle. This was finishing power of the highest order. Amazingly, I was watching this quality display from the club derided as 'hopeless' Hastings.

Harry Haslam was an easy-going, jocular character but his teams were always strongly competitive. His class of '62 was no different. Increasing pressure was applied to the Hastings goal. Fortunately, Tonbridge's finishing was less competent than their approach work. With just a few minutes remaining, though, Hastings were undone by Ronnie White's star turn. Hastings captain Keith Tucker recalled, 'I knew Ronnie at Charlton. He had bags of skill. One minute he was playing on the Hackney Marshes, the next he was playing for Charlton in Division One. It was incredible. He could do fantastic things with a ball.'

Ronnie was positioned around 20 yards from goal and hemmed in but somehow created a slither of space in which to chip the ball over keeper Agate. I still replay that goal in my head, although its execution is becoming slower with age. The ball arcs lazily over the heads of our defenders. Agate's upward leap is silhouetted against the pallid glow of the floodlights. The ball eludes him, dropping gently just below the bar and into the net. There is a momentary stillness both on the makeshift terracing and in the upper tier of the ancient pavilion. Then, in a snap second jubilation explodes, with the Tonbridge fans around me leaping, screaming and waving their arms in the air. I am left motionless with disappointment in the eye of this storm. I had to concede, though, that it was a worthy end to a terrific game.

Almost 60 years have passed since that day. Upon emerging from Tonbridge station, the London–Hastings train passes the site of the old Angel Ground. But the only connection with the past is the name of the shopping complex – the Angel Centre – which stands where the ramshackle ground once was. The adjacent sidings have become a car park. The steam locomotive shed now houses track maintenance stock. The throaty roar of the diesel has been superseded by the smooth, quiet acceleration of the electric train. Perhaps there are now less than 100 people who can recall this compelling contest. Soon all memories will be erased. The only remains of that game will be a dog-eared programme or two and a rarely examined press archive in the local library. That is the fate of parochial passions.

With neither side having further FA Cup commitments, Ted Ballard invited his friend and former 'Saints' team-mate George Curtis to bring his senior Brighton team to Hastings for a friendly on the following Saturday. Although Brighton had fallen upon hard times, I expected their first team to be too strong for my resurgent side. Not so. Apart from a combative display from their left-half, Bill Cassidy, sluggish Brighton were beaten comprehensively. Gordon Burden murdered the Brighton right-back Sid Jest, setting up a host of chances for his colleagues. Reserve right-winger Alan Back scored a brace in the opening half hour, the first coming in under a minute. Hastings's superiority was much greater than the 2-0 result suggested.

However, just two days later reality bared its teeth. Hastings were paired with Premier Division Chelmsford City in a second-round Southern League Cup game. Expensively assembled City used this home tie to celebrate the turning on of their new floodlights. And they made sure that nothing would spoil their party. Hastings were thrashed 5-1. All the Chelmsford first-team players were full-timers. Up front they had Tony Nicholas, formerly of Brighton and Chelsea, on £28 per week – more than he earned at Brighton – and Bobby Mason, the former Wolves star, on £35 per week. These two were two or three times better off than anyone in Ballard's side.

Ambitious Chelmsford proved far too strong. They had greater skill, with Mason pulling the strings at inside-forward, threading a succession of exquisite passes through Hastings's back line for Nicholas and others to exploit. Collectively, City had greater pace, too, although Burden caused the home defence some discomfort. More significantly, City had greater stamina, a product of their full-time status. Chelmsford's fourth and fifth goals came late in the game when Hastings were running out of puff, having spent 80 minutes doggedly chasing their opponents. If Hastings had any pretensions of reaching the Football League, this was the daunting standard they would have to meet. Saturday's victory over Brighton now seemed pyrrhic. However, Ted Ballard soon had his lads geed up again. Five league victories followed with 22 goals scored. It seemed that Hastings were on course to seize the Southern League First Division title. Life was sweet. Then on Boxing Day 1962 a savage blizzard swept across Britain. The town slipped and slid under the weight of successive snowfalls. Ash, cinders and brown salt pocked the treacherous ice sheets, but the wan winter sun could not loosen the icy grip. From late December until March, Hastings United, like 10CC's cold lasagne, was 'suspended in deep freeze'.

Brighton & Hove Albion v Halifax Town

Football League Division Three, 2 February 1963

'Please Please Me'

GEORGE CURTIS'S Brighton began life brightly back in Division Three, reaching third position before the end of August. It was a false dawn, though. By the end of November they were in the drop zone.

Following Albion's demotion, George Curtis had rung the changes. Out went full-backs Joe Carolan to Tonbridge and Bob McNicol to Gravesend; midfielders Alan Brown to Hastings and Tony Sitford to Gravesend; forwards Tony Nicholas to Chelmsford, Ian McNeill to Southend, Bobby Laverick to Coventry, Mike Tiddy to Penzance and Joe Caven to Raith Rovers.

These players had cost the club over £50,000 in transfer fees, yet almost nothing was recouped from their departures. More worryingly, Brighton were developing few of their own players. Only wing-half Robin 'Nobby' Upton and goalkeeper Brian Powney had emerged as promising home-grown talent, although young centre-half Norman Gall, brought in from

Gateshead, seemed a good prospect. Once again cash-strapped Brighton were forced to spend.

George Curtis recruited goalkeeper Bert McGonigal from Glentoran; Jimmy Collins, a Scottish inside-forward, from Spurs at a cost of £8,000; Bill Cassidy, a Scottish wing-half, from Rotherham for £6,000; Peter Donnelly, an inside-forward, from Swansea for £6,000; plus both Jim Cooper, an outside-left, and William Bailey, a centre-forward from Airdrie. The new recruits lined up alongside surviving regulars Bobby Baxter at left-back; Jack Bertolini, Roy Jennings and Steve Burtenshaw, the well-established half-back line; and Johnny Goodchild up front. Despite shelling out £20,000 on new signings – probably collectively worth around £20m today – Curtis was unable to improve Brighton's performances.

Embarrassingly, Brighton were dismissed from the League Cup by a visiting Portsmouth side largely comprising reserves. Despite winning 5-1, Portsmouth received a £50 Football League fine for fielding an under-strength team! A shocking 2-4 home loss to Reading followed on 6 October. Reading were one of the worst travellers in the division, yet they were far too good for the Albion. This defeat dumped Brighton into bottom spot. With many Brighton fans losing patience with Curtis, only 6,556 turned up for the Albion's 1-0 win over Carlisle three days later. Even an unexpected 5-1 win at Bradford Park Avenue in early December failed to allay supporters' concerns about George Curtis's management. But while chairman Gerald Paling remained in charge, Curtis enjoyed a stay of execution. After all, Curtis had been Paling's appointment. Instead of being shown the door, Curtis was given more money to spend on new players. In came Orient's versatile forward George Waites and Bury's inside-forward Alan Jackson, a former understudy to Jimmy Murray at Wolves. Jackson was a devout Christian who objected to playing on Good Friday. Swansea's tough-tackling right-back Alan Sanders was added to the squad, too, for a £6,000 fee. But with the disgruntled fans exerting mounting pressure on the Brighton board, Paling's days were numbered. So were George Curtis's.

Curtis received his cards on 1 February 1963. A dismal 0-0 home draw with Southend in the Goldstone snow was the final straw. Gerald Paling and senior director Cyril Clarke departed, leaving directors Eric Courtney-King and the wealthy Harold Paris in charge. They would eventually provide the investment needed to reverse the Albion's calamitous decline.

After Curtis departed from Brighton, trainer Joe Wilson took temporary charge until Archie Macaulay was appointed in April. His first game in charge was on 2 February against fellow strugglers Halifax Town. The Goldstone surface was still covered with snow and treacherous underfoot. With the nation starved of football on account of the prolonged freeze, the BBC screened extensive 'highlights' of the game in its Saturday evening *Sports Special* programme. I remember the occasion well. The game was a farce. None of the players could keep their feet, save one, Halifax's keeper Peter Downsborough, who was magnificent, producing a succession of jaw-dropping stops to deny Brighton. With the surface uneven and unreliable, there was no point in attempting a passing game. 'The big boot' was the order of this frozen day. Roy Jennings spent more time in his opponents' box than in his own, as he endeavoured to capitalise on the long, lofted balls pumped into the Halifax area. While finding the target on several occasions, Downsborough was always in the right place to frustrate him. Jennings's exasperation was magnified when Halifax broke away to grab the only goal of the game. It was Halifax's solitary chance in the game, and their only victory on the road that season. Six years after his indomitable snowman display, Downsborough produced another heroic performance for Swindon at muddy Wembley, in the 1969 League Cup Final against Arsenal. He grabbed the chance with both hands as the Robins completed one of the most momentous giant-killing feats in 20th-century football, winning 3-1 after extra time.

George Curtis's period as manager at Brighton was an unmitigated disaster. Of the 74 league games he was in charge, less than a quarter were won. He had greater success subsequently in Norway, guiding Rosenborg to the Premiership title in the late 60s. But even here the fans complained about his sterile, defensive tactics. He was less successful, though, as Norway's national coach. As several Brighton players confirmed, George Curtis was at his best in a coaching capacity. Former Arsenal and Scotland keeper Bob Wilson had a very high opinion of him, saying, 'George had a wonderful manner and fantastic knowledge. He was a truly outstanding coach and a real gentleman.' George continued to coach youngsters until dementia blighted his later years.

George Curtis, Ted Ballard and Alf Ramsey were awestruck by the quality of Brazilian football in 1948. But what they took from this chastening experience was quite different. While Alf Ramsey sought to neutralise gifted players, George Curtis sought to improve them, borrowing ideas from the Brazilians such as head-tennis and throw-in routines. However, George proved less capable than his two colleagues in converting this intelligence into winning football. Although Ted did not share Alf's distrust of flair players, endeavouring to produce entertaining teams, he could only utilise his managerial abilities at a non-league level.

Arguably, George Curtis's most important contribution to Brighton's later revival was his signings of Spurs inside-forward Jimmy Collins for a song, and versatile Bill Cassidy from Rotherham, another bargain acquisition. Both men played a crucial role in Brighton's promotion from the Fourth Division under Archie Macaulay.

Jimmy Collins recalled, 'George was a bit of a flash character and that's why I liked him. When we met to discuss the move, he rolled up a copy of the *Daily Mirror* and showed me how one of the Hungarian stars of the time, Hidegkuti, did a trick. That convinced me to come.' But once he had signed, Jimmy realised what a mess the club was in. Discipline was poor and player relationships seemed strained. On his own admission, Jimmy did not help on either score. He told Brighton *Evening Argus* reporter John Vinicombe, in 2001, 'Some of the players were dreadful and I made myself unpopular by letting them know that. They had some good ones, of course, like Roy Jennings and Jack Bertolini, but I found the style in which the team played such a contrast to the fluid passing and movement they played at Spurs. Albion just hoofed the ball and chased it a bit like Wimbledon. It upset me.'

Jimmy confessed he even had a punch up with some team-mates. There was an early set-to with Scottish winger Jimmy Cooper. Jimmy explained, 'The fights occurred during five-a-sides. I had a bit of a temper. I was a bit of a miserable little so and so. I was always moaning and snapping at my team-mates on the field and was probably made captain because I had the biggest mouth. I was anti-establishment, a rebel. I regret being like that. It's not nice to make yourself unpopular and it meant I didn't enjoy my football like I should have done. I've now become more tolerant.' Jimmy enjoyed a drink, too. He said, 'I was keen on off-the-field action. I sought out the nearest pub. I had, as I've said, a bad attitude.'

Temporary manager Joe Wilson was given rare cause for cheer after a 5-4 victory at Reading on 23 February. Although Reading were 2-1 up at the break, Brighton fought back strongly, with inside-forward Alan Jackson and centre-half Roy Jennings scoring a brace apiece. Even defender Steve Burtenshaw chipped in with a rare strike. Not only had the country frozen over, so had hell, it seemed.

Joe Wilson's permanent replacement was Archie Macaulay. Macaulay had considerable success at Third Division Norwich, steering them to an FA Cup semi-final in 1959, and then to promotion a year later. In October 1961 he was appointed as manager at West Bromwich with a substantial wage increase. Macaulay struggled, though. In his first season in charge, only a late five-match run of victories rescued the Baggies from trouble. His second season was the club's worst in eight years. With the Hawthorns' average gate dropping by 4,500 – a massive fall of 20 per cent – Macaulay left the club in April 1963, to be replaced by ex-Sheffield United star and Peterborough manager Jimmy Hagan.

Archie was a tougher character than George. He had no qualms about laying down the law. Several Brighton players had run-ins with him. Even with better discipline in place, Macaulay had little time to turn around Brighton's fortunes, having arrived just before Easter 1963. His first signing was Keith Webber, a Welsh 20-year-old reserve striker at Everton, who cost £7,000.

Macaulay's first game in charge gave cause for hope – a 1-0 win at highly placed Notts County. But it was a false dawn. A week later, on Good Friday, free-scoring Northampton Town came to the Goldstone Ground and crushed Brighton 5-0. Successive defeats by Bournemouth and by Northampton in the return fixture left the club 'hanging on a prayer'. Albion won just once in their last eight games. Their victims were Bradford Park Avenue, whom they had thrashed at Park Avenue in December. The Yorkshire side followed Brighton through the trap door.

The 3,000 reduction in Brighton's average gate also worried their new board of directors. This meant that the average Goldstone crowd had dropped by more than half since the Albion's first season in Division Two in 1958/59. Moreover, a further £30,000 had been paid out in transfer fees during this vexed season of ice, snow and postponements, which concluded with a 25 per cent loss in revenue and further relegation. Put together, the club had paid out around £100,000 in transfer fees since the 1958/59 season. Very little of that expenditure had been recouped in transfer receipts. And the club was two divisions worse off.

Hastings United v Hinckley Athletic

Southern League Division One, 9 March 1963

'Rhythm of the Rain'

A MAJOR topic of discussion during the 1962/63 English Football League season was 'blanket defence'. Respected football journalist Ivan Sharpe commented in the *News of the World Football Annual 1963/64*, 'Perhaps it was because defensive tactics played a prominent part in the 1962 World Cup. This may have been the reason why English football developed this bugbear and menace last season. Perhaps it was because English league and cup honours have become so important. Whatever the cause, the trend is regrettable, especially as this dulling effect on the game as a spectacle arrived at an inopportune time. The sponsors of Manchester City's five half-backs formation denied that this was primarily a defensive system, but improved attack, was not discernible in their team's performance. Such a system might prove attractive if the right players were available – mobile, nippy, versatile; able to advance or retire as the flow of the game demanded, players who have had experience at both forward and half-back. But this essential element was not there when I watched the City.' City manager McDowall played a 3-5-2 formation, with the five midfielders employed primarily as a defensive shield for three at the back. It was hardly a success. One hundred and two goals were conceded by Manchester City during the 1962/63 season, with West Ham administering six of the worst in both games, and Wolves thrashing them 8-1 at Molineux.

Leicester had some success with their defensive tactics, although it won them few friends. When the Foxes shut up shop, having taken the lead against Liverpool in an FA Cup semi-final, the press were highly critical. One paper described this tactic as 'Leicester City's cul-de-sac'. Another derided it as 'a 10-1 system as sound as a castle dungeon'. Defeated Liverpool manager Bill Shankly carped, 'This can never be football. It is bad for the game and the best way of emptying the terraces.' Leicester manager Matt Gillies shrugged off the criticism, maintaining, 'We have players, not forwards or defenders.' But having secured a Wembley place, he promised, 'You have my assurance that Leicester will show just what we can do in the final.' He needn't have bothered. Manchester United's attacking prowess made his pledge irrelevant.

The Potteries pair, Stoke City and Port Vale, were criticised, too, for their defensiveness. Nottingham Forest had their detractors, as well, including many of their own supporters. Forest fans took exception to manager Andy Beattie selecting an extra centre-half, Peter Hindley, instead of a centre-forward.

My first acquaintance with the new defensiveness was when Hinckley Athletic visited Hastings United in March 1963. Hinckley was a hosiery manufacturing town with a population of no more than 40,000. Its football team suffered, being squeezed between nearby Leicester, Coventry and Birmingham. It rarely attracted more than a few hundred supporters to its home games.

During the 1962/63 season, the tiny club was managed by Dudley Kernick, a former Birmingham City and Torquay player, and a qualified FA coach. Like Ted Ballard, Kernick knew how to bring the best out of a small squad of players. Assembling a number of cast-offs from local league sides,

Kernick turned his little club into unlikely promotion contenders. He made them hard to beat, reducing the number of goals they conceded by a half. He was helped by having a vastly experienced captain in Peter Aldis. Aldis had played 262 times for Aston Villa, starring in their controversial FA Cup victory over Manchester United in 1957. He had been well regarded by Villa boss Joe Mercer. Aldis had the distinction, too, of scoring with a 35-yard header. This was a world record until 2009. It was Aldis's only goal in competitive football. More importantly, Kernick could rely upon Aldis to organise a tight defence.

Saturday 9 March 1963 dawned stormy and sopping. Having been frustrated by the Arctic occupation for over two months, an accumulation of Atlantic fronts made up for lost time. Congregating impatiently at the Western Approaches, they roared in one after another, flooding the thawing land and leaving oozing sludge where the crumpling snow had previously lain. Hastings United's Pilot Field pitch was turned into a hissing quagmire before the game began.

From my untutored perspective, Hinckley's strategy seemed timid. Whenever Hastings gained possession, eight or more of their players clustered behind the ball. Hastings mounted attack after attack, only to find their route to goal barred by a double rank of defenders. With Hinckley's defensive tactics drawing Hastings forward, the visitors found gaps to exploit on the break. *The Hastings & St Leonards Observer* reported, 'Before the interval the visitors scored twice, although Hastings's goalkeeper Agate was at fault for their first, being caught in no-man's land as Mellor nodded in. Hinckley centre-half Aston then extended his side's lead by heading in from a poorly defended corner.'

And yet it seemed inexplicable that Hastings should be two goals down at half-time having had so much of the ball. Failing to recognise what I had seen, I put this down to bad luck. Yet despite the slithering conditions, the sheeting rain and buffeting wind, I thought the game could still be saved.

I was wrong. Hastings pressed forward and even managed to pull one goal back. But Hinckley were calm and skilful in defence, never resorting to aimless clearances. As soon as they won possession, their alert forwards scampered off, ready to plunder the gaps in Hastings's back line. While Hastings attempted to play through their midfield, with their players dragging their tiring legs over the churned, glistening surface, Hinckley let the ball do the work, employing the most direct approach to goal. However, they were indebted to another Agate error in restoring their two-goal lead. Ex-Wolves forward Stan Round scored Hinckley's third after Agate had dropped the greasy ball. Round wore the number-11 shirt and yet he appeared to be the Hinckley centre-forward. In fact, several Hinckley players occupied positions at odds with their shirt numbers. I was bewildered. I had yet to see Cassius Clay's demolition of the colossus Sonny Liston. I was still under the misapprehension that all-out defence signalled impending defeat. I was at the base of a new learning curve.

Despite losing again on another claggy surface at Cheltenham on 14 March, Hastings then excelled with a 7-1 victory at Burton Albion, with recalled centre-forward Dai Davis recording a hat-trick and Terry Marshall snatching a brace. Burton's beleaguered goalkeeper was Peter Taylor, once of Middlesbrough, later becoming Brian Clough's partner in their glory days at Derby and Nottingham Forest. He would also manage Brighton during the mid-70s.

Subsequent wins against Canterbury (4-0), Tunbridge Wells (3-0), Folkestone (1-0), Sittingbourne (3-1), Ashford (3-1) and Barry (3-1) kept Hastings well on track, while their crucial triumphs over promotion rivals Tonbridge (1-0), Hinckley (1-0) and Nuneaton (3-0) took them to the top of the table at the end of April. Nevertheless, unexpected setbacks at Ramsgate (0-2), Kings Lynn (0-1) and Corby (0-1) not only toppled them from pole position, they threatened to wreck their promotion prospects. Hastings's season hinged on the result of Dover's final game at Nuneaton. Thankfully, Dover did not win, meaning that Hastings squeezed into the fourth promotion slot on goal difference. After enduring so much failure, success was difficult to take in.

Gus Hunneman was Hastings United's mascot for many years. He seemed a good, kindly man. As another Hastings fan aptly observed, bearded, bow-tied Gus looked like Colonel Sanders of KFC. Before most home games, he ran on to the pitch adorned in a claret-and-blue jacket and a top hat. He carried a bell and a claret-and-blue cane. His pre-match ritual comprised tapping the posts and the crossbars with his cane and then blessing both penalty spots with his bell, which he rang lustily while he ran from one end of the pitch to the other. I have no problem with naked superstition. After all, I fed sizeable proportions of my limited pocket money into the church collection in the hope of persuading God to grant better results. Behaviourists reckon that compliance is best achieved through irregular gratification. God knows this, too, as do gambling addicts. Anyway, I was prepared to subscribe to this mercenary piety while there was hope. Gus, on the other hand, was a hex, pure and simple. He annihilated hope. For two years I had watched him perform his ridiculous pre-match ritual, glumly recognising that it signified certain defeat. He was devaluing my divine investments. That's why I began arriving bang on kick-off, demanding that my friends conceal from me whether he had been seen.

Bobby Smith at Victoria Station on 14 May 1964 on the way to Brighton to sign for the Albion. Although an instant success, he fell out with Archie Macaulay, leading to his move to Hastings United.

Manager, Archie Macaulay, shown here holding 'Scampi', rejuvenated Brighton after successive relegations. In his second season in charge, Brighton were promoted as Fourth Division champions.

The Albion's promotion party on 26 April 1965. Back row from the left: Collins, Gall, Jack Smith, Cassidy, Turner, Goodchild, Burtenshaw. Front row: Bobby Smith (with bottle) Gould, Hopkins, Powney, director & film comedian, Norman Wisdom, Bertolini, Baxter. Macaulay is in a dark coat. (photo: Brighton & Hove Albion)

Hastings United's squad for the 1964/65 season was too small to compete in the Southern and Kent Floodlight leagues. Wage cuts, injuries and impetuous dismissals made the situation worse. By spring 1965, many of the players seemed burnt out. The drop appeared inevitable.

James Humphreys, Hastings United's highly controversial director and chairman 1965–68.

Player/manager, Sid Bishop (5) repelling an Ashford Town attack in August 1965. Hastings won 2-0. (photo by kind permission of the Hastings & St Leonards Observer).

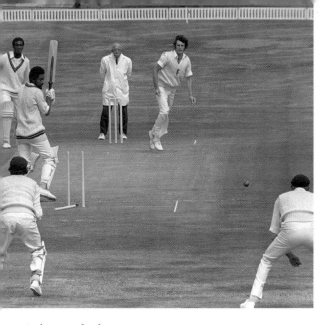

Sussex and England fast bowler, John Snow clean bowling Michael Holding at Headingley in 1976. Snow decimated 'the Windies' at Hove in June 1966, taking 7-29 on day one. Snow and Tony Buss shared eight wickets on the second day, dismissing the tourists for 67 in a nine wicket victory.

In his comeback innings against Kent, at Hastings in July 1968, Ted Dexter smote a double century. It was a fitting farewell for him and for me also, as I was soon to leave Sussex, never to live here again.

My farewell shot of Hastings pier. For most of my youth it reflected a thriving seaside resort. Leaner times lay ahead, though, for the town, its pier and its premier football club. (author's collection)

Kit Napier (left) and Willie Irvine. Kit and Willie established a strong partnership up front, helping Albion win promotion to Division Two in 1972 (photos: Brighton & Hove Albion & Willie Irvine)

Promotion-winning Brighton and Hove Albion in 1971/72. From left to right; Back Row: Goodwin, Irvine, Piper, Powney, Dovey, Templeman, Sheridan, Kit Napier Middle: Saward (manager), Gall, Spearritt, John Napier, Turner, Duffy, Murray Front: Henderson, Stanley, Boorn, O'Sullivan.

*Brighton's promotion-winning side of 1978/79.
Alan Mullery is far right (middle row) and
chairman Mike Bamber, in a red shirt, is in the
middle of the front row with captain & leading
goalscorer, Brian Horton on his right. Mark
Lawrenson is two along from Mullery. (photo:
Brighton & Hove Albion)*

*Peter Ward was an ex-Rolls
Royce apprentice who became a
Brighton 'hot shot' scoring 79
goals in 178 games.*

*Burly Peter Sillett helps his goalie, Bill Robertson, thwart Wolves's Jackie
Henderson at 'The Bridge' in August 1958. Then aged nine years, this was my first
top flight game. With Jimmy Greaves scoring five goals in a stirring 6-2 victory, it
was a day I would never forget.*

Mushtaq Ahmed takes the final Worcestershire wicket, enabling Sussex to win by an innings and 14 runs and claim their third County Championship trophy in five years.

Sussex captain Chris Adams celebrates with team-mate Mushtaq Ahmed after winning the 2007 County Championship. Mushtaq was the competition's leading wicket-taker with 90 wickets.

The Amex stadium pays tribute to two of Albion's highly respected, former players.

The Sussex County Cricket Ground, Hove. It's still my haven of peace.

Why I am blessed to have grown up in Sussex by the sea. (photo by Brendan Rumbold)

A winter sunset over Pevensey Bay, taken from St Leonards-on-Sea's promenade. An appropriate image, perhaps, with which to end this nostalgic journey. (author's collection)

Sussex CCC v Worcestershire CCC

Gillette Cup Final Lord's, 7 September 1963

'It's All in the Game'

THE YEAR 1963 also saw the birth of the Gillette one-day tournament after a prolonged six-year gestation. The tournament represented the first major stage in the commercialisation of English cricket which would ultimately challenge the authority of its traditional administrators in determining the game's destiny. The one-day competition of 1963 began on a wet day at Manchester in early May, almost unnoticed. It ended with the cup final at Lord's on 7 September in front of a 20,000 crowd, including partisan followers of Sussex and Worcestershire, sporting favours. The Sussex banners had Dexter's photograph at its centre, while the green Worcestershire banners had the inscription 'Worcester for the Cup'. It was a scene quite unparalleled at Lord's. It confounded the sceptics who derided or dismissed one-day cricket as 'frivolous', 'not a true test of skill', or a travesty of 'the noble game'. As the various rounds were played during a summer uncommonly blessed with fine weather, captains became progressively astute in their selection of the tactics required for victory. Indeed, the one-day game demanded greater tactical acumen than the three-day version.

There was no way a three-day game would have proceeded in the gloomy conditions which prevailed on Cup Final day, though, but with both captains fully aware of what was at stake, with thousands turning up from the west midlands and south coast, they were prepared to forgo normal rules. The final was certainly not a 'crash, bang, wallop' affair. It was a cagey contest throughout, more attritional than adventurous. Sussex managed 168 from their 60 overs, while Worcestershire scraped together 14 less. But the game was never less than absorbing. After Hastings's promotion and Sussex's success, I felt bountifully blessed in 1963.

Ted Dexter's Sussex won this trophy in successive years, not just because of Dexter's and Parks's batting brilliance, but because of their abundance of proficient seam bowlers in Ian Thomson, Don Bates, Tony Buss, John Snow and Dexter himself. Collectively, they were capable of bowling consistent, tight, back of a length seam-up to defensive fields. Not that Dexter was without misgivings at his side's success, warning that if the one-day game flourished, the stereotyped medium-pace bowler would prevail at the expense of the spinner, signalling the disappearance of slow bowling in the English first-class game. Ironically, then, Worcestershire left-arm spinner Norman Gifford bowled superbly in the inaugural final, but in a flat, containing style that any medium-pacer would have been proud of. And for his impressive efforts in a losing cause, Gifford was deservedly awarded 'Man of the Match'. I must add that given the stuffiness of cricket administration during the preceding years, I never thought I would see an English county captain holding a winning trophy aloft in front of a baying crowd as if this was Wembley not Lord's. If there was any doubt, then, that cricket belonged as much to the innovators as to the traditionalists, the entrepreneurial Australian tycoon Kerry Packer would tip that balance decisively in favour of the former within the next decade.

1963 A Year of Living Pruriently

'Louie Louie'

PHILIP LARKIN'S sardonic take on the Profumo Affair started with the whimsical reflection that it was then when sexual intercourse began, arriving between the ban of DH Lawrence's novel *Lady Chatterley's Lover* and the Beatles' first album. Although embattled Prime Minister Harold Macmillan insisted, 'I was determined that no British government should be brought down by the action of two tarts,' he was forced to resign a few months later due to ill health. The satirical magazine *Private Eye* had a field day mocking the Tory slogan 'Life's better under a Conservative' and spoofing Macmillan's 1957 boast with, 'We Have Never Had It So Often'.

The Profumo Affair was first and foremost a political scandal. John Profumo, the Conservative Secretary of State for War, had an affair with Christine Keeler, a young woman who was said to have had an intimate relationship with a Soviet naval attaché, Captain Ivanov. Profumo attempted to conceal this security risk by lying to Parliament about the affair, denying he had compromised British security. However, it was the affair's salacious details which absorbed most people. These exposures were carried each week in the *News of the World* and *The People*. As a pubescent boy in a hot house, single sex school it was a joy to pore over their prurient revelations.

It was difficult to imagine the two young women involved, Mandy Rice-Davies and Christine Keeler, being anything other than sexually alluring. So, when Millicent Martin, the TW3 chanteuse, parodied 'People' from *Funny Girl* singing 'People who read *The People* are the muckiest people in the world,' Dad was so offended he immediately cancelled both papers. Thanks a lot TW3!

With John Profumo forced to resign from his cabinet post, the morally discredited Tories were figures of fun. Despite Alec Douglas-Home's best efforts, electoral defeat beckoned. Contrasted with Harold Wilson's implied promise of a 'white heat' technological revolution, Douglas-Home's grouse moor tweeds seemed musty and bygone. The spectacular summer event, though, was the West Indian cricket tour.

Their series victory showcased brilliant, vibrant, black Caribbean talent to a nation still consumed with racial bigotry. The supremely lithe Sobers epitomised grace and power; Kanhai melded stridency with style; Butcher boasted brawny belligerence; Gibbs exhibited guile and potency; and Hall and Griffith possessed fearsome strength and speed. Their collective efforts refuted black inferiority and deference. And how the *Windrush* generation rejoiced.

Frank Worrell was the man of the series. He lifted his team and the Caribbean diaspora above divisive inter-island rivalries, conferring an esteemed identity that they could all share – essentially a West Indian one. And yet his charisma was not expressed in pumped-up gestures or eloquent oratory. He used words sparingly, often contenting himself with a smile or a frown, a nod or shaking of the head, deporting himself with languid calm and genial confidence. His authority was unquestioned. He restored stability to an historically fragmented team. Whereas the English selectors chopped and changed their team ruinously, ten members of Worrell's side played in all five Tests.

By the summer of 1963, shrieking Beatlemania had swamped Britain, but there were young detractors, too.

Swimming doggedly against a tsunami of popular acclaim, a friend of mine was unconvinced by the Beatles' 'tinny love songs', preferring the reverberating twangs of US surf guitars and feral garage rock. He abhorred 'She Loves You', paying homage instead to The Trashmen's frenzied 'Surfin' Bird' and Link Wray's resonant 'Rumble'. But it was The Kingsmen's 'Louie, Louie' that bowled him over, describing it as 'a superb celebration of gutter glory'. The song's insinuating organ phrase grabs you instantly, but it is the clattering drumbeat, the chopping guitar and the rasping vocals that announce a rawer, rabid sound. From Elvis Presley to Public Enemy, rock music has often been castigated as subversive. The FBI even investigated supposedly corrupting lyrics of 'Louie Louie'. It not only presaged the Kinks' abrasive debut but the anarchic overdrive of hell-raisers MC5 and The Stooges, as well as pioneering punk sensibilities for the 70s and beyond.

Hastings United v Chelmsford City

Southern League Premier Division, 26 December 1963

'Glad All Over'

HASTINGS STARTED uncertainly in the higher division. A 1-1 draw at Hereford seemed a satisfactory result given the wealth of international experience in the home side, but Hereford soon found that illustrious reputations are no guarantee of success. Relegation awaited them in May. The U's first home game against Bexley United was a rugged, feisty affair that left the battered and bruised home side grateful for a 2-2 draw. Four days later, on a serene summer evening, visiting Bedford Town raced into a three-goal lead before half-time. Although Marshall's sizzling drive enabled Hastings to pull one back, Bedford deservedly won.

Despite an improved display against visiting Wisbech, it was not good enough to prevent the Fenmen from claiming their customary victory (1-3). Depressingly, this seemed to be a reprise of 1960/61. But a pair of brilliant goals from Marshall and winger Back at Bexley revived our flagging spirits, only for a crushing 2-5 FA Cup defeat by arch-rivals Tonbridge to dampen them once again. The star of the show was hat-trick hero Gerry Francis, who performed magnificently, turning Keith Tucker, Hastings's experienced left-back, inside out.

A workmalike victory at Dartford followed, but a feeble 0-2 loss at Rugby was a missed opportunity. Nevertheless, Hastings did well to hold would-be champions Yeovil to a 1-1 draw on 5 October. Their poor home form was beginning to impact on gate numbers, though. The attendance for the Yeovil game was 1,880; 800 less than the 2,658 at the Bedford match. A 0-1 home defeat by title contenders Romford on 9 October hardly helped, although the 1,402 crowd was artificially low on account of a 4:15pm midweek kick-off. Hastings eagerly awaited use of their new floodlights.

Two of the next three games were lost, the 0-2 defeat at sunny Margate being the most disappointing. But a 2-1 win at fellow promotion winners Nuneaton was an unexpected bonus. It seemed ironic that Hastings's impressive away record was keeping them afloat. Under Tim Kelly, an away victory was rarer than a dodo.

It was not until 2 November that Hastings gained their first home victory. But it came only after Gary Brown, the Wellington keeper, sustained a serious injury, requiring his immediate transfer to hospital. Oddly, Jack Bentley, father of Morecambe's Jim, was chosen to deputise in goal. Bentley was a prolific goalscorer, racking up 431 goals in 835 appearances for the Shropshire club, also netting in this game. Hastings had difficulty in capitalising upon Wellington's misfortune, though, winning narrowly 3-2. During the second half, Hastings's newly installed floodlights were first used. However, at Cambridge, a week later, Hastings let a good first-half performance slide into a sloppy second when they conceded three soft goals (0-3).

Changes were made for the home game with Guildford, played on a bright, crisp 16 November. Arnold Eckersall, a new acquisition from Sittingbourne, was selected to lead the line, while pugnacious Derek Razzell, a direct right-winger, came in for only his third game. It was a full-blooded contest in sticky conditions. Neither side gave any quarter and it took a Terry Marshall penalty to tip the balance (1-0). The Hastings fans were well satisfied. The gate of 2,029 was the best since September.

This figure would not be exceeded until Good Friday, when 2,325 turned up. Despite Hastings's improving form, their average gate was ten per cent less than in 1962/63.

On 23 November Hastings headed off to lowly Merthyr Tydfil. Ted Ballard reported, 'The game at Merthyr turned out to be a real battle as, after gaining a three-goal lead in 20 minutes, with Ron Wright (twice) and Arnold Eckersall (once) scoring, and playing like champions, we had the misfortune to have Roger Carter kicked in the muscle. He was little more than a passenger, hobbling at centre-forward, for the rest of the game. This would still have been a comfortable position had the referee been impartial. Never in my career have I encountered such an official. Nevertheless, the entire side worked very hard, and despite the heavy rain and mud, their spirit was very high.' Hastings won 3-2, rising seven places to tenth.

But Hastings could not extend their winning run when Worcester City visited on a grey 30 November. Despite dominating the early play, Hastings failed to convert the many openings they created into goals. They were repeatedly denied by Worcester's keeper Ball, who was in superb form. Worcester then countered strongly with their ace marksman John Fairbrother snatching the lead. Deflated by their inability to strike back, United became increasingly disjointed, leaving Worcester's right-half McEwan to seal the game (0-2).

A week later, frustration turned into elation as Hastings won 3-1 at Guildford, completing the double over their Surrey rivals. Ballard said, 'Guildford are never an easy side to beat, as any club in the Southern League will tell you, but having a little run of the ball, that we never seem to have at home, we were comfortable winners. Joe White came in for injured Eckersall and got two goals with his head, while Guildford inhabitant Ron Wright got one and had a very good game. I suspect he had a very nice week at the Guildford GPO where he works!'

It was difficult to understand Ted Ballard's reluctance to play Joe White more regularly. The big, brave, brawny centre-forward was a part-time fisherman in a local fleet owned by his family. Like Gerry Boon, he had been foolishly dismissed in Tim Kelly's clearout in the summer of 1960. White scored 16 times during Hastings's 1962/63 promotion push. But as much as Ted appreciated White's barnstorming performances, he liked his centre-forwards to sparkle with their feet, too.

Hastings's 7-0 victory over ten-men Hereford on 14 December was a personal triumph for Joe's replacement Arnold Eckersall, whose aerial strength brought him four goals, as Hastings routed Hereford in the Pilot Field snow. Although Hereford lost their Welsh international right-back Thomas in the second half, they were then already five goals in arrears. Sadly, only 1,120 were there to see this scintillating display. Disappointment followed a week later, though, at icy Bedford where an impressive defensive display counted for nothing after a controversial late goal.

Consolation followed on a grey Boxing Day. The U's produced a devastating display of attacking football against their fifth-placed visitors Chelmsford City. Leading the line for Chelmsford was their record goalscorer Tony Butcher, who netted 286 times for the Essex club. He was well supported by free-scoring inside-forward Wesley Maughan, and fast wingers Tony Nicholas, formerly with Brighton, and ex-West Ham wide-man Andy Smillie.

Chelmsford started brightly but were repelled by beefy centre-back Ray Brand and his vigilant cohort of defenders. 'Spider' Brown at right-half had a storming game, repeatedly dispossessing the City forwards with his exquisitely timed tackles. Although the heavy conditions were not conducive to speed, the cloying mud did little to impede the scorching pace of Marshall and Burden as Hastings counter-attacked sharply.

Within the first half hour, Marshall had put Hastings two up, twice nipping in between the hesitant Chelmsford defenders to beat keeper Medlock with a brace of crisp drives. Eckersall was unassailable in the air and assured on the ground. He poked in a third just before the interval.

The second half began as the first ended, with Eckersall heading in emphatically at the near post. A year after outclassing Hastings, Chelmsford were facing a rare drubbing. However, Hastings overreached themselves, allowing Chelmsford to pick them off on the break, prompted by the speed of Nicholas and Smillie. Goals from the irrepressible Butcher and Maughan restored respectability to the scoreline, but Hastings's supremacy was not in doubt. The 1,750 attendance was about par for Hastings in 1963/64, although 450 down on the previous season's average. And given that at least 200 fans were from Chelmsford, a turnout of only 1,500 home supporters was disappointing, especially for such a high-quality, festive game.

Perhaps the missing hundreds had a sixth sense of the pyrotechnics elsewhere. For on 26 December 1963, English football went 'goal crazy'. Thirty-nine Football League matches produced 157 goals, 66 of which were in the First Division. The biggest win was Fulham's 10-1 defeat of Ipswich and Blackburn's 8-2 win at West Ham. John Cobbold, the Ipswich chairman, cracked, 'Only our goalkeeper was sober.' Two days later, many of these freak results were reversed. So was Hastings's 4-2 Boxing Day victory.

Ted Ballard remarked, 'I am sure Chelmsford's most faithful supporters would say they were very fortunate as we were most unlucky to have a penalty awarded against us for accidental hands, a very harsh decision, with the score at two all. We pressed very hard for the equaliser and in an all-out effort we were caught a little open in the last minute, allowing Chelmsford to get a fourth, which made the score out of all proportion, for I thought we played even better there than we did here in the first game. Such is football! Besides losing the game, we had Arnold Eckersall limping after 20 minutes with a strained muscle.' Sadly, the injury proved to be much more serious, a career-ending cruciate tear.

Hastings continued their upward momentum in the new year. Dartford were thumped 4-0 on 11 January, on another day of heavy snow. Marshall scored twice, but wingers Back and Burden stole the show. Unfortunately, barely 1,000 were there to appreciate another memorable display. A week later, the tables were turned as, on an icy pitch, Wisbech's forwards ruthlessly exposed deficiencies in the Hastings defence (1-4). Although relegation-pointed Hinckley were beaten 3-2 in the next home fixture, it was a lacklustre display against a side that had declined markedly since winning promotion a year before. The U's were back to top form, though, when Rugby Town arrived at the Pilot Field on 8 February. Rugby were torn apart in a 6-0 goal rush, with wingers Back and Burden running riot with a brace apiece. Languishing Kettering put up a better fight under the Pilot Field lights on 12 February, but Hastings still prevailed 2-1. Arch-rivals Margate were perilously positioned near the drop zone when they came to the Pilot Field on 22 February. Hastings's 3-0 victory was more a reflection of Margate's inadequacies, though, than of Hastings's superiority.

United returned to form on 29 February at league leaders Romford. In front of a bumper 3,462 crowd, Hastings more than matched their hosts. Ted Ballard reported, 'Having conceded an unlucky own goal early on, we looked the better side in the second half, with Gordon Burden scoring a beauty.' It certainly was, for Burden curled a shot into the far top left-hand corner of the net from 25 yards out, leaving Dunbar, the Romford keeper, a helpless spectator (1-1). A week later, on a bitterly cold 7 March, with faint whispers of snow, Hastings overcame a first-half deficit to beat sixth-placed Weymouth. Back's outstanding wing play was rewarded with a crisp equaliser, while Marshall seized the points with a composed late penalty.

A week later, the ice had turned to heavy rain as Hastings made the long journey north to Wellington, now known as Telford. Ted Ballard remarked, 'Last week's journey to Wellington was quite an adventure for we had torrents of rain there and back, with plenty during the game as well, and although the ground was in first-class condition before the game, it was in a very sorry state afterwards. It seemed as if the "All Blacks" had been playing. Despite playing one man short for 50 minutes, the remaining ten worked tirelessly to bring the points back (2-1). Our missing player, Gary Griffiths, was very severely dealt with when the other player involved in the angry confrontation received only a caution.'

Against a scrapping Cambridge United side, Back added two more to his bulging tally in an impressive 3-2 home win, helped by a goal from redeemed wing-half Gary Griffiths. Once again, Hastings were depleted with an injury to left-back Keith Tucker, which incapacitated him for the whole of the second half. Despite moving into fifth position on the back of this fine victory, the game was watched by only 1,509 supporters. It was small wonder that Ted Ballard became so frustrated. A much healthier 2,325 crowd turned up on Good Friday for another sunny 3-2 win, this time over Cambridge City. Having recovered from a 1-2 half-time deficit with Back on the money, the game was won with a towering header from tall wing-half Alan Brown.

On Easter Saturday, though, Hastings succumbed to a leggy defeat at lowly Kettering (1-2), before completing their Easter programme with a 0-0 draw at Cambridge City on Easter Monday. It was a game which Hastings should have won. When relegation candidates Merthyr visited on a wet, icy 4 April, Hastings were still in fifth place. The visitors shocked Hastings, though, with an early goal from inside-left Davies, and although Marshall and Burden turned the game around by half-time, Merthyr's greater doggedness in the mud, sleet and snow resulted in a rare victory (2-3). Only 1,204 local fans braved the inclement weather to witness one of Hastings's worst performances of the season.

Unabashed, Ted Ballard's side finished the season strongly, winning 3-2 at Worcester, beating third-placed Bath 2-0 at Twerton Park before drawing 1-1 with the West Country team in the return fixture. This meant Hastings had played 42 Premier Division games in 1963/64: winning 20, drawing 8 and losing 14; scoring 75 goals and conceding 61. The 48 points they won were just two behind former runaway leaders Romford. Marshall was top shot with 17 goals, followed by Back and makeshift centre-forward Carter with ten apiece. A final position of sixth was a superb achievement for a club that had been on its knees just 18 months before.

1964 'Youthquake'

'My Generation'

IF THE popular press were to be believed, the summer of 1964 was scarred by seaside violence, perpetrated by warring gangs of Mods and Rockers. The moral panic aroused was largely without justification, although the bold Mod and Rocker youth cultures did challenge restrained middle-class society. The cessation of National Service was a significant factor in their growth, as was an extended period of full employment. Baby Boomers, notably those from working-class families, like me, benefitted enormously from the higher disposable income and resulting freedoms denied to previous generations.

Mod and Rocker cultures were defined by contrasting choices of fashion, music and wheels. With her eye-covering fringe and long hair, Cathy McGowan of *Ready Steady Go* was a Mod role model. Other Mod girls had short cuts like model, 'Twiggy'. Shift dresses with round collars were the rage, worn with white stockings and stack-heeled shoes, although tights replaced stockings once miniskirts became fashionable. Make-up was minimal and lipstick was out.

But Mod guys were equally fastidious. Mod boys liked a middle parting with puffed up, lacquered tops and backs, their girlfriends supplying the lacquer. If you can remember Steve Marriott of the Small Faces, you will know the look.

Many were fond of small-brimmed blue beat hats. As for the rest of the gear, it wasn't cheap. Ivy League suits – three buttons, narrow lapels, and two vents – cost £30, in excess of £600 today. To get the picture, watch the video footage of The Righteous Brothers singing 'You've Lost that Lovin' Feelin'' or The Zombies performing their breathy, jazzy single 'She's Not There'. Then there were the trousers with 17-inch bottoms and imitation crocodile or python shoes with rounded toes, although many of the cheapskates settled for desert boots. Blue suits were popular too. For Mods who could afford wheels, this meant a Lambretta or Vespa scooter, bristling with lamps and wing mirrors. Scooter wear was an olive-green parka with a fur-trimmed hood.

Then there was the music. Blue beat, rock-steady artists like Prince Buster were Mod favourites until abrasively energetic bands like The Who and the Small Faces emerged. The Who's centrepiece was 'My Generation', completed with a frantic trashing of their instruments.

As for Rocker fashion, this was strictly retro, caught up in the 50s beat – driving rock 'n' roll, grease, leather gear and roaring bikes. The Rocker girls wore leathers too, with flat shoes, lacquered bouffants and thick make-up. They were keen on Elvis pendants. While Rockers remained faithful to the jive and the twist, the Mods were strictly blue beat, knees stiff, arms flailing all over the place. I watched all of this from afar, in my hermit's cave of football and cricket obsessions, observing this remote world through my TV screen – the coy Lad of Shalott.

Guildford City v Hastings United

Southern League Premier Division, 7 November 1964

'Downtown'

THE START of the new season was riven with internal strife. There were rumours that Ted Ballard wanted to leave after being refused promised resources for team strengthening. He was deeply frustrated by this, given that he had lifted United into the top 20 of English non-league clubs. Ballard, therefore, cast his eyes on the vacant Dover job. Although a hot favourite for this post, the Hastings United board of directors refused to release him. The job went instead to ex-Brighton full-back Roy Little. Despite being granted leave to purchase prolific goalscorer George Francis from Gillingham for a four-figure fee, Ballard remained disgruntled. This season would be his last, not only at Hastings, but as a football manager per se.

Hastings began the 1964/65 season promisingly, though. A strong second half display at sunny Cambridge United resulted in a worthy 1-1 draw. A 2-2 home draw with Cheltenham followed, although Hastings missed copious chances to put the game to bed. The U's also had the better of a 1-1 draw with Worcester City, a side brimming with former Football League stars, including Colin Webster, an FA Cup finalist with

Manchester United, and Norman Deeley, a top performer in Wolves' Championship-winning teams of the late 50s. Terry Marshall's second-half equaliser secured the U's a share of the points. Hastings's leading performer in these opening games was right-winger Alan Back, who displayed sting and style in equal measure. However, Ballard's frustration at his side's wastage of scoring opportunities caused him to ring the changes for the ensuing matches, away at Ramsgate and at home against Margate. It was to no avail. Both games were lost.

Hastings broke their duck with an impressive 3-1 victory at Cheltenham on 16 September, but after crushing Eastbourne United 7-1 in an FA Cup qualifier, and drawing 1-1 at newly promoted Folkestone, home blues returned when Kings Lynn visited on 26 September. Hastings should have taken charge after Francis's fierce, rising drive had given them a first-half lead. However, once again they failed to capitalise while on top. The longer the game went on, the more disjointed Hastings became. With the momentum shifting towards the visitors, Bobby Laverick snatched a late equaliser. Fired up by Ted Ballard's sharp tongue and their own exasperation, Bedford were put to the sword four days later. Burden's devastating wing play and Marshall's scorching drive set up an emphatic 3-0 home win.

A subsequent 0-3 defeat at Tonbridge in the FA Cup was set aside quickly with an admirable 2-2 draw at champions Yeovil, followed by a superb 4-1 home victory over Folkestone on a glorious russet afternoon on 17 October. Back was again the pick of the bunch with an outstanding display of pace, power and penetration that utterly bewildered his distinguished marker Eddie Lewis, formerly of Leyton Orient. Back celebrated his five-star performance by hammering home his second goal shortly before the close, to raucous acclaim from the home fans in the 1,813 crowd. After such a splendid display on a sumptuous afternoon, I was reluctant to leave. While the crowd slowly dispersed, I remained on top of the grassy bank, taking in the view of the bay: the distant sea, opaque in the dimming light; the shadowed Downs, set against a limpid sky, streaked with old gold and crimson. God, this is a lovely place, but I sensed my time here was shortening. Soon I would sit my GCEs. My unexpected success led me north where I found a life happier than I ever thought possible. Yet Hastings made me. Its legacy is the enduring hold that Sussex by the sea has upon me. This day of euphoria tinged with poignancy will remain with me for as long as I live and retain capacity.

A week later, Hastings recovered from a 0-3 deficit at Chelmsford to earn a remarkable 3-3 draw. Burden snatched a point in the last minute, having latched on to Marshall's fizzing cross. It was enough to lift Hastings into seventh place. Alas, this was as good as it got in this star-crossed season.

In his programme notes for the home game against Cambridge City on 31 October, Ted Ballard wrote, 'Last weekend saw the Southern League side gain a very good point from Chelmsford City. With various knocks suffered against Gravesend midweek in the Kent Floodlight League, we were hard put to field a fit side. George Francis played, but was only 75 per cent fit. Further injuries were then sustained in a KFL game at Margate in the lead up to the home fixture against Cambridge City.'

Once again, money was in short supply. Although helped by a local benefactor, the directors had to find around £4,000, about £80,000 today, for replacement floodlights, which were installed in late 1963. It hardly helped that attendances were falling. Although the average gate for the entire 1964/65 season was almost 1,300, it was less than 1,000 between January and May. Seven home fixtures attracted three-figure attendances. Compare that with an average gate of 1,770 during the previous season, and 2,200 in the one before. The decline in attendances since 1962/63 was over 40 per cent.

The slide in the U's fortunes began on 31 October when Cambridge City pulverised hobbling Hastings. City's lively inside-left, Alan Gregory, formerly with Accrington and

Burnley, snatched two goals in their 3-0 victory. George Francis was one of several players carrying incapacitating knocks. They were pressed into playing because Ted Ballard did not have good enough reserves to deputise. As a result of the club's summer austerity drive 16 players had been released. On top of that a 50 per cent wage cut was imposed. This was bound to impact upon player morale, as did their onerous workloads and the injuries they were asked to carry.

Matters came to a head at Guildford on 7 November. On a cold, cloudless, dazzling autumn day, formidable Guildford City ripped Hastings apart 3-0. The scoreline did scant justice to the host club's superiority. Leading the charge for the Surrey club was their all-time top goalscorer Dave Barrett, who would notch 149 goals in 309 appearances for the Joseph's Road club, before moving to Cambridge United a year later for a substantial sum. He had extraordinary ball control, poise, speed and power. He always scored against Hastings, so it was merely routine when he rifled in the opening goal. What was flabbergasting, though, was that Hastings were ostensibly still in the game at the interval when the score was 0-1. But brawny centre-forward Stevens quickly snuffed out an improbable revival by thumping a header past Agate soon after the resumption. Home right-winger Bennett then hammered in the final nail. As the downcast Hastings players slouched off the pitch, we made for the coach which we shared with Ted and some of his team.

Hastings centre-half Alan Crudace told us that Ted was so incensed by his team's lack of fight that three players were sacked on the spot – stalwart wing-half Eddie Stone, midfielder Bela Olah and deputy centre-forward Alan Selway. This reduced Ballard's 'fit' first-team squad of 15 to 12. Three former first-team players – Boon, Eckersall and Wright – had already left the club, while Francis and centre-half Brand were recovering from injuries. In Brand's case, this was a long-standing one. Moreover, Ted had no reserve goalkeeper, compelling him to restore veteran keepers Bill Farnfield and already retired Alf Bentley to fill in for some Kent Floodlight League games. Farnfield also substituted for Ian Agate occasionally in the Southern League.

With numbers so short, Olah was later reprieved, and although Stone returned, becoming Hastings's 1965/66 player of the year, he did not come back until Ballard had left. Ted was prone to impetuous outbursts when stressed, but he usually relented before any lasting harm was done. Here, his actions were reckless. A shaken Crudace said that some of the players retorted by blaming Ted for providing them with an inadequate pre-match meal – a round of toast each. They complained that the Cambridge City players had been given steak before the previous home game. It sounded petty. Steak was the gold standard for 60s footballers despite offering them no immediate dietary benefit. Toast wasn't that bad as an alternative. Pet Clark's hit single 'Downtown' was playing on the coach radio. Outside, Guildford's cathedral was silhouetted starkly against the embers of a tingling winter sunset. The good times were sinking from view.

In his programme notes for the Wellington game seven days later, Ted wrote, 'The team was not only lacking in ability, but endeavour as well. With the injury list as it is, it showed that their deputies are very much below the standard required for Premier Division football. Thought must be given to this immediately, before we sink into the depths.'

But the club felt unable to loosen the purse strings. A month later the chairman announced that the club was £3,000 in debt, around £60,000 today, a sum which was roughly the same as its annual wage bill. £75 was being lost each week, about £1,500 per week today or £78,000 annually. The Hastings United Supporters' Club made a one-off donation of £50. Although well intentioned, it was a token gesture. The lottery scheme was stalling, too, placing more strain on the shrivelling revenue stream. Although an embargo was placed on incoming moves after George Francis's signing in August, Hastings's growing injury list and Ted Ballard's cull forced a change of heart with the signing of local right-half Nick Howe. Howe played 36 times, scoring five goals. Left-half Graham Sawyer also joined in the new year.

The heavens opened on 14 November. In front of 886 drenched fans, Hastings held free-scoring Wellington in a madcap game that ended 3-3. As expected, Jack Bentley scored once for the visitors. Thankfully, George Francis was declared fit, because without his powerful, far-post headers, Hastings would surely have lost.

Much to our relief, Hastings got the show back on the road when they visited Bexley a week later. Marshall's late strike proved decisive in an entertaining, switchback game. Visiting Dartford then upset my birthday celebrations by inflicting a third home defeat upon the U's. It was another nip-and-tuck affair on a mild, grey afternoon. A contingent of young Hastings supporters chose to deride Dartford's prematurely greying right-winger, inundating him with cat calls of 'granddad'. Twenty-three-year-old Richie Ward was no slouch, though. He was quick, slick and incisive, playing a major role in Dartford's win. Why do fans try to wind up opposing players? It usually backfires. I'm sure Ward enjoyed his riposte.

On 5 December Hastings wasted a gilt-edged opportunity to bury the Wisbech jinx. Alan Back's hat-trick gave Hastings a 3-1 lead in just 16 minutes. But on a treacherous, half-frozen pitch, Hastings made the cardinal mistakes of dwelling on the ball and rushing into uncontrolled tackles. Wisbech capitalised, winning 4-3.

Heavy rain returned to the south coast on 12 December. While Hastings prevaricated, Cambridge United struck ruthlessly. By half-time the muscular visitors were three up and totally in control. Their bulldozing style was ideal for such a saturated, sapping surface, and while Burden got one goal back Cambridge United's strapping centre-forward Peter Hobbs retaliated instantly by blasting an unstoppable shot past Agate (1-4). Hastings's cause was not helped by having to deploy two of their players in unfamiliar defensive positions while also calling upon inexperienced Nick Howe.

A Boxing Day defeat at Nuneaton did little for Christmas cheer but in the return fixture Hastings once again revelled in the snow, beating their Midlands opponents 3-1 with goals from Francis, Marshall and new boy Nick Howe. Certainly, this impressive performance deserved more than a 986 gate. Ted Ballard wrote despairingly, 'It makes all concerned wonder whether good class football is really wanted in Hastings. It is so difficult to look to any future for the club.'

Yet when champions-elect Weymouth arrived on a cold, grey afternoon on 9 January, Hastings unexpectedly beat them 2-1. This was only Weymouth's fourth defeat of the season. While Weymouth had greater class, Hastings had doggedness and resilience, and in Back and Burden they had the best players on show.

Bath City's fall from grace had been even more precipitous than that of Hastings. They completed the 1963/64 season in third place but were rock bottom when they came to Hastings on a bright, mild 23 January, having managed to accumulate just 11 points in 22 fixtures. In a very scrappy game, Francis, Marshall and Howe were again on target in a 3-1 win. Although Hastings's away form had disintegrated – as exemplified in their 1-7 thrashing by avenging Weymouth – their home form continued to improve. Subsequent home wins over Romford (2-0) and sixth-placed Yeovil (1-0) gave Hastings a realistic chance of averting the drop. Sadly, Hastings's second slide was steeper and terminal. After beating Yeovil on 20 February 1965, they had 27 points from 28 games. However, only five points were taken from their final 14 fixtures with no victories. Relegation became a formality.

The rot set in on a bright, freezing 6 March 1965. Once again, the Pilot Field was covered in snow. Previously, Hastings had performed well on such surfaces, at least at home. Chelmsford City seemed there for the taking. City struggled to keep their feet in the early stages, allowing Hastings to take a two-goal lead. Crucially, though, the visitors pulled one goal back just before the break. With Hastings's confidence still fragile after a 0-5 rout at Worcester on 22 February, Chelmsford turned the game around, winning 3-2. Only Back performed well for the U's.

Meanwhile, doubts about the future sustainability of Southern League football were resurfacing. In February 1965 Ted Ballard had called a meeting of 16 south-eastern non-league clubs to consider the possibility of forming a regionally based league. Hastings's sharp loss of support was not unusual. Southern League attendances had been falling at many clubs during the second half of the 1964/65 season, although Hastings's gates after New Year were among the lowest in its Premier League, alongside Rugby and Wisbech.

What troubled most south-eastern clubs was the expensive long-distance travel on top of rapidly declining home gates. This had been debated in 1961 with all Southern League clubs, without a radical solution being found. With so many Southern League Premier Division clubs, such as Telford/Wellington, Worcester, Cheltenham, Weymouth, Bath, Yeovil, Rugby, Hereford, Nuneaton, Cambridge City and United, Wisbech and Kings Lynn, situated far from Kent and Sussex, there was a growing appetite among south-eastern clubs for a more local competition. Because of mounting costs and reducing revenue, some Southern League clubs had not paid their players for several weeks, Deal being a prime example.

Of course, Football League gates had dropped, too, by almost 40 per cent from the post-war high in 1949/50. Alarmed at the sharp fall in gate revenue, the Football League briefly considered re-imposing a wage ceiling. But, with the cork out of the bottle, nobody could jam it back in. Nevertheless, Tom Finney was just one of several former stars who regretted the abolition of a wage ceiling. He wrote an article called 'Pampered and Overpaid': 'I was one who fought against the maximum wage, arguing that footballers should be paid what they are worth. But today, when the sky's the limit,

I'm afraid the trouble is that many are paid too much for too little. I could not name 50 players, or indeed a dozen, who are worth £100 a week. And too often, I fear, this fantastic sort of money goes to their heads rather than to their feet.'

Remember, this was written in 1964 not 2019! Not that many Southern League salaries were anything like £100 per week. In 1964 Hastings centre-forward George Francis was reputedly on around £14–15 per week. He was one of Hastings's highest-paid professionals in recognition of the 144 goals he had scored for Brentford, QPR and Gillingham.

With six games left there was a flicker of hope that Hastings could avoid the drop, despite losing 0-1 to relegation rivals Bexley in a home game that the U's had dominated from start to finish. Three of their remaining fixtures were against sides also in relegation peril.

On 16 April, three days after the Bexley fiasco, Hastings were at Tonbridge for a Good Friday fixture. A lot was at stake for Tonbridge had relegation worries, too. It was a warm day of glittering sunshine. After two minutes Hastings were ahead after unmarked Francis headed Back's cross past Fred Crump. How we cheered while the 1,700 or so Tonbridge fans were reduced to morose silence. Frustratingly, it took our hosts only another 11 minutes to equalise when Hastings's wing-half Alan Brown deflected a fierce drive into his own net. The hard, rutted surface created problems for both sides. But with Tonbridge gaining confidence after the break, Kemp put them 2-1 up, prompting an almighty roar from the home fans. Just as we were preparing ourselves for another disappointment, Alan Back salvaged a point in the final minutes with a cross shot that hit the far post and ricocheted in (2-2).

Next day, hope vanished as winter superseded spring. Second-from-bottom Wisbech Town beat us yet again (2-4), having mastered the rain and sleet and the slushy Pilot Field surface with aplomb. Francis's second Eastertide goal was merely irrelevant. When Guildford called four days later, there were only 849 people present as Hastings were crushed

1-4 by stronger, quicker and more incisive opponents. The visitors brought many fans with them, overwhelming the sparse home support.

Roger King, a long-standing Hastings supporter, was at the critical Rugby match on 24 April. He recalled, 'The match was best forgotten as United were 0-3 behind, and mathematically down, inside 30 minutes. I got back to my relatives in Birmingham to find that I could have been at St Andrew's watching the Division One game between Birmingham City and Blackburn, which ended in a 5-5 draw!'

Roger King continued, 'The Rugby home game was squashed in on the evening of Friday 30 April. I think everyone would have been happy not to have had another game just then. It turned out to be another 2-2 draw. The gate was so awful that it did not feature anywhere, even in the Supporters' Hut window, but basing my calculation on the published season's average for all 21 games, it was 551.'

The last game of the 1964/65 season on 1 May was the return fixture against Tonbridge. Roger King remembered, 'It was another disappointing game as United led 2-0 through goals from Sawyer and Marshall, the latter coming from a goalmouth scramble, only for Jones and Wright to even things up in the second half. The *Sunday Express* reported, 'Sawyer completely missed from three yards in the final few minutes.' It was one of many United misses in that woeful season. The gate was 717. After the match, my friend Pip and I went to see Gordon Burden presented with the Player of the Year award – the first time this award had been made at the club. We then got caught in a late evening thunderstorm!' A season which began with optimism, at least among the fans, as reflected by the 2,343 and 2,143 attendances for the first two home games, ended in despondency with gates of 551 and 717.

The last home programme for the 1964/65 season carried a list of first-team appearances, including those in cup and the Kent Floodlight League competitions. These figures confirm the excessive load carried by the first-team players. Player of the year Gordon Burden made 71 appearances, scoring 31 goals. Alan Back made 71 appearances with 20 goals. Defender Bill Cockburn made 68 appearances with five goals. Francis made 64 appearances with 25 goals. Marshall made 61 appearances with 16 goals. Olah made 56 appearances with eight goals and Simpson made 52 appearances with one goal. Talk about flogging the dead horses.

Three of Hastings's best players undertook almost two seasons' work, while two more were laden with a workload only marginally smaller. These commitments were at least 40 per cent higher than during the previous season when the playing squad of 34 was twice the size of that in 1964/65. While reserve appearances in the Southern League team aggregated 106 in 1963/64, in 1964/65 there weren't any. In 1964/65 the term 'reserves' was a misnomer, for it referred to the amateur young hopefuls who played principally in competitions designed for youth teams, such as the Thames & Medway League. Although one or two did occasionally represent the club in the KFL, there was only a handful of appearances. The Thames & Medway League standards were significantly inferior to that of the Metropolitan League.

With eight crucial Southern League fixtures crammed into April at the end of a gruelling season, it was no surprise that Hastings performed well below their capabilities. While the directors were keen to maximise the earning capacity of the club's new floodlights, their decision to enter the Kent Floodlight League was bound to end badly, given the small size of the first-team squad. Their estimate of the revenue to be accrued from participating in this competition was way off beam, with average KFL gates no higher than that at Metropolitan League games, around 500.

Towards the end of the season, Ted Ballard's son, Ken, came in for half a dozen games, playing in midfield, while Hastings's other new recruit, Graham Sawyer, was converted into an inside-forward. Here, he scored seven times in 15 first-team appearances in 1965. His time would come during the next season, when he scored 34 senior goals, helped by the space Bobby Smith and Jim Ryan created for him.

Ted Ballard resigned as manager of Hastings United after the Tonbridge home game. Apart from spending a brief spell as a Hastings United director and caretaker manager, he left football for good, becoming a local publican. According to his sons, Ken and Alan, Ted became very disillusioned with the game. Ted told Roger Sinden, author of *Hastings United Through Time*, that he did not think the Hastings directors were 'football people'. Ted recalled that he was once addressing the board on important playing issues when he noticed a director distracted by something on the floor. Ted stopped to enquire what the problem was. The director in question had apparently dropped a sixpence and was more concerned with retrieving it than with listening to Ted.

In his final programme notes, Ted Ballard wrote, 'The lads themselves gave all they had but it wasn't enough [Guildford excepted, presumably]. But can we blame this on "Lady Luck" or is the real reason to be found elsewhere? As manager, I must take a certain amount of the blame, as also must everyone else connected with the club.

'Our 0-4 defeat at Rugby completely sunk any hope we had of saving ourselves. It was typical of all the matches we played this season, we had the majority of the play, especially during the second half, with more than enough chances to have won the game, but we were unable to finish.

'When a club starts to struggle financially as we have, right from the start of the season, with players leaving and the rest having wage cuts, our position gradually deteriorated, with little hope of drafting in new blood. So, we have struggled on through the season. At times we have looked a good side and clubs wonder why we have been at the bottom, while in other games, especially at home, we have been really bad.

'I feel I now have no big part in the club's new plans. The club will always be an important part of my past and I will always be available for any assistance I can offer. I sincerely hope I have not let anyone down and take this opportunity to thank all those who have made my job that much easier and do hope you will continue to give even more help to my successor. I know the club has a future but only if we regain the faith of you, the supporters, which can only be done by sheer hard work and this must be done by all connected with the club. If they are not prepared to do this, or have not the time, I SAY GET OUT, make way for someone who will, but these people must come forward, not just criticise the person or persons in office. Let everyone now do that little bit more to help.'

Ted Ballard could have done with a rich benefactor with deep pockets but there was none to be seen, at least until James Humphreys arrived in the summer of 1965. But his story comes a little later.

Brighton & Hove Albion
v Darlington

Football League Division Four, 26 April 1965
'Ticket to Ride'

WHILE HASTINGS were struggling, Brighton were prospering on the back of renewed investment. During the 1963/64 season, Brighton's boss, Archie Macaulay, assembled the nucleus of a side that would storm out of Division Four a season later. Among his key signings was Dave Turner, a young, dynamic wing-half who had been playing in Newcastle's reserves. After arriving in December 1963, Turner quickly found his feet in Archie's side. Industrious utility player Bill Cassidy was shifted to inside-left to accommodate him. York's goalscoring winger Wally Gould was also brought in, as was Swindon's skilful inside-forward Jack Smith.

Helped by Macaulay's additions and blessed with a more settled team, Brighton's 1963/64 season was more successful, accumulating 19 league wins to reach a comfortable eighth spot in Division Four.

With centre-half Roy Jennings's Football League career coming to an end, young Geordie defender Norman Gall was given the chance of regular first-team action, initially at left-back. Norman told Paul Camillin, author of *Brighton: Match of My Life*, 'During Archie's first full season in charge, 1963/64, I played 41 games. We had a decent season. But for an awful run of form through the winter months of December and January, we could have been in the promotion shake-up.'

The most eye-catching Macaulay signing, though, was that of 32-year-old former Spurs and England centre-forward Bobby Smith, in May 1964. John Vinicombe of the *Brighton Argus* remembered, 'Just imagine Michael Owen joining Albion. That was the impact Bobby Smith made when he quit Tottenham Hotspur for the Seagulls in May 1964. Smith remains arguably the biggest name ever to sign for the club. Smith had similar superstar status to Owen. He was a top-flight icon, a cup-winning hero and a renowned England goalscorer. More Didier Drogba than Owen in style, he was a barnstorming centre-forward, a prolific marksman with a touch of flair.'

Smith began his Football League career at Chelsea, where he scored 30 goals in 86 games before moving to White Hart Lane in December 1955 for £16,000. The Brighton programme for the opening game against Barrow in August 1964 contained an article about Smith which added, 'There have been few more courageous wearers of an England shirt than Smith, who on 20 November last year was a national hero after Northern Ireland were crushed 8-3 at Wembley. Yet that was to be Bobby's last international appearance. He couldn't have ended on a finer note. It will not take long for Bobby's fame to stir the Goldstone and lead Albion back into the higher class of football that Brighton and Hove deserve.'

Brighton chairman Eric Courtney-King was bursting with pride at his club's capture of Smith. Seizing the slot that is normally reserved for the manager's notes, Eric wrote, 'This signing shows just how eager we are to climb to our rightful place in the Football League, and we all wish Bobby a happy and successful stay with us. I am seldom courageous enough to make predictions about professional football, but this is an occasion when I am inclined to do so. I believe there will be a larger number of fans at this, our first match of the season, than we have seen at the Goldstone Ground for quite a long time.'

But there were those who had doubts about Smith. Some queried why he had fallen so far, so quickly. What was the back story here? Was he carrying significant injuries? Was his gambling an embarrassment to Spurs? Was he not staying in shape? John Vinicombe of the *Brighton Argus* questioned Smith about his gambling several years later. Smith replied, 'I liked a flutter. You won some, you lost some. I was happy doing it, as long as I didn't get into any trouble. But I never did.'

Daily Express journalist Norman Giller disputed this. He recalled the time when Spurs were checking out of their hotel after the away leg of their European Cup first-round tie against Feyenoord in 1961/62. Bill Nicholson found out that the hotel telephone bill was ten times what was expected. Nicholas railed, 'Somebody has been taking liberties calling home!' Nicholson knew the culprit, though, prompting Smith to snap: 'All right, all right. Keep your hair on. I'll pay it when I get home.' Smith had been on the phone to his bookie in London throughout the trip.

Significantly, perhaps, Smith joined the Albion via a bookmaker. He said, 'I knew Georgie Gunn who was a bookie who supported Brighton. He rang me up and said come down. He was a nice fellow and Brighton were interested so I said yes.' But Smith insisted to Vinicombe that he had not left Spurs under a cloud. Smith explained, 'I left Spurs because Bill Nicholson told me he was going to replace me. I thought I can't stay somewhere where I'm not wanted. Bill Nick let me go for a small fee to help me get a move more easily as a reward for what I had done for the club.'

Giller was aware that Smith had played regularly while in pain following his disclosure to Giller shortly before the 'double-winning' 1961 FA Cup Final. As for being out of shape, Giller was at Brighton in July 1964 when Smith weighed in at

16st 9lb. Giller knew that Smith had weighed 13st 9lb while at Spurs. When Macaulay heard that Smith was three stone overweight, he was apoplectic, demanding that Smith follow a strict exercise and dietary programme to bring him back into shape, a tough regime which Smith fully cooperated with. Giller remembered that his newspaper highlighted the issue with a headline piece on its back page with the caption 'Blobby Smith'. But soon Bobby was making the headlines for the right reasons.

Some 20,058 supporters turned up on a scalding 22 August to see Bobby Smith score two goals, including a stunning diving header, and Jimmy Collins, one, in a 3-1 victory. The attendance more than doubled the average gate for the previous season of 9,300. It was the largest Goldstone crowd since 1958/59. Archie Macaulay wanted Brighton to succeed playing stylish, attacking football. Barrow might not have been great shakes. They had been forced to seek re-election having finished the previous season in 92nd spot.

Nevertheless, Archie's selection of five attacking players showed the strength of his conviction. Supporting centre-forward Bobby Smith were two free-scoring wingers in Wally Gould and John Goodchild, plus creative inside-forwards Jack Smith and Jimmy Collins, both of whom had an eye for goal. As for the rest, Mike Hennigan, a new signing from Southampton, was chosen at centre-half, assisted by Alan Sanders at right-back and Norman Gall at left-back. Jack Bertolini and Dave Turner filled the wing-half berths. In goal, Brian Powney was preferred to Bert McGonigal.

Stirred by Brighton's immediate success, an even bigger crowd of 22,697 was attracted to the midweek home fixture against Oxford United on 25 August. Oxford were a much tougher proposition than Barrow. It had taken Oxford boss Arthur Turner seven seasons to transform a mediocre, suburban non-league side, previously known as Headington United, into a forceful, scrapping Fourth Division outfit capable of overturning strong First Division opposition.

If Turner was responsible for setting up the club, his forthright skipper Ron Atkinson drove it forward. Ron Atkinson was known as the 'Tank' or 'Oil King'. He exposed as much of his thick, muscular thighs as was decent, coating his legs in olive oil so that they would glisten in the floodlights. Before each game he wound himself up into a frenzy of aggression. Handicapped by an arm injury to new centre-half Hennigan, Archie's archers could not pierce Arthur's armour (0-0). Come April, Arthur Turner's side would accompany Brighton into Division Three with the second meanest defence in the Football League. This was another team on a mission.

Despite beating a strong Rochdale side 3-0 on a sunny 5 September, with goals from Collins, Jack Smith and Goodchild, Brighton's early form was erratic. Archie Macaulay was not happy. He wrote in the programme for the Rochdale game, 'At Hartlepools, our lads were well below form and disappointingly gave away a very silly equalising goal in the closing seconds (1-1). This would suggest a repeat of last season. The players had been instructed to keep the defence solid in the closing minutes. We had four defenders in our six-yard box against one Hartlepools forward. Norman Gall was carrying out my instructions, "When in doubt, kick out" and attempted to do just that. Unfortunately, he mis-kicked, which put Dave Turner off balance and their incoming forward, challenged by Alan Sanders, was hit by the ball, with the ball rebounding into the net. Here was a case of players being in position but an individual mistake costing a goal.'

A subsequent 0-2 league defeat at Millwall would not have improved his mood. In fairness, Brighton had been asked to play two midweek games. First, there was a long trip to Newport on the Monday (1-1). Then, they had the Millwall League Cup replay on the Wednesday. In fact, the fixture congestion was such that the Albion had to play five games in 11 days! Modern professionals complain vociferously about a much less crowded fixture list. It was no surprise that Brighton had to contend with a growing injury list. Archie was forced to make six changes for the return home game with Newport County. Young Peter Knight and Peter Donnelly, a George Curtis purchase, came in for first-choice wingers Gould and Goodchild. Bill Cassidy replaced Jack Smith at inside-left. Norman Gall was shifted to centre-half and young Robin Upton took Dave Turner's place at left-half.

Archie was impressed with the Welshmen. In the return fixture on 15 September, Gall performed well at centre-half, successfully subduing Newport's dangerous centre-forward Laurie Sheffield. In front of a disappointing midweek crowd of 13,980, Jimmy Collins's goal decided an even contest. This win lifted Albion two places to sixth spot. It wasn't clear why the attendance was so low. Albion's stuttering form had not helped, but it was recognised that the bumper crowds in August were possibly boosted by tourists.

In 1964 we had a wonderful Indian summer. September delivered day after day of basking sunshine. Pullovers and cardigans remained on our shelves. The warm seawater continued to glitter invitingly as if it was still August. The weather was so enticing that the Brighton programme contained adverts for late coach holidays in Devon, Edinburgh and the Trossachs. The Carrington Marriage Bureau also advertised itself as the place where 'a wonderful match may begin' and 'where many a happy home team has started'. There was no messing about at the Carrington.

On 19 September Bobby Smith scored twice against 91st-placed Bradford City. But even with fleet-footed Peter Knight adding a third, this was not enough to beat the determined Bantams (3-3). Archie became even more alarmed after Brighton lost two successive games at Chester (1-3) and York (1-2). Brighton had fallen to 13th position. This wasn't what the board of directors had in mind.

Brighton's form in October was much better, helped by the signing of 29-year-old former Spurs and Welsh international full-back Mel Hopkins for £8,000. Four victories came on the bounce, against mid-table Torquay (3-1), York (3-1) and

Notts County (6-0), while Lincoln were defeated 1-0 at Sincil Bank. Archie's five-star attack was beginning to fire on all five cylinders.

If Bobby Smith was the celebrity performer, Jimmy Collins was the team's driving force. A Brighton programme described him thus: 'Jimmy, 26, has proved to be one of Albion's best inside-forwards since the war. He was easily one of the outstanding players in the Fourth Division last term and would have stood out in better company. Northampton Town fancied him and there were other clubs who noted the trickery and cunning of Albion's skipper. Since the end of last season, Jimmy has married a local girl and is keener than ever to settle down in Brighton and Hove.' Collins played 221 games for Albion in a six-year stay at the Goldstone, scoring 48 goals – a tremendous return for a midfielder. Having scored 17 league goals during the 1964/65 season, Jimmy is remembered fondly as the feisty Scot who inspired Brighton's promotion success.

Jimmy Collins told *Brighton Argus* reporter John Vinicombe 36 years later, 'If I hadn't have met Wendy, I'd have ended up a fat alcoholic blob. She straightened me out. Meeting and marrying Wendy was the best thing I ever did. Brighton had big crowds for a club in the lower divisions. Archie did a good job and it was an exciting season. Six of us got into double figures that season. I don't think that will ever happen again. It was unbelievable. I remember I got the first goal against Barrow and the hundredth, thanks to the lay-off by Bobby Smith, against Darlington. I remember Archie turfed me out of a snooker hall once. He didn't like his players in snooker halls. I think he became a traffic warden. I find it difficult to go past where the Goldstone used to be and see Toys 'R' Us in its place.'

On 24 October Doncaster Rovers came to town. Although Bobby Smith had been injured in the midweek 4-0 rout of visiting Lincoln, Brighton were confident of extending their winning run at home to five games. But Archie exercised a measure of caution, singling out Rovers' danger man Alick Jeffrey in his programme notes. Archie wrote, 'Jeffrey is one player who is contributing much towards Rovers' revival. You will recall he received a serious broken leg injury. It was thought that his career was ended but through sheer guts and determination this young player has brought himself back to fitness, and our lads will have to be on the alert to contain this fine forward'.

In 1954 Jeffrey seemed destined for greatness. Stanley Matthews described him as a 'football genius'. Manchester United coveted him, believing him to be as talented as Duncan Edwards. By the age of 18 he was an established player, having scored 34 goals in 71 league appearances. However, a leg fracture during an England under-23 international ended his career. Or so he thought, until international coach George Raynor devised a special rehabilitation programme for him. After a year spent rebuilding his strength, stamina and speed, he found that he was good enough to return to full-time professional football. He was offered a further contract with Doncaster Rovers. Time had not been kind to the Rovers. In the intervening years, they had fallen from the Second Division to the Fourth. Jeffrey made a tentative return – 20 senior games; four goals. But it did not take him long to remind us of what we had missed. During the 1964/65 season, he played in each of Doncaster's 46 league games, scoring an incredible 36 goals. He would net 95 goals for 'Donny' in his second spell with the club. Jeffrey never cursed his ill luck. When others commiserated, he'd say, 'Don't weep for me, think of those lads in Munich. If I hadn't broken my leg, I would probably have been on that plane.'

On a bright, warm Saturday, 24 October, Jeffrey was a real menace. Brighton were hard-pressed to contain him. He led the charge as Doncaster pushed forward while veteran Bill Leivers and his fellow defenders restricted Brighton's free-scoring attack to just one goal – netted by Bill Cassidy. With Bobby Smith incapacitated by a groin injury and his namesake suffering from a badly gashed ankle, Brighton could not summon enough firepower to subdue 'Rovers' (1-1). But the draw was good enough to raise Albion to third position, their highest placing so far.

Hampered by injuries to key players, Brighton performed inconsistently during the following month, dropping out of the promotion places. The top-of-the-table clash with Bradford Park Avenue on 7 November proved to be a big attraction. 20,722 came to the Goldstone on a bright, raw afternoon to watch an exciting 2-2 draw. Bradford's attack was led by the prolific goalscorer Kevin Hector, who would score 113 goals in 176 appearances for Park Avenue before moving to Derby County in 1966. He and fellow striker Jim Fryatt kept the Brighton defence at full stretch. Although both Jack and Bobby Smith scored for Brighton, it wasn't enough to seal victory. Nevertheless, Brighton went up one place to fourth.

Archie's FA Cup ambitions disappeared at the first hurdle at Ashton Gate on a day of gusting wind and slanting rain. Wrexham bore the brunt of Albion's anger at the Goldstone a week later. Once again, the gate was lower than hoped. 14,477 came along on a grey afternoon to see goals from Goodchild, Bobby Smith, Cassidy (2) and Gould secure an easy 5-1 victory.

Promotion-seeking Tranmere had more of a bite in Wallasey, though. Goals from Bobby Smith and Cassidy were in vain as Brighton lost 2-4. But rejuvenated by a free weekend – a legacy of their early FA Cup exit – Brighton visited Barrow on a glowering, wet Saturday afternoon on 12 December. The Albion turned on a scintillating display in the Holker Street mud, winning 4-1 with goals from Bobby Smith (2), Gould and Goodchild. It was their biggest away victory of the season. One Barrow supporter was so impressed with Brighton's performance that he wrote to Archie Macaulay saying, 'I would be a regular attender at football if I could see a display like this every Saturday.'

Back in their stride, Brighton hammered Hartlepools 5-0 at a freezing, foggy Goldstone on the Saturday before

Christmas. Bobby Smith and Gould scored a brace apiece while Collins added a fifth. Perhaps Christmas shopping duties were to blame for the 12,667 attendance, the lowest home gate of the season. But the shivering cold probably played a part, too. Snow then fell over the Christmas period. However, both games with Halifax went ahead. Albion won the Boxing Day game at the Goldstone 2-1 with goals from Gould and Cassidy, loudly cheered by the delighted 19,000 Albion supporters. Bill Cassidy's match-winning goal was the icing on the cake.

Bill Cassidy was a Goldstone favourite. He always gave his all in Albion's cause. He made people laugh, too. *Brighton Argus* reporter John Vinicombe wrote, 'Bill played every game as though it was the cup final. The highly charged 90 minutes that he put in, either at wing-half, inside-forward or occasionally centre-forward were particularly effective in the lower divisions where the need to fight for the right to play was paramount. Moreover, Bill knew full well that he had to make up for a lack of pace by extra physical effort. A tackle from Cassidy did not contain an option of coming back for more, although there was not a bad bone in his body and a joke was never very far away from a stream of Scottish oaths. Being a good pro, Bill took his football very seriously but was blessed with an intuitive knack of relieving tension by a timely quip or gesture. When Bill donned the cap and bells it did more for morale than a torrent of invective from manager Archie Macaulay. Flagging spirits soared when Bill was up to his pranks. Archie, a fellow Scot, valued his joker in the pack. He knew full well that a happy dressing room can often be the launch pad of a successful side. This proved to be the case in 1964/65 when Bill's ten goals in 24 was a most acceptable ratio amid so much competition for places. It used to be said in the old days of pre-overseas imports that a manager needed to guard against getting too many players from north of the border at one time in case they formed a too powerful group. That was not a problem for Archie. After all he was one of them, although he tended to treat some of the players like a laird might boss his tenants.' Jimmy Collins, his closest friend at Albion, told Vinicombe, 'A man couldn't have had a better friend. He had his down spells, but he made you laugh. I loved that man.'

Archie was very happy with his festive returns. He wrote in his programme notes, 'For the first time for many seasons, the lads gave the directors, myself and the supporters a real Christmas box in the shape of five points out of six, nicely positioned in fourth place in the table to make an all-out effort for promotion, and it is satisfying to note that Albion are seven points better off than this time last season, and what is most important to supporters, of the 58 goals scored to date, no less than 57 have been scored by the forwards, and that is crowd-drawing stuff.'

Brighton's 3-1 home win over Crewe in January saw the debut of the ill-fated Barry Rees at right-half. Tragically, Barry was killed in a road accident just before Albion won the Fourth Division championship in April. He played just 12 times for Brighton but left a lasting memory with all who saw him play.

A storm-tossed 4-4 draw with Chester on 6 February was the only time that Brighton failed to win in a sequence of seven games. Promotion rivals Millwall were beaten 2-0 at the Goldstone on 16 January and struggling Southport were beaten at Haig Avenue a week later in front of a miserly 2,286 crowd. Then, with Robin Stubbs, the leading Fourth Division marksman, well marshalled by Norman Gall, Torquay were beaten 1-0 on a day of dappled sunlight at Plainmoor. According to John Vinicombe, Archie Macaulay was so pleased with the result that he converted the return trip into an almighty bender. John wrote, 'To say [we] were sloshed would be an understatement. We were all very nearly paralysed.'

Nevertheless, Brighton were back in shape in time for the following week's trip to Meadow Lane, where Notts County were beaten 2-1 on a day of grey, damp, penetrating cold. Once again, Jack Smith was on target, as was Cassidy. A hat-trick of victories ensued, including a 5-0 romp against Chesterfield at the Goldstone. Goodchild grabbed two goals and Gould one, but in answering the case for the defence, Mel Hopkins joined in the fun with a debut goal. A crowd of almost 21,000 clapped and cheered. Brighton seemed well ensconced in third place.

Brighton's 11-match unbeaten run came to an end in the mud and snow at a bright, blustery Belle Vue, Doncaster, on 6 March. Here, Alick Jeffrey inspired Doncaster to a 2-1 victory in front of a 10,000-plus crowd. Despite Bobby Smith scoring on his return to action, Bradford Park Avenue proved no more hospitable two weeks later (0-2). Although this was a promotion battle, only 6,300 locals considered it to be worthy of their interest. Five years later, Park Avenue ceased to be a Football League club, having been voted out in preference of Cambridge United.

On the following Monday came another promotion four-pointer. This one was at Spotland, Rochdale. Norman Gall recounted his experience of this fiery game to author Paul Camillin in his *Match of My Life* book. Norman said, 'This was a cracking game. It was quite a tetchy affair, not helped by some poor refereeing. Kevin Howley awarded Rochdale a penalty, claiming an Albion defender had punched the ball out when in fact it had been our goalkeeper, Brian Powney. We were livid, and all the more so when the penalty was converted. We fought back to equalise through Johnny Goodchild, only for Rochdale to take the lead again. Jimmy Collins equalised for us a second time, before the incident occurred which makes the game stand out in my mind as certainly the most eventful of my career.

'Me and Rochdale forward Bert Lister, a big stocky six-foot-plus centre-forward, were chasing a loose ball towards the byline in front of the main stand. As we were running towards the ball, I knew what he was going to do; I knew he wasn't going to go for the ball so neither did I. I stood my ground and we both barged into each other. He went into the wall and I went over the top and into the home supporters. As I went into the crowd, I felt a blow to the back of my head. As I got to my feet, still in the crowd, I found everyone was trying to hit me. I had my head down and couldn't see much and I put my hands up to protect myself, instinctively pushing out at the baying mob. I managed to get away from the crowd and back on to the side of the pitch, but then Lister started wrestling with me. We were both on the ground for a few seconds before the other players ran in to separate us and stop us fighting. Howley came over and straight away sent us both off. Lister went off being cheered by the Rochdale fans, and I was told by Jimmy Collins, the captain, to go down injured so they could buy some time and reorganise the defence. That upset the crowd even more. Howley then ordered me to get off and by then I was getting some real stick from the crowd.

'Archie Macaulay came out to put his arm around me and console me, but as we were walking off the pitch towards the tunnel we were pelted with rubbish, fruit, pies and all sorts by their fans. At that point Archie bailed out and left me to walk back to the dressing room on my own, taking sanctuary in the dug-out. I took the brunt of the supporters' pelting as I left the field of play and I remember looking down at my shirt. It was covered in rubbish but at the same time I was thinking how important the point could be.'

Macaulay was not angry with Norman, and nor were his team-mates. They were simply relieved to come away with a vital point. Norman duly served a seven-day suspension, meaning he missed the 3-1 home win over Southport on a Friday evening, on 26 March, in which Collins (twice) and Gould were on target. He missed the tense 2-2 draw at promotion-chasing Oxford, too, in front of a 13,429 crowd at the Manor Ground. Here, Jack and Bobby Smith were the marksmen.

The sending-off incident rumbled on, though, after a Rochdale supporter complained to the police that Norman had assaulted him during the off-the-pitch melee. Norman was summoned to court in Greater Manchester but was found not guilty. Outside the courtroom he made his peace with the Rochdale supporter. They parted quite amicably, with Norman inviting the chap to the Goldstone for a drink.

Brighton entered the final straight in good shape. A midweek 2-1 victory at Wrexham on 3 April, with goals by Jack Smith and Gould, moved Brighton into second spot. Despite losing 4-1 at lowly Bradford City on Friday 6 April, the damage was immediately repaired with a crucial 2-1 midweek home win over promotion rivals Tranmere. Norman Gall recalled, 'We went top of the league by beating Tranmere. Tranmere had gone 1-0 up after I made a mistake with a short back pass which let in their striker to score, but Bobby Smith drew us level with only 15 minutes remaining and I then headed in a corner in the final minute at the South Stand-end. Wally Gould picked me out from the left and I got above the Rovers defence and headed home. That win took us to top spot with four games to play.' 24,017 supporters attended this game, making it Brighton's biggest gate of the season, thus far.

All that remained were the three Easter games plus a re-arranged game with Darlington at home at the end of April. First up was the Good Friday game at Edgeley Park, Stockport, played in warm spring sunshine on a bone dry, rutted surface. Urged on by a large contingent of Albion fans in the 10,000-plus crowd, Brighton cruised to a 4-1 victory with goals from Goodchild, Bobby Smith, Gould and Collins. However, winter then made a sudden and unwelcome return with temperatures plummeting overnight.

Easter Saturday dawned icy and wet with the persistent rain turning to snow. Brighton lost their footing at Feethams, where Darlington won comfortably by 2-0. Despite this setback, Brighton managed to cling on to pole position. The conditions for the return game with Stockport on Easter Monday were scarcely better, but Brighton had little difficulty despatching their opponents 3-1 with goals from Collins, Jack Smith and Goodchild.

Now, only five points separated the seven teams contesting the four promotion places. But for Brighton, the equation was simple. If they won their final home game against Darlington on Monday, 26 April, they would be promoted as champions.

It was in late afternoon that my friend Tony and I decided to go. Having pooled our depleted resources, we had just enough for our rail fares and admission. We hurriedly set off barely two hours from kick-off. Our electric train seemed to saunter sadistically along the coastal line, meaning that the whale-backed downs approached with infuriating slowness. Outside, the verdant marshland celebrated a succulent spring growth. The golden evening sunlight dazzled in the criss-cross dykes. Fresh foliage fluttered on a serene breeze. A scent of cut grass wafted in at each of our interminable stops. The evening's beauty clamoured for attention but kick-off preyed on our minds. We changed trains at Lewes and Brighton, scampering between the platforms, trying to catch the fastest connection.

By the time we had arrived at Hove station, the game had begun. The sound of the crowd had a shuddering impact, even as far away as the Hove platform. We sprinted over the footbridge and then down the eerily empty street to the first set of turnstiles. Once inside, we were confronted with a heaving crowd, later reported to be in excess of 31,000. With the Eastern terrace full to bursting, we headed towards the South Stand, making our way along the well between its upper and lower sections. There seemed to be no space at all. But a sudden spilling motion granted us a narrow ledge which we seized. With the crowd recoiling we had to defend our slender foothold staunchly, grabbing at a stanchion to prevent us from toppling backwards. Thereafter, we were forced to stand mainly on tiptoe. But still our vision was obstructed. We couldn't see the goal immediately in front of us. It was the one that the Brighton lads were attacking in their blue facings and white sleeves.

We could see Jimmy Collins, though, deep in midfield; busy, buzzing, bustling; angrily brushing off his obstructive opponents, twisting one way, then another, looking for an opening with prickly resolve. But we had to rely upon the crowd to know whether one of his raking passes had found its mark. A sudden crescendo, like the ignition of a jet engine, signified that it had. And then, with the added thrust of an afterburner, there seemed to be a chance of a goal. But the cascading sound, like surf surging over the pebbles, suggested that the opportunity had been lost. It was pointless asking what was happening. We had no way of hearing one another above the din. And besides, those around us had no better idea of what was happening than we did. We had to content ourselves with snatched glimpses and audio clues. We could see the Brighton wingers at the start of their runs. There was Gould upright, composed and direct, shrouded in the shadow of the West Stand. On the opposite flank, there was Goodchild, hunched and scurrying, catching the full glare of the setting sun. But sight of them would be lost as soon as they approached the box or veered towards a corner. Stretching upwards as far as we could go, we could just see the Darlington keeper at the height of his leap, grasping the ball, under pressure from the heads of the Brighton forwards. But that was as good as it got.

We continued to be storm-tossed, as if caught in an Atlantic squall. Urged on by the increasingly vociferous crowd, Brighton cranked up the momentum. Darlington were pushed further and further back. At least, that was the implication. Certainly, sightings of the Darlington players in advanced positions became rarer. The visitors had not come to pay homage, though. They were determined to compete – by fair means or foul. Judging by the crowd's mounting anger it seemed as if they were opting for the latter. The Brighton trainer made several sprints towards the 'Darlo' end. His appearances were accompanied by shrill whistles, so piercing that we had to cover our ears. It was as if he was the culprit. With boos also bellowing out at regular intervals, we presumed that the 'Darlo hit men' were hard at work.

Then it happened. It simply had to. The crowd's strength appeared overpowering. It seemed as if the ball was being sucked into the Darlington net by its collective gasps. We discovered later that Bobby Smith had put Jimmy Collins in on goal and Jimmy had finished clinically. The resulting roar was volcanic. The South Stand shook with so many bodies pogoing in no space at all. A chaotic, tumbling surge followed, giving us a brief glimpse of Collins being hugged by his team-mates. It was his 17th league goal of the season and Brighton's 100th. Soon afterwards, we gathered that Jack Smith had added another. The mayhem of the first goal was repeated with even greater fervour. With the Darlington defence unravelling, Brighton were home and dry. When the third went in – Gould's 21st league goal – the promotion party began. Brighton's three years of hurt had been gloriously expunged. Perversely, the third goal seemed to spark a Darlington revival. A balding wing-half called Ray Yeoman began to stride forward purposefully, but to no avail. Although their tall centre-forward scored with a rasping shot in front of the North Stand, Brighton's title was safe.

As the final whistle blew, thousands of fans clambered over the perimeter wall and on to the pitch. But Tony and I decided to leave quietly. I was pleased at Brighton's triumph, of course. I had followed them for seven years, reading their match reports avidly, always looking out for their results and periodically going to their games. I wanted them to do well. But this didn't feel like my night of joy. Instead, I felt like a party crasher. I had thought that Brighton's promotion might have compensated for Hastings's sad decline. It didn't. I was beginning to learn what monogamy means.

The 1964/65 triumph was another feather in Archie's cap. He had brought together a team that had, for the most part, performed superbly. It was also a vindication of the investments made by the board of directors under Eric Courtney-King. The signing of Bobby Smith was a huge success.

Smith enjoyed the company of the directors like comedian Norman Wisdom. He recalled, 'Norman asked if he could join in training one day at the Goldstone. We put him in goal and for a bit of fun I hit a volley so hard Norman got knocked into the back of the net. He laughed and said, "I'm not staying in goal for more of that." He was a good lad.'

But Smith's relationship with manager Archie Macaulay was far from cordial. While Smith refuted that he was suspended for a fortnight because he reported back for pre-season at an overweight 15 stone, he was adamant that it was a money row with Macaulay that saw him sacked three months later. Smith said, 'I was writing an article for *The People* and getting £500 for it. Macaulay wanted £400 and said if he didn't get it he would terminate my contract. He was due to leave. I had been asked to take over as manager, but the board told me they had to go with his decision to sack me. I was annoyed. I thought, "That's me finished with pro football." It was not a nice way to go.'

Bobby Smith left Brighton in the summer of 1965. It was a premature departure. Team-mate Robin Upton observed, 'I thought Bobby Smith was a terrific player at home. You didn't see much of him away.' But Smith might have served Albion well for a further year or more. Instead, he chose to join newly relegated Hastings United in October 1965. The former Orient centre-half Sid Bishop had recently replaced Ted Ballard as Hastings's boss, playing as well as managing. Smith and Bishop had apparently been friendly when they were both playing in London. It was reputed that Smith was offered £65 a week to play for Hastings – a huge sum, worth around £68,000 per year today – for a club said to be in financial difficulty. Regrettably, the move was not a success. But more of that comes next.

Seventeen months later, I went to the Goldstone Ground to watch Brighton take on Northampton in a Third Division game. It was a bright, blustery late September afternoon. Brighton were becalmed in the third tier while Northampton had been relegated recently from Division Two, mustering only 30 points. Even the return of previous talisman Frank Large could not prevent a further fall.

On 30 September 1967, Northampton arrested their slide by winning 2-0 at Brighton, with goals from Large and Hall. It was a wretched game. Neither side could deal with the ball's erratic course in the swirling wind, not helped by the Goldstone's rock-like surface. For the Albion, former Cobbler Charlie Livesey was partnered up front by ex-Workington starlet Kit Napier. Future Leeds and England boss Howard Wilkinson was expected to keep them in business, but his 'dog with a balloon' display meant that he wasn't much of a wing commander, to the derision of the home fans. Although the Cobblers hung on to their Third Division status at the end of this season, a year later they were back in the basement, where they had been eight years before. Their average attendance had slumped to under 7,000. Just six years after competing in the top flight, Northampton had to apply for re-election to the Football League. Their ten-year 'Grand Old Duke of York' journey was complete.

Improbable success, as Northampton achieved, often becomes a rod with which to beat those who have dared to dream. We raise the expectations of modest performers at our peril. Nevertheless, Joe Mercer credited Northampton's rise from the bottom to the top flight as one of the greatest achievements in the history of British football, bigger than Ramsey's World Cup triumph in 1966.

James Humphreys:
Hastings United's 'Mr Big'?

'Keep on Runnin'

QUESTION: WHAT do the following have in common
– Hastings United; the 1996 BBC drama *Our Friends in
the North*; large-scale corruption in the Metropolitan Police
force and the *Oz* obscenity trial of 1971? Answer: Mr James
Humphreys.

Hastings United author, Roger Sinden, recalled: 'In
January 1966 the new chairman of United was James
Humphreys, whose major passion was greyhound racing at a
time when there were moves afoot to bring racing to Hastings.
He had joined the board in June 1965 and was chairman by
mid-season.'

It was understandable that Jim Humphreys should have
been received so cordially by the club. Humphreys seemed a
personable chap, ostensibly charming. More importantly he
had a viable plan for reviving Hastings United's fortunes: dog
racing. He planned to use the Pilot Field's perimeter space,
vacated by the defunct town speedway team, for a dog track.
The club were hard-up. Humphreys seemed to be a successful
businessman. He wasn't short of cash, it seemed, having an
impressive spread at nearby Northiam. He was experienced in

the gambling business. It looked as if a local dog track would benefit himself, the club and, maybe, the town, too. According to those closely connected with the club, nothing was known about the shadier aspects of Mr Humphreys' life when he became a director in 1965.

As for the football team, former Orient centre-half, Sid Bishop, replaced Ted Ballard as Hastings's boss, also retaining a playing role. But according to Ken Ballard, Ted's son, Sid was not suited to management although he was still a good player. Ken, who played under Sid, thought that the former Orient 'stopper' wasn't disciplined enough, leaving the players too much to their own devices. Sid's results were erratic with emphatic victories over Bexley (4-2) and Tunbridge Wells (7-0) juxtaposed with disappointing defeats at Hillingdon (1-2), Stevenage (0-1) and Tonbridge in the FA Cup (0-3).

However, on 14 October 1965 former England international Bobby Smith signed for Hastings United almost certainly bankrolled by Humphreys. Smith signed a two-year contract with a wage reputed to be £65 a week. It was considerably less than that – probably under £40 per week but this was still a massive outlay for a small non-league club – equating to an annual wage now worth around £40,000. Although Smith later claimed that the club reneged on a promise to pay him a £1,000 signing-on fee, he seemed initially happy with the deal, stating that he was looking for a club near to his Brighton home. He also said he was pleased to be playing alongside Hastings's player-manager, Sid Bishop, who was described as an 'old friend from his London footballing days'. Smith explained: 'I'm not really match fit because I haven't been able to train for several weeks but it won't take me many days to get in condition again. I'm a big man and I have to watch what I eat and so on, but too much has been made of this overweight business. That was not really what the business at Brighton was all about.'

Ken Ballard remembered the build-up to Smith's signing. He said: 'We knew something was in the wind because right out of the blue Sid Bishop told us he was laying four of us off. He made no bones about it. He needed our wages. So, off we went. George Francis was on about £14–15 per week (worth probably £20,000 today). He went to Hillingdon. I went to Stevenage, under George Curtis. We heard that a £500 signing was to be made. Then in came Smith. It was a bit of a shock. George hung around for a few more weeks but knew his time was up.'

Roger Sinden, author of *Hastings United Through Time* wrote: 'None of the Hastings team had met Smith before, let alone trained with him, and the speculation grew in the dressing room as to whether he would turn up. Before his first game at Ashford, Kent on 18 October, there were traffic jams in the town, contributing to Smith's delayed arrival, and Ashford's average gate of 650 was increased to 2,875. Hastings midfielder, Bela Olah recalled that Smith sauntered into the dressing room eventually, with his football boots wrapped in newspaper under his arm.

'After a brief introduction Smith proposed tactics to Olah. Smith suggested that if there was a cross from the wing, it should not be at him but placed three or four feet in advance for him to run on to.' Apparently, Bela Olah questioned whether Smith would be able to reach such a cross – perhaps indelicately, given concerns about Smith's weight and fitness – but Smith assured him that this would be fine if it wasn't hit too hard.

According to Roger Sinden, 'Bela found Bobby Smith a down-to-earth person, with no airs and graces. Smith was disarmingly modest about his previous international successes, saying all of that was in the past. Bela was quick to scotch any rumours about Bobby Smith's off-the-field drinking and said that he never saw any evidence of this. His interest in betting is well evidenced, though, and Sid Bishop once had to drag Smith out of a betting shop to make sure that he started the game on time.' The reality was that Smith had a gambling addiction. He desperately needed cash to clear gambling debts which were mounting exponentially, thereby reinforcing his addiction.

Smith started well, scoring with a header against Ashford and then netting two goals with nonchalant ease in his first home match against Dover. But the business strategy did not go to plan. Club chairman, Cecil Catt, expected a crowd of up to 5,000 to greet Smith's first appearance at the Pilot Field, whereas on a damp, grey afternoon only 3,223 turned up, no more than for a local derby with Tonbridge. Thereafter, Smith's appearances became increasingly fitful. He excused his absence on health grounds. Some claims seemed genuine, but according to the club, others were not. Crowds – home and away – lost patience with him. So did the Hastings management. There were three suspensions – one by the club and two by the FA. These were usually followed by frank, heart-to-heart discussions between the player and the club, leading to new, but short-lived resolutions. In May 1966, the club thought they had gone far enough and decided to sack Smith only for the Southern League to uphold his subsequent appeal.

Nevertheless, after Humphreys had signed Jim Ryan, a Welsh under-23 international centre-forward in November, he and Smith established a formidable spearhead. Hastings United suddenly fired into life as Christmas approached. A 12-match unbeaten run followed, containing crushing victories over Ramsgate (6-0); Deal (9-0); Gloucester (6-2); Kettering (7-3) and Canterbury (4-1). An incredible 46 goals were scored during this purple patch. Promotion seemed assured. However, a 1-4 defeat at Bath on 31 January caused Bishop's team to falter.

Having been elected club chairman in January 1966, Humphreys responded to this setback by appointing Stan Berry, once of QPR, as his general manager, supposedly leaving Bishop freer to manage team affairs. But Berry immediately strayed into Bishop's area of responsibility, bringing in two half-backs, John Blake and Peter Phillips, plus veteran QPR striker, Bernard Evans without conspicuously improving United's performances. Hastings won just eight of their final 20 Southern League games, a lapse in form that caused them to miss promotion by three points, despite scoring over 100 league goals. As Hastings's form deteriorated dressing room tensions increased. Bobby Smith's erratic appearances hardly helped.

Ken Ballard's younger brother, Alan, remembered Smith's brief appearance against champions-elect, Barnet, in February 1966. He said: 'There were only a few minutes to go before kick-off when Smith's car roared into the ground. He strode into the dressing room with his boots under his arm. He didn't stay too long, either, dismissed for having a right go at a linesman. When I told dad about it, he was really angry. He had no time for anyone not committed to the club.' Hastings lost 2-4 with stand-in goalkeeper, Dickie Guy, gifting Barnet a goal. Eight years later, Guy performed heroically in Wimbledon's FA Cup run, denying both Burnley and Leeds.

Hungarian midfielder Bela Olah was critical of Sid Bishop, complaining that he had a problem with foreigners and never seemed to have a good word for him. Some fans got wind of this, protesting publicly at Olah's exclusion from the team at Sittingbourne on 12 March 1966. Bishop was stung into retaliation. In his 'Manager's notes' for the Hillingdon home game on 19 March, Bishop's anger was palpable: 'At Sittingbourne last week I was ashamed that there was a group of supporters chanting and yelling their heads off about something of which they obviously knew nothing. So, I would like to say right now for the benefit of this little group, that the reason why Bela Olah was not in the side was that if I had played him, he would not have stood a cat-in-hell's chance of being fit for our Southern League Cup semi-final against Yeovil four days later.' Bishop clearly felt under pressure.

Jim Humphreys was strong-minded and ambitious. Quester, the *Hastings & St Leonards Observer*'s football correspondent wrote after Humphreys' election as club chairman: 'That is the man at the helm of United. And we will know he's there, believe me!' Although Humphreys' over-riding ambition was to establish dog racing locally, he had not neglected the football club, as evidenced by the various signings he had appeared to finance.

With Hastings falling short in the promotion race, Sid Bishop resigned, joining Guildford City as a player. He remarked darkly: 'The wrong type of people were running the club at Hastings and I wasn't at all happy there.' While there was growing unease about James Humphreys' background, his shady dealings were not fully exposed until concerted investigations revealed the extent of corruption within the Metropolitan Police Force.

In 1996, Colin Wills of the *Sunday Mirror* wrote an article about this scandal at the launch of the BBC TV serial *Our Friends in the North*. He wrote: 'BEHIND the sex and sleaze of TV's newest crime blockbuster lies a real-life story of police corruption. The drama served up in *Our Friends in the North* paints a glamorous picture of Soho in the Sixties. But millions of viewers will be unaware that it is based on true accounts of the blackest period in police history when hundreds of Britain's policemen were on the payrolls of gangsters. The parallels between the TV characters and real people are astoundingly close. Pornographer, Bennie Barratt, played by Malcolm McDowell, is drawn from Jimmy Humphreys, the Mr Big in Soho at the time. The "crusading cop", Roy Johnson, is the double of Frank Williamson, a senior police officer drafted in by then Home Secretary, Jim Callaghan to clean up Scotland Yard.' Wills said that Humphreys thought the drama was 'very accurate'.

Coincidentally, in 1971, the editors of the 'hippie' magazine, *Oz*, were prosecuted under the obscene publication laws for producing a 'School Kids issue'. Among the magazine's features was a comic strip of an unusually libidinous Rupert Bear. There was a public outcry, led by John Lennon and a young John Birt, against the jail sentences handed out to

Oz's Richard Neville, Felix Dennis and Jim Anderson. The convictions were subsequently overturned on appeal, but only after Lord Chief Justice Widgery had conducted some investigations of his own. He was said to have sent his clerk to Soho to buy £20 worth of the hardest pornographic material on open sale. The contents of the offending *Oz* magazine paled by comparison. Lord Chief Justice Widgery then realised the *Oz* prosecutions were indefensibly discriminative.

According to Alan Travis, in his *Guardian* article of 13 November 1999, the collapse of the *Oz* trial prompted new Home Secretary, Reginald Maudling, to enquire why the Metropolitan Police Obscene Publications Squad had targeted *Oz* when there was more lurid material on open sale. Maudling was concerned not to discriminate against the 'alternative society' particularly when the Obscene Publications Squad had targeted other 'underground' magazines, namely *International Times* and *Frendz*. Maudling was not at all reassured by the answers he received from DCI George Fenwick, the head of the 'dirty' squad. Meanwhile, Lord Longford's enquiries revealed that seven porn merchants were bribing police officers. Humphreys was named as one of these. But Maudling's subsequent investigations came up against a wall of silence. According to Travis, 'Flying Squad' boss, Commander Kenneth Drury, then compromised himself by spending a two-week holiday in Cyprus with James Humphreys in February 1972. Drury attempted to excuse his presence there, claiming he had been looking for Ronnie Biggs, the escaped train robber. Not hot on geography, then.

Within weeks of this exposure, Maudling appointed Robert 'Mr Clean' Mark as the new commissioner of the Metropolitan Police Force. The hawk-featured Mark was also known as the 'Manchester Martinet' and the 'Lone Ranger from Leicester'. He was a fierce moral warrior. Despite Drury's exposure, Mark made little headway in uncovering the other culprits caught up in the supposed web of corruption.

Humphreys' evidence was vital in the success of Robert Mark's clean-up campaign. Not renowned for his stand-up turns, Mark remarked: 'A good police force is one that catches more crooks than it employs.' He added: 'The real fear of pornographers was not of the courts but of harassment, either by strong-armed men seeking protection money or by the police doing, in effect, the same thing'.

Historian Alwyn Turner observed: 'The Sweeney might show Flying Squad officers mixing with criminals, but there was nothing in that TV series to indicate that James Humphreys was a suitable guest at an annual Flying Squad dinner.'

Dave Underwood, a former Watford, Fulham and Liverpool goalkeeper, replaced Bishop as Hastings manager in 1966. By this time Stan Berry had left the club together with his three recruits. With Humphreys exercising much greater financial caution, five players were added to replace the seven who had or were about to leave. These were: QPR's Irish international centre-half, Ray Brady; former QPR and Ashford centre back, Keith Rutter, who replaced the departed Bishop; Peter Knight, a winger, formerly with Brighton, who replaced the popular Gordon Burden; Willie Smith an attacking Scottish wing half, originally with Celtic, replacing Bill Goundry; Jim Strachan, a Scottish defensive midfielder, who replaced 1965/66 'player of the year', Eddie Stone after Stone's move to South Africa in the autumn of 1966.

Although Dave Underwood had a reputation as being a 'Jack the lad', his team played with greater discipline than under Bishop. Liam Brady's elder brother, Ray – a Rolls-Royce centre back at this level – performed superbly with Keith Rutter in a tightly organised defence, also featuring the versatile full backs, Bill Cockburn, Dave Coney and Ken Nicholas, while Underwood's former Watford colleague, Tony Gregory, an FA Cup finalist with Luton in 1959, was signed in October to cover the loss of right winger, Alan Back. Gregory provided versatility and extra punch up front.

Despite an embarrassing FA Cup defeat at Horsham, Hastings joined the promotion places during the autumn of 1966 and remained there all season, losing just five times. Horsham was Smith's last full game for Hastings. Although his claims of injury and sickness were treated with scepticism by the club and the fans, Smith was often in pain as a result of injuries sustained while with Spurs. Smith told Giller how, on the morning of the 1961 FA Cup Final, he made two secret journeys from the team's Middlesex hotel to see his GP near his home in Palmers Green for painkilling injections for his knee. Smith said: 'If our manager Bill Nicholson had known the pain I was in, he would have left me out. This was the game of my life and I was determined not to miss it.' Smith played through the pain and scored the first and laid on the second in a 2-0 victory over Leicester City that clinched that historic FA Cup/Football League 'double', the first of the 20th century.

1966 Swinging Britain

'Tomorrow Never Knows'

BY JULY 1966 British pop music sat alongside Ramsey's 'wingless wonders' at the top of the world. Inspired by Dr Timothy Leary's mantra 'Turn on, tune in and drop out,' The Beatles recorded their first 'trippy' song, 'Tomorrow Never Knows', in this year. Less than three years before, the mop-haired 'Fab Four' were still peddling soppy love songs such as 'I Want to Hold Your Hand', but by 1966 they had become beaded, bearded hippies intrigued by notions of cosmic love and metaphysical meanderings. In 'Tomorrow Never Knows' a spectral-sounding John Lennon emerges from a droning swirl of instrumental distortion, agonised seagull-like cries and a pounding Indian drumbeat, to insist it was time to leave reality behind and drift listlessly downstream. The narcotic age of pop had arrived.

'Tomorrow Never Knows' set the pace for a swathe of psychedelic compositions from both sides of the Atlantic, as exemplified by Jefferson Airplane's 'White Rabbit', The Jimi Hendrix Experience's 'Purple Haze', The Velvet Underground's 'Heroin', Pink Floyd's 'See Emily Play' and, of course, The Beatles' later composition 'A Day in the Life'. It was left to the iconoclastic Kinks to deconstruct the venal vapidity of mid-60s pop culture, mocking Carnaby Street-style narcissism in 'Dedicated Follower of Fashion', scorning parvenu decadence in 'Sunny Afternoon', graphically itemising grinding poverty in 'Dead End Street', and satirising fond sentiments of Imperial glory in 'Victoria'. Hogarth might well have been impressed. Meanwhile, in his sardonic 1966 film *Blow Up*, Italian film director Michelangelo Antonioni scoffed at the vacuity of swinging London values.

While the froth of 'swinging Britain' suggested a thriving UK, its economy was far from sound. In *Anatomy of Britain Today*, esteemed political commentator Anthony Sampson wrote, 'It is hard to see how Great Britain can quickly break out of its supine contentment without the challenge of the Common Market. Its quasi-aristocratic society has difficulty in generating dynamic movement. Much of its current energy comes not from the English but from the immigrant, particularly in the fastest growing industries – electronics, television, hire purchasing or advertising. This monopoly must be broken if Britain is to make proper use of her brains and her energy. The public schools and richer colleges not only perpetuate an anachronistic class system, they project a view of Britain which is out-of-date and often irrelevant.' Our productivity was being outstripped by the former Axis adversaries. While we were constructing our final steam locomotive, *Evening Star*, in 1960, Japan was developing its ultra-swish, much faster 'Bullet Train'. No wonder we consoled ourselves with preposterous *James Bond* tales of British supremacy.

With British manufacturing in retreat, the Labour government faced a huge imbalance of payments which soon led to devaluation. The country, particularly the industrial north and west midlands, remained sullied by slum, derelict and shabby prefabricated housing. Too many people were without basic amenities, adequate shelter being the most pressing need. The BBC Wednesday play *Cathy Come Home* would ram that point home better than any government inquiry. Beneath the vapid gloss of swinging Britain there was a grim, grimy reality, much nearer to the abject poverty of *The Whisperers* than the atavistic preening of *Darling*, closer to the austerity of *Z Cars* and *Softly Softly* than the cosiness of *Dixon of Dock Green*.

Sussex CCC v West Indies

County Ground, Hove, 11 and 13 June 1966

'Monday Monday'

THE WEST Indians' triumphant tour of England in 1966 was not without its setbacks. I was to witness the first of these at Hove on a sparkling, humid Saturday on 11 June. England had just capitulated haplessly inside three days at Manchester. In almost a replica of their one-sided victory there in 1963, Hunte (135) and Sobers (161) enabled the tourists to compile an unbeatable first innings total of 484 runs. Then, on a newly prepared surface that increasingly favoured spin, Gibbs twice ran through the hesitant England batting order, taking ten wickets for 106 runs. England lost by an innings and 40 runs.

This abject defeat signalled the end of Mike Smith's period as England's captain. As MCC's captain at Lord's, in May Smith had made an aggressive century against Sobers's side, but he had been given easy pickings by the West Indian left-arm spinner Rawle Branker, who generously fed his penchant for the sweep. However, at Old Trafford, just two weeks later, Smith struggled to cope with the pace of Griffith and Hall and seemed confounded by Gibbs's sharp turn. According to Colin Cowdrey, who replaced Smith as captain, in the next Test at Lord's the selectors were alarmed that the bespectacled

Smith might incur fearful injury as he appeared to be late in picking up the line and height of fast, short-pitched bowling, although it was Gibbs who sealed his fate, dismissing him twice for single-figure scores.

Since the second Test was only five days away, the astonishing events I witnessed at Hove on 11 June had no bearing upon the selection of the England team for Lord's. Geoff Boycott was preferred to Eric Russell and Tom Graveney was belatedly recalled, replacing Smith in the middle order, while Basil D'Oliveira made his debut in place of off-spinner David Allen, and Essex all-rounder Barry Knight was included instead of the Warwickshire 'quick' David Brown. England's tail had been too long at Manchester, but this revamped side batted down to Titmus at nine. The crucial omission, though, was that of Sussex fast bowler John Snow.

Sussex appeared to pose little threat to Sobers's unbeaten touring side. They had completed the 1965 County Championship second from bottom and managed only two victories in their opening ten county fixtures in 1966. Sussex's batting order was highly suspect. Even with Jim Parks, Ted Dexter, Alan Oakman and the Indian Test captain the Nawab of Pataudi junior in their side, they had been shot out for just 69, two weeks before, by the Lancashire seamers, Statham, Higgs and Shuttleworth. With Dexter apparently turning his back on first-class cricket, Sussex's veteran left-handed opener Ken Suttle would top their County Championship averages in 1966 with an unexceptional 29.36 runs. And while Tony Buss and Don Bates gave admirable seam support to Snow, Sussex were almost entirely reliant upon the part-time off-breaks of Alan Oakman in the spin department.

Sussex's captain Pataudi won the toss and put the West Indians in to bat. It was rumoured to be a generous decision to indulge the 10,000 spectators, many of whom had been attracted by the prospect of bold West Indian stroke-play. But Pataudi knew the recently replaced square was unreliable, and given its greenness and the steamy weather, bowling first seemed to be the sensible option. Besides, he was disinclined to expose his fragile batting line-up to Griffith, Cohen and Sobers in helpful conditions. Moreover, the Hove crowd proved much more patriotic than was envisaged. With the World Cup finals beginning shortly in England, perhaps there were many there relishing a salty David versus Goliath contest. Whatever the cause, this crowd treated the occasion as if it was a feisty football derby.

Snow began the proceedings, bowling up the slope from the sea end, and immediately made the ball fly off a length forcing wicketkeeper Parks into a series of leaping takes. Parks and his slip cordon promptly retreated a few yards. The West Indian opening pair, 'Joey' Carew and Easton McMorris, looked ill at ease at Snow's daunting pace and seam movement, but there was little respite at the other end where Tony Buss, with his pumping approach, was achieving extravagant swing. Carew and McMorris were made to look like novices as they groped unconvincingly outside their off stumps, with each failure to make contact greeted by a rowdy 'ooh' or 'ahh' from the crowd. Frustrated at his attempts at laying bat on ball, McMorris flashed rashly at a wider, climbing delivery from Snow, slicing a catch to Pataudi at backward point (14/1). An explosive roar greeted his dismissal, obliterating the customary sense of decorum. This was not an occasion for polite applause.

Urged on by the excitable crowd, 'prize fighter' Snow let rip at the incoming batsman, Seymour Nurse. The moody and introspective Snow was not a Freddie Trueman. His aggression was less volatile, more an expression of smouldering menace.

Snow had been bitterly disappointed at his exclusion from the Ashes squad of 1965/66, but he had spent the winter wisely, perfecting his approach on the true wickets of South Africa. Dexter had first noticed that when Snow was bowling over the wicket, he made an involuntary step to the left at the point of delivery. This left him too open-chested and confined to bowling in-dippers. In South Africa, Snow practised straightening his approach, bowling close to the stumps, and bringing his torso around into a more sideways profile, giving him greater accuracy and the ability to swing the ball away from the right-hander's bat, although the lateral movement he achieved was principally due to his use of the seam.

Snow's considerable speed and lift owed much to his six-foot height, his wiry elasticity and shoulder power. Upon reaching the crease from a relaxed, loping run, Snow swayed slightly to his right, bringing him as close to the stumps as possible, flinging his guiding left arm across his chest, as if mimicking a crossbow, before cocking his right shoulder with a hunched gesture, propelling the ball with lithe fury. As he matured, Snow learnt to vary his pace and conserve energy better, relying more upon swing and seam movement, but here he was on trial against fearsome opponents. Having ambitions of an England recall, there was to be no letting up.

While the damp surface encouraged Snow's darting seam movement, the steamy atmosphere assisted his colleague's threatening swing. Somehow, the West Indian opener, Joey Carew, survived Snow's early onslaught, albeit with a succession of false shots that repeatedly sent the ball scurrying to the third man and fine leg boundary. Meanwhile, Carew's new partner, the strapping Seymour Nurse, began to play him and the probing medium-pacer Tony Buss studiously and with growing assurance. But just as Nurse appeared to be mounting a solid recovery, Sussex's first change seamer, Don Bates, castled him with a late swinging delivery – West Indies were 45/2 with Nurse out for 24 runs.

Pataudi then brought Suttle into the attack with his bustling, restrictive left-arm spin, in order to give Snow a well-earned breather. Suttle did more than contain, though, trapping Basil Butcher (12) in front of his stumps when the tourists' score had reached 60. Butcher's departure brought the great Gary Sobers to the crease. Surely, he would throw off the shackles and transform the course of this game? Sobers would complete the summer's five-match Test series with a 'Bradmanesque' average of 103 runs. But here Sobers stayed for less than five minutes as he was dismissed for a duck after edging a wide delivery from Bates to Parks. The roar that went up must have been heard over a mile away at the Goldstone Ground, where, as a wing-half, Don Bates had served Brighton & Hove Albion with distinction, helping the Seagulls achieve promotion to Division Two in 1958. The West Indies tottered in to lunch, four down for 70 runs.

Immediately after lunch Pataudi recalled Snow, prompting a cacophony of well-lubricated hectoring and hollering. Snow did as he was rowdily demanded and simply blew away the remaining West Indian batting, uprooting Lashley's and Gibbs's stumps in spectacular, cartwheeling fashion. The West Indies were dismissed for 123 in less than four hours' batting. Carew was the only West Indian to make a substantial score, having ridden his luck outrageously. Snow dismissed Carew also, leg before wicket for 56, achieving his best first-class bowling figures of seven wickets for 29 runs off 16.5 overs.

Although the incensed West Indian fast bowlers Griffith and Cohen reduced Sussex quickly to 40/6, the county recovered slightly, closing the day on 122/7, with Pataudi contributing 32 of these. The Sussex batting hero, though, was to be 20-year-old Peter Graves, who batted with brave resilience and skill, supported stoutly by a lower order comprising Oakman, Buss, Snow and Bates. Graves's innings of 64 runs, which was then his highest first-class score, eventually helped Sussex to an unexpected 62-run first innings lead on the Monday morning. Equally remarkably, Sobers failed to take a wicket in these seamer-friendly conditions.

If the West Indians' paltry first innings score was merely an aberration, their second was a humiliating calamity. In heavily overcast, humid conditions, the tourists were dismissed, within two-and-a-quarter-hours' play, for 67 runs with Buss and Snow sharing eight wickets and Bates adding a further two. Sobers avoided the indignity of a pair but made only eight before being clean bowled by the estimable Buss, who took four wickets for 18 in 11 overs, almost identical figures to those of John Snow who bagged 11 West Indian wickets in the match.

Sussex needed just six runs to win. Griffith was beside himself with rage. During Sussex's first innings he had held himself in check. Although still menacing, he chose not to strive for that lethal extra yard of pace which had attracted so much controversy. He was mindful that he had been called once for 'throwing' just prior to the first Test at Old Trafford and had no wish to excite the umpires' critical attention with the second Test so close. However, with an angry Sobers tossing him the ball at the start of the Sussex second innings, and then placing nine men behind the bat, with the tenth at short leg, Griffith knew exactly what was expected of him. It was the fastest, most deadly over I have ever seen. Griffith's first ball flew off just short of a length, chinning Suttle as he imprudently tried to hook. Suttle staggered from the crease and was quickly despatched to hospital where mercifully the x-ray confirmed only severe bruising. Suttle later quipped that Griffith must have slowed up, claiming that when he was hit by him in 1963 he had been hit *before* making a stroke. Here, he had completed the stroke before being felled.

The first innings hero, Graves, was promoted by Pataudi to hit the winning runs but Griffith's first ball to him hissed past his ear before he could blink. There was a call of 'no-ball' but this was for over-stepping, so there was to be no reprieve. Graves's second ball was his last. A spearing yorker crashed into his right boot, leaving him hobbling in great pain. As he looked up, he was relieved to see umpire John Langridge, a former Sussex stalwart, raise his finger. Parks then replaced Graves and immediately faced a brute of a delivery that grazed his ear. The fourth was shorter and flew over his head as he ducked. The fifth was another lightning yorker which Parks dug out just in time while the sixth flashed past his forehead barely seen. Parks swivelled around to see the ball still rising as it reached Hendricks, 20 yards back, the West Indian wicketkeeper leaping frantically to stop it flashing to the boundary. Parks and Griffith exchanged glares. It was only then that Sobers relented. He had made his point and calmly allowed Lenham and Parks to score the five runs they needed for victory from his part-time bowlers Solomon and Lashley, who had been the only West Indian batsmen to reach double figures in their wretched second innings.

From a lumbering run and a laboured, wheeling action, Griffith stunned his opponents with a deadly diet of venomous 'throat balls' and sizzling yorkers. Moreover, Griffith managed to produce his lethal lift off a good length, surprising many unwary batsmen. This had been the fate of the Indian captain, Nari Contractor whose skull was cracked, almost fatally, by a Griffith thunderbolt in 1962. Contractor never played Test cricket again.

Unlike Hall, whose pounding, wild-eyed sprint to the wicket presaged extreme speed, there was nothing in Griffith's trundling approach to suggest how menacing his deliveries would be. It was a common assumption then that Griffith could not generate such lightning pace legally. In fact, he had already been called for throwing by West Indian umpire Lopez Jordan in the match in which Contractor almost died. Ted Dexter was adamant that Griffith 'threw every ball', claiming that Frank Worrell said as much during the 1959/60 MCC tour of the Caribbean. Richie Benaud later joined the chorus of disapproval, stating that Griffith was an 'embarrassment' to his team-mates, many of whom were certain that he threw. Australian umpire Cecil Pepper was equally convinced of Griffith's guilt, having officiated in an exhibition match between an England XI and a West Indian one in 1964. However, MCC merely noted Pepper's concerns, and thanked him for avoiding any 'unnecessary unpleasantness' by not calling Griffith.

Griffith maintained his innocence, though, in his autobiography, whimsically entitled *Chucked Around*.

Although 'called' only twice during his first-class career, once by Lopez Jordan and once by English umpire Arthur Fagg, his protestations of innocence failed to remove the suspicion that he 'threw', particularly when striving for extra pace.

Wisbech Town v Hastings United

Southern League Division One, 29 April 1967

'Release Me'

HASTINGS SEEMED to be a happier, better side under Dave Underwood. Much of that can be attributed to the ex-Watford, Fulham and Liverpool goalkeeper's breezy management and tactical acumen. Ricky George played at Oxford, Hastings and Barnet before becoming an FA Cup hero at Hereford in 1972. He told Roger Sinden, 'Dave had a face like an old-time prize fighter; a broken nose, swollen lips. He also talked with a lisp. I was always notoriously late for games and I remember one Sunday we were playing the inmates of Ford Open Prison and Dave told me the kick-off was two o'clock. At five to two on the dot I rushed in breathlessly to find an empty dressing room. About a quarter of an hour later, big Dave strolled in with the rest of the players grinning fit to burst: "Whoopth-a-daithy", he says, "I've thuthed you out Ricky, alwayth late. Kick-off'th at free." I loved the man, I truly did.' Underwood became club chairman at Barnet between 1977 and 1982. There, he signed Jimmy Greaves, who later thanked him for helping him in his struggle with alcoholism.

Chirpy Dave Underwood wrote his programme notes for the opening home game against Gloucester City: 'Overall,

I feel we will have a good season. The board of directors, staff and players are determined to give their all to try and win the championship, but we must have your support. Remember, someone has got to win the league so why not us?' Despite Dave's entreaties, only 1,364 turned up. Perhaps the scorching weather had enticed the missing hundreds to head for the beach. In truth, many of those present were not only comatosed by the extreme heat but also distracted by *Test Match Special* reports of an improbable last wicket partnership at the Oval, for Sussex's John Snow and Lancashire's Ken Higgs put together 128 runs against the all-conquering West Indies, failing to break the world Test record for a last wicket stand by just two runs. Both Snow and Higgs reached maiden half-centuries. For much of the game many supporters had transistor radios pressed to the ear. Even the surprising return of Bobby Smith did little to shift the crowd's interest back to the football.

Alan Back eventually broke the deadlock before the interval but soon after had to be stretchered off with a double fracture. In the inaugural season of the substitute, Bill Cockburn deputised. Even with Bobby Smith and Jim Ryan up front, Gloucester proved surprisingly resilient and drew level midway through the second half. It looked as if we would have to put up with a disappointing draw until Jim Ryan scored with a diving header in the final minute. On 24 August newcomers Banbury United also frustrated Hastings in their first visit to the Pilot Field but were undone by Peter Knight's winner.

Hastings had never won at Ramsgate but seemed on course to break that duck on a sunny 27 August when Bobby Smith headed them into a first-half lead. But just before the break, Sid Jest equalised with a free kick outside the box. And although Jim Ryan had seemingly secured victory with a second goal, a wickedly spinning ball touched right-back Coney on the arm and a penalty was awarded, which Riggs converted. Hastings were also aggrieved at the outcome of the games at Stevenage and Banbury on 10 and 13 September. In both games a legitimate goal was disallowed, depriving Hastings of three points. At Banbury Jim Ryan equalised twice, the second with a blistering shot from 30 yards, but his third 'equaliser' in the final minute was incorrectly ruled out by a mistaken linesman.

There was no argument about Hastings's elimination from the SL Cup by Margate, though. The Kent side won 6-1 on aggregate! It was pleasing, too, that Hastings finally defeated rivals Tonbridge in an FA Cup tie. Other FA Cup wins over Ramsgate and Canterbury set up a winnable away tie at Horsham with the first round proper beckoning. Unfortunately, Hastings played poorly against geed-up opponents who capitalised on their greater pace and brawn on a heavy surface, winning easily. Bobby Smith's late headed goal from Knight's perfect cross merely emphasised Hastings's deficiencies for much of this game.

Their league form was encouraging, though. Gravesend (5-2), Merthyr (4-2) and Ashford (2-0) were swept aside at home with male model Ryan responsible for seven of the 11 goals, notching a hat-trick against Gravesend.

He also scored one of the two goals that defeated dogged Dunstable on 19 October, with ex-Luton FA Cup finalist Tony Gregory scoring the winner. Trowbridge were the only side to interrupt this impressive run. At the Pilot Field Hastings fought back courageously in the last few minutes to snatch a point, thanks to midfielder Ken Nicholas and right-back Dave Coney, whose freak, looping, long-range effort somehow eluded the Trowbridge keeper and found goal, with the referee about to blow the final whistle. The Trowbridge players slumped to the ground in dismay for they had completely outplayed their hosts and taken a deserved 2-0 lead. However, Trowbridge won the return match with ease (1-3), although Ryan was once again on target.

Ryan was a menace to opposing defences. At over six feet tall and weighing almost 13 stone he was a hefty proposition. Capable of holding the ball up in advanced positions, he created openings, using his bump-and-grind ability to pull defences apart. Although packing a vicious shot, it was his aerial strength that confounded his markers. Even in a scrum he jostled successfully for space, levering himself above the melee to put away towering headers, while his upper body strength enabled him to connect with any cross pumped into the box, high or low. It was these capabilities that resulted in Gravesend suffering a heavy defeat on 5 October. Performers like Ryan command instant attention, whatever level they play at. This is borne out by the 1,500 fans who turned up for an evening of floodlit fun. With his goal standard rising exponentially, over 2,000 were at the Pilot Field seven days later to see him shoot down Ashford. Of course, victory is a product of teamwork, but two goals decided the game, and he was responsible for both. During this autumn period Ryan appeared unstoppable.

Republic of Ireland international centre-back Ray Brady, an older brother of Liam, was recruited from QPR to stem the concession of avoidable goals. His signing proved to be a masterstroke.

But the sale of 1965/66 top gun Graham Sawyer was greeted with dismay. Sawyer scored 34 senior goals in the previous year but struggled to replicate that hot streak, not helped by the absence of wingers Back, to injury, and Burden, who was sold to Margate for £150. With Sawyer requesting a move nearer to his London home, Underwood negotiated an exchange deal with Hillingdon Borough which resulted in versatile inside-forward Jim Whitehouse coming to Hastings. Whitehouse had considerable Football League experience with Coventry and Reading. Meanwhile, Bexley's skilful striker Tony Gregory was brought in, too. Like Whitehouse, Gregory could be deployed in a variety of forward roles, having had substantial top-flight experience with Luton. Gregory made an auspicious Pilot Field debut against Tonbridge on an overcast 22 October. Almost 1,800 fans looked on as Gregory scored a brace and Bobby Smith, one, in a 4-0 drubbing of our traditional rivals. This would be Bobby Smith's final Southern

League goal for Hastings. Dave Crush, a Hastings favourite in the early 80s, was playing for Tonbridge on that day. He told Hastings fan and writer Roger Sinden, 'I had a lot of respect for Bobby Smith. He was in a different class to the others. The games were a lot more open then and players were encouraged to play like individuals. More sophisticated formations had yet to emerge. Teams were still playing with the WM set-up with traditional full-backs, wing-halves and inside-forwards. Had Smith been on our side, we might have won.'

The thinness of Underwood's squad was emphasised at Dover a week later, where a patched-up Hastings side battled with the current league leaders. A novice amateur, Davis, had to be drafted in for the absent Bobby Smith, while injuries to Ryan and Gregory required full-backs Cockburn and Nicholas to play unaccustomed roles in midfield and up front. Incredibly, this threadbare team scrapped so well that only a late goal from Dover's Ray denied them a deserved victory (2-2). Bill Cockburn received special praise for his pugnacity as a makeshift forward, capping his brave showing with a goal. What this performance emphasised was how closely knit and determined this team was under Dave Underwood's management.

November featured two 1-1 home draws and two 1-0 away victories, the second of which at Rugby was achieved with ten men. 3 December 1966 was a red-letter day for me as I witnessed Hastings's first victory over Wisbech in eight games. The skies fell in on Wisbech, literally so, as they folded, not only from a constant barrage by the voracious Hastings forwards, but also because of a savage blizzard. Ryan scored two in a 5-1 victory. A healthy crowd of 1,375 braved the elements to see Hastings retain a third-place promotion slot.

Hastings then obtained a creditable 0-0 draw at promotion rivals Margate on a grim, grey 10 December. Ryan came closest to breaking the deadlock, but we were pleased that our defence comfortably contained the threat posed by Margate's prolific goalscorer Dennis Randall.

However, I was disturbed to find the following excerpt in the Margate programme on my way home. It read, 'Unfortunately for Hastings, all their star signings have not resulted in a marked increase in their income. To compensate for the expenditure, a few weeks ago they were forced to place their entire staff on the transfer list in an endeavour to recoup their losses. Once again bad luck beset them in that no non-league clubs could pay the fees required, although there is a possibility that Ryan will be transferred to Exeter City.'

Sadly, that possibility became fact. In the Boxing Day home game with Tunbridge Wells Rangers, Ryan scored his last goal for the club. It was his 17th league goal that season in 22 appearances. That was the scale of his loss. It was hard to deny Ryan's wish to resurrect his Football League career, though, having played so ably for us. His first shot at League football was not a success despite netting eight goals for Second Division Charlton in 16 games and being capped for the Welsh under-23 side. A crowd of 1,820 wished him well. However, his sale did little to reduce the club's debts. The fee turned out to be considerably less than the £1,000 figure originally quoted. Regrettably, the move was not a success. After scoring five goals in 20 appearances he moved to Dover where he scored eight times for them in the following season. He returned to the Pilot Field at Easter 1973 with a Metropolitan Police side but was a pale shadow of the player he once was. His time at Hastings was the highlight of his truncated career. What a waste!

After the comparatively lavish expenditure of the previous season, money was scarce. Adult admission prices were raised to 4 shillings, forcing chairman Jim Humphreys to justify the decision in the local press. But life went on. Jim Whitehouse rescued Hastings from a humiliating defeat in the return fixture at Tunbridge Wells, played on a surface akin to a hippo watering hole. Ramsgate were beaten 2-1 on New Year's Eve, with Whitehouse again proving the difference. He netted neatly, too, in a polished 3-0 home victory over another promotion-chasing side, Stevenage.

Gravesend interrupted the sequence of wins by grasping a late point at Northfleet. Underwood was injured shortly before the game, requiring full-back Dave Coney to deputise. Tony Gregory's blistering 30-yard drive had appeared sufficient until Tosh Chamberlain's powerful intervention (1-1). Unabashed by a midweek defeat at Ashford, second-placed Kettering were seen off 3-1 with a wonderful cameo goal from Peter Knight. Also on target was new boy from Dunstable Bill Meadows. He scored again on the following Saturday at the club he had just left (1-1).

Like all good managers, Dave Underwood used his networks well. Although the club was in a financial mess, he was permitted to bring in centre-forward Bill Meadows, a former team-mate. Meadows had been a junior at Arsenal before spending several years at languishing Clacton. But at Dunstable he proved to be an excellent goal poacher. On first sight, he looked ungainly. He ran with a stiff-legged gait, and yet he was deadly in front of goal. During Hastings's 1966/67 run-in, he scored 14 league goals at almost a goal a game. Like Ricky George, Meadows was destined for greater things. Both played leading roles in Hereford's FA Cup run of 1971/72, which included a staggering defeat of First Division Newcastle United.

Three games were then won on the trot: at home to Barry (2-1) and upwardly mobile Crawley (2-0), against whom local amateur Mick Cullen deputised superbly in the Hastings goal, and at Canterbury (3-1), played in a raging gale. I recall the Canterbury game with great clarity, having recently been prescribed spectacles. Everything stood out so sharply, as if on narcotics – the blades of grass quivering in the squally wind, the weave of the net at the opposite end, the players' facial features. I had missed so much in my myopic haze. Talk about 'Tomorrow Never Knows'. At Canterbury, Alan Back returned from injury and celebrated with an absurd, wind-assisted goal, struck from 40 yards. Although Tonbridge avenged their 4-0 defeat at Hastings by reversing that score at the Angel ground, the crowded Easter programme was an outstanding success.

Sittingbourne were thrashed twice, 7-1 on Good Friday, with Meadows recording a hat-trick, and 5-0 on Easter Monday, while new league leaders Dover were beaten 2-1 on Easter Saturday with a brace from Gregory in front of a bumper 3,005 crowd. Hastings did not lose again.

Off the field, the financial problems persisted. Director Ted Ive resigned just after Easter, insisting that the club's debts of £6,000 were unsustainable. He claimed the club was 'not ready for Premier Southern League football and that it needed to take drastic action to stop the financial drift'. James Humphreys made a board statement which read, 'The football club has liabilities in excess of £34,500. The only course of action that appeared open was for a 50 per cent cut in wages and salaries to be made, together with other economies.'

Meanwhile, Underwood continued to be embroiled in the Bobby Smith problem. In January 1967 San Francisco offered Smith $12,000 per year – over £80 per week – to play American soccer with them, also dangling a $2,000 signing-on fee. Smith announced he was 'keen for a fresh start'. The national press quoted him as saying, 'I would be only too happy to put English football well and truly behind me. I have had enough.' He didn't discuss the offer with Underwood first, though, prompting his manager to declare angrily, 'Smith has been very quick to speak to the national press but though I have sent telegrams galore I have heard nothing from him and I am disgusted with the whole business.' As it happened, the US deal did not go through. Smith also expressed interest in becoming Cheshunt FC's player-manager, after his former Spurs team-mate Terry Medwin left the job, but his application was unsuccessful.

Smith was chosen to play in the home game against Wisbech on 3 December but did not turn up. Smith claimed it was due to a breakdown in communication. However, after Ryan's departure for Exeter, he was picked for the Southern League game at Crawley on 3 January 1967, which was abandoned because of ice. He was also picked, too, for the home fixture against Stevenage on 14 January but cried off with a cold. In mid-February he was given two weeks' notice for continued failure to report for training. He appealed, but on Monday 13 March his appeal was turned down by the Southern League, bringing his United career to an end. In Smith's chequered 17-month spell with Hastings he made 34 starts in all competitions, scoring 16 goals. Despite his excessive weight, he was still a formidable footballer – too talented for second-tier Southern League football.

After leaving Hastings, Smith became a painter and decorator, also driving a minicab, before the disabling injuries sustained playing football caught up with him, not helped by a fall through a manhole that damaged his already wrecked legs. Norman Giller said that Smith had to take a disability pension after suffering heart problems and having a hip replaced. His 1961 FA Cup winners' medal, which had vanished from his house, suddenly turned up in an auction, where it was sold for £11,200. 'I think it's disgusting,' said Smith. 'It's only football. How can prices like this be justified?' Even after the abolition of the maximum wage in 1961, Smith earned only £65 per week – worth about £1,360 today – while with Spurs during the most successful period in the club's history. He said, 'I was always made very welcome at White Hart Lane, but my first club Chelsea went further, sending me a cheque for £1,500 each Christmas – [worth nearly £30,000 today] – as they did with other members of their 1954/55 championship-winning side. And I hardly got a kick because manager Ted Drake hated my guts!' Giller believed if Smith had been playing today, a striker who 'mixed cruiserweight strength with subtlety on the ball', he would have been revered as much as Alan Shearer and rewarded with the riches his ability warranted, but Smith played in 'the soccer slave era'. His rewards were 'pain in the limbs, much of it self-inflicted, and poverty in the pocket'.

On 29 April 1967, the Hastings team travelled to Wisbech Town. Dad and I went with them. We had resumed our football partnership just in time to bid a joint farewell to Southern League football. How fitting it was that Wisbech should be our opponents; for the Fenmen had been the visitors when I resumed my interest in Hastings United in 1960. When I was young, it was Dad who took me to games. In no time at all, I would begin taking him. In this brief interlude we went as a pair. This game would mark my release from Hastings – not only from the club but the town also, as first university and then work took me to the opposite end of the country. I did not know this then, but this was almost a valedictory journey.

It was a magnificent spring day of soporific warmth. We were hopelessly late by the time we reached Cambridge. Three players clambered out and shot off across the Fens in a taxi, forgetting that their kit was in the coach boot. Meanwhile, our lifeless driver progressed at a funereal pace along the straight Fenland roads. The prairie-sized fields of black, silty soil stretched out for mile after mile, interrupted by regimented lines of trees and sludgy, algaefied dykes. The sun dazzled in a huge cloudless sky while the horizon shimmered like a mirage, its haziness fed by the languidly drifting smoke from the smouldering field fires.

We reached Wisbech's ground half an hour late, where we were greeted with a weary jeer. The home fans seemed more bored than angry. One of them itemised previous latecomers. It was a long list. The drawn-out, dreamy drive stripped the game of any urgency or atmosphere. The first half was just a scrappy, lethargic midfield stroll.

After the interval Hastings showed greater appetite and verve, probing the home defence. But it was a laboured effort. It would take a highly controversial refereeing decision to spur this dull contest into life. Wisbech's left-back had sustained a nasty ankle injury and limped off the field. At that moment Hastings's defender Keith Rutter punted the ball towards Bill Meadows, positioned just inside the Wisbech half. The home defenders pushed up to catch Meadows offside. Meadows dawdled on the ball, expecting the referee's whistle. But upon hearing our frantic calls to make for goal, he twigged. Even Bill was too quick for his markers when given a ten-yard start. Being at his best in one-to-one challenges, he rounded ex-Peterborough keeper Jack Walls and slammed the ball home.

All hell broke loose. Former Birmingham forward 'Bunny' Larkin led the charge, almost going head-to-head with the referee, demanding that he rule out the goal. The referee remonstrated he had not given their full-back permission to leave the field. He had played Meadows onside. Larkin was not appeased. His incensed tirade resulted in a booking. It might have been worse. Larkin was considered a 'stormy petrel' after his spectacular set-to with Tony Nicholas at St Andrew's. The intervening years had not dimmed his fire. The game degenerated into a squally spat, littered with crunching tackles and petulant abuse. The mood was hardly improved when Wisbech's left-winger Spelman was denied a blistering equaliser 16 minutes from time. It wasn't clear what the infringement was. In a fizzing, feisty finale only desperate goal-line clearances from Ray Brady and Keith Rutter kept Hastings's lead intact. While the Hastings players hugged one another excitedly at the final whistle, believing that promotion was almost in their grasp, their opponents trudged off grumpily. Before this season, Pye's team had won nine games on the spin against Hastings. Arguably, Wisbech would never be as good again. As for Hastings, promotion was confirmed a week later but it proved to be a pyrrhic victory.

Ted Ive was right. Hastings were not strong enough for Southern Premier League football. Bill Meadows suffered a cartilage injury, leaving the club without a centre-forward. Two players with First Division experience were signed. Tommy Harmer, once of Spurs, who played in only a handful of games, and Derek Leck, formerly with Brighton and Northampton, but they did little to prevent the club's freefall. Hastings were duly relegated having accumulated just 16 points.

New manager Reg Flewin, previously a First Division title winner with Portsmouth, pleaded, 'We have only 13 registered professionals on our books and one, Bill Meadows, is injured and unlikely to be available for selection for several weeks [actually, it was months]. Our wage bill for players and staff is about £350 per week [almost £300,000 per year today] and overhead charges are approximately £100 per week. Our Tote Improvement Fund brings in about £90 per week and our gate money is between £200 and £250 per fortnight. Our income is therefore approximately £215 per week and our expenditure is £450 per week. We are launching a new ticket scheme in addition to the Tote and we must sell approximately 4,500 each week to break even.'

Reg Flewin was looking for 5,000 local people to donate £1 each week. Many potential punters did the weekly football pools in the hope of winning much greater riches. There were those who liked a flutter on the horses. This was a time of economic hardship, too, with devaluation just around the corner. Hastings was no longer a prosperous town. The holiday trade was flagging. Local jobs were harder to find. There was little chance that Flewin would achieve his goal.

The only saving grace from the wretched 1967/68 season was the discovery of Kevin Barry, a talented 19-year-old Hastings Grammar School boy. Barry would later become the uncle of Gareth Barry, an England international midfielder. At school, Kevin was a burly, free-scoring centre-forward, good enough to be selected for the England grammar school squad, but he found himself overshadowed by the greater capability of Alan Gowling, who later played for Manchester United, Huddersfield, Newcastle United and Bolton. Kevin and I were previously at Grove secondary modern school, once sharing the opening bowling in a school cricket match. I always found him affable, accessible and grounded. After returning from the England squad, Kevin spoke to me of his disappointment with his performances against an Amateur FA XI, the Welsh Schools FA XI, and the Scottish Schools

FA XI, but appreciated being given the experience. I admired his maturity.

Kevin was strong in the air and quick and powerful on the ground. He was a prodigious goalscorer at school with an explosive burst of pace that troubled the experienced Yeovil defenders in his Southern League debut on 21 October 1967. In the 1968/69 season he was converted into a centre-back but switched back to a striking role in the following season when he scored 22 Southern League goals and 30 in all competitions. He netted 21 times in Southern League games in the following season, too, which brought about his transfer to Chelsea in July 1971 for a £2,000 fee.

This was not a successful move, so he returned to Southern League football with Margate, who paid a 'substantial' fee for him. He was enticed back to Hastings, though, in September 1973, for a four-figure fee. He scored ten goals for his parent club in 1973/74 before reverting once again to a centre-back role. It was in this position that he captained Hastings to promotion to the Premier Division at the end of the 1976/77 season, under Bobby Drake. Although very talented, Kevin never let success go to his head. Les Riggs, his former Margate manager, described him as 'one of the easiest men to handle I have ever known'.

A *Hastings & St Leonards Observer* reporter described him as, 'One of Hastings United's most liked and well-known players over the years,' and in their article Kevin's former United team-mate Dave Nessling said, 'He was a wholehearted and very, very strong player, but a genuinely nice bloke. Everybody liked Kevin and the supporters really took to him at Hastings.' Another former team-mate, Sidley manager John Lambert, told the paper, 'He taught me so much about defending, so much about football and how to conduct myself.' But when Kevin objected to the appointment of Cyril Jeans in place of Bobby Drake in 1979, the club banned him. Sadly, Kevin died in 2011 after losing a brave battle against cancer.

The 1967/68 season was my last as an avid supporter of the club. It was also Jim Humphreys' last as chairman. His dog track proposal had not won any favours. Football was not his main preoccupation. In attempting to draw a bigger crowd, he experimented with pre-match jousting, to be staged before Hastings's opening home fixture with Weymouth. A local knight was found, complete with lance, shield, and chain armour. A suitably robed steed was obtained, too. But Weymouth declined to bring a jouster of their own. Maybe space was at a premium. In any event, the solitary Hastings jouster was confined to the cinder track given the torrential rain. Poor man. He was left to ponder upon life's futility while the rain ran solemnly down his armour. Never in the field of medieval conflict was so much embarrassment felt by so few. While this experiment was not repeated, one-hit wonder The Crazy World of Arthur Brown was engaged for a raucous rendition of 'Fire' and sundry other compositions at a Pilot Field rock concert.

Thereafter, Hastings United experienced a fate that befell many non-league clubs after an immediate post-war surge of interest. While passionately supported by a few, they became ignored by the majority. After the mid-60s boom, four-figure crowds at the Pilot Field were rare, although during Peter Sillett's period in charge, in the early 80s, there was a brief reminder of better times.

However, the two promotions to the Premier Division led by Bobby Drake, son of Ted, in 1977, and by Peter Sillett in 1982, did not bring back the crowds of the mid-50s and early 60s. Bar a few high-profile games, attendances rarely reached 1,000. With Jim Humphreys investing substantially in the club in 1965, bringing in prolific goalscorers such as Bobby Smith and Jim Ryan, Hastings's average attendances almost doubled, rising to 2,181 in the 1965/66 season, but as was the case at many other non-league clubs, a steady decline set in thereafter. Although Hastings were promoted to the Premier League under Dave Underwood in 1966/67, with Humphreys' magic money tree withering, the average gate fell to 1,671. The disastrous season that followed resulted in a sharper drop to 939. While the next two seasons back in the First Division did not produce much change – 937 in 1968/69 and 987 in 1969/70, when a late surge lifted Hastings to sixth position – the 70s saw a more rapid decline: 633 in 1970/71; 402 in 1971/72; 449 in 1972/73; 387 in 1973/74. These were the years of three-day weeks, power cuts, petrol shortages and runaway inflation. United's chairman George Dicker said in 1975, 'In these days of inflation it has become increasingly difficult to financially support football without the benefit of substantial income from other resources.'

After the 60s, the best gate at the Pilot Field for a Southern League game was in November 1977, when 1,115 turned up, expecting to see Jimmy Greaves play for Barnet. I returned from the North especially, hoping to see my boyhood hero before he bowed out. It seemed appropriate since I first saw him at the beginning of his career. On my first visit to a Football League ground, in August 1958, the precocious teenager scored five goals in a 6-2 thrashing of champions Wolves. But my long journey south was in vain. Greaves did not play.

With unemployment worsening in the early 80s, there was further pressure on attendances, not helped by the rising hooligan problem. By the mid-80s the average gate in the Conference was around 800, pitifully low given that automatic promotion to the Fourth Division was introduced in the 1986/87 season.

1967 My singular 'Summer of Love'

'Respect'

I DID not get a 'Summer of Love'. I didn't try too hard. San Franciscan radiance seemed an anathema to sour, de-flowered Hastings. Besides, I had winter in my blood. My compass pointed resolutely northwards. Lancaster was on my radar and independence was on my mind. In the meantime, I settled for the womb-like warmth of the local chess club, heavy with the scent of polish, tea, toasted teacakes and cigars. Here, an ancient gas fire popped and flared all day, every day, whatever the weather. It was an ideal bolthole for the socially lame. Little was said, just a brief exchange of courtesies, followed by hours of silent, furrowed concentration to the accompaniment of so many ticking clocks. An elderly woman, clad in heavy woollens, shuffled mutely in and out of the oak-panelled room with trays of refreshment. It was a place untouched and unnoticed by the passing years. Here, the liturgy of chess was respectfully recited – the Queen's Indian, the Ruy Lopez, the Sicilian – in its musty imperial, consular glory.

But if I was an equivocal subscriber to the present and a bashful advocate of the past, I was not alone, not by a long chalk. For instance, take The Beatles. As much as they pushed the margins with 'Tomorrow Never Knows' and 'Day in the Life' they seemed, as George Melly observed, 'at their happiest when celebrating the past'. George Harrison's dismissive take on the trippy, hippie San Francisco scene was 'a load of horrible, spotty drop-out kids on drugs'. Their *Sgt. Pepper's Lonely Hearts Club Band* album, released in 1967, evoked a fading image of greasy, cobbled, streets, travelling circuses and raucous music halls. The Kinks championed the past with equal enthusiasm with their 1968 album *The Kinks Are the Village Green Preservation Society*. It was almost as if, like novice swimmers, we needed to remain at a safe depth as we tentatively entered uncharted waters. With the nation in love with the televised *Forsyte Saga*, and Victorian fashions revived by Biba and Laura Ashley, this pervasive ambivalence about releasing the past and embracing a florid yet uncertain future was more pervasive than 60s caricatures suggest.

In the Kinks' 1967 single 'Autumn Almanac', Ray Davies sang of traditional working-class routines such as Saturday football, the Sunday roast and Blackpool holidays. How this sentiment resonated with British photographer Tony Ray-Jones. In his posthumous exhibition *Only in England*, his visits to fading English resorts in the summer of 1967 are depicted in stark monochrome. Here, we find images that are alternately surreal, tender, melancholic and hilarious. Above all, they remind us that these were still conservative times despite their permissive reputation. The decade began with the 'Chatterley' ban and concluded with the *Oz* trial. In between, the musicians' union refused to allow the Stones to perform their new release, 'Let's Spend the Night Together', on the Eamonn Andrews TV show.

I was familiar with those who refused to swing. I recall their arrivals, hardy holidaymakers from another age, transported in their Zephyrs, Wolseleys and Anglias. They often huddled together on the tar-struck shingle in their utility plastic macs, sheltering behind flapping windbreaks, gazing dubiously at the foam-flecked sea and the leaden sky, while sipping stewed Thermos tea. Holidays were a solemn duty. Fun was a beauty pageant or dog show, perhaps a penny arcade, a children's parade or a choppy trip around the bay.

Sussex CCC v Kent CCC

Central Cricket Ground, Hastings, 20 July 1968

'Jumping Jack Flash'

AS THE vital Leeds Test match approached, Cowdrey realised he was short of top order batsmen. He had pulled a muscle while scoring his 21st Test hundred at Edgbaston and was unlikely to be fit. Boycott and Milburn were also ruled out with injuries. Cowdrey therefore rang Dexter asking him whether he might be interested in playing again for England. Dexter was very interested. His business affairs were apparently boring him. He missed the cut and thrust of international competition but wondered whether he could recover his touch in time, given his two-year absence from first-class cricket.

Besides, the knee that Charlie Griffith had damaged at Lord's in 1963 was still causing him pain. He was unsure whether it would stand up to another five-day examination. But in Milburn's absence, Cowdrey needed a batsman of Dexter's calibre to force the pace and create an opportunity of victory, which was essential if England were to have any chance of regaining the Ashes at the Oval. Cowdrey counselled Dexter that if he played well at Hastings, he would recommend his selection for the Leeds Test.

Realising what was at stake on Saturday, 20 July, I decided to attend the opening day's play. I had spent a considerable time at the Central Cricket Ground during my teenage years watching club and county cricket and practising in its nets. Since I was about to leave Hastings for Lancaster University, it seemed appropriate to make a farewell visit. As farewells went, this one was special.

Unless appearances were deceptive, Dexter seemed relaxed about his trial. His long-standing team-mate Jim Parks was amused to see Dexter arrive with a tattered cricket bag that had not been touched for two years, the contents having gathered mould in the meantime and his bat untreated. Dexter seemed to have had little difficulty in switching off when a game was in progress, at least when he was not central to the action. So, his minimal preparations were not surprising. However, once at the crease his fierce competitiveness and supreme technique made light of the shabbiness of his kit.

I suspect, but do not know, that Sussex captain Mike Griffith – son of MCC's Billy – chose to bat upon winning the toss because of Dexter's need to prove his worth. The green, still wet wicket hardly commended batting first. He must have regretted it when, after an hour of play, four members of his top order were blown away for only 27 runs. Crucially, Dexter survived.

Kent's stocky, genuinely quick bowler David Sayer, or 'Slayer' as he was known by his team-mates, justified his nickname by ripping out Mike Buss's stumps with only one run on the board. Like Ken Higgs, who also made a waving gesture at the point of delivery, the muscular Sayer generated sharp pace off a short run. His opening partner was the giant Northumbrian medium-fast bowler Norman Graham, whose trudging approach and laboured action belied his mastery of seam, swing and bounce. Graham had been in the selectors' minds when they picked an MCC team of England hopefuls at the start of this season, but unfortunately for Graham he became the only member of that side not to play at Test level.

On this humid morning, however, he was too good for the hardened battler Ken Suttle. Graham located the edge of the Sussex left-hander's bat and Knott took the catch, throwing the ball up exultantly (6/2). Derek Semmence also struggled to add to his solitary run before being caught by Denness, off Graham (17/3). His dismissal brought Dexter to the wicket, bearing the disdainful expression he reserved for his toughest challenges.

Dexter's partner was the 6ft 6in tall Tony Greig, a promising young South African-born all-rounder, abrasive and brash, who relished playing front-foot drives on the rise, unleashing thrashing power. Cannily, Kent captain Alan Dixon turned immediately to Underwood, believing that Greig and Dexter, both confident and belligerent players of pace, might find sharp spin more difficult to play. Greig duly obliged, presenting Underwood with a simple catch off his own bowling as he played a rashly expansive on-drive (27/4).

With Sussex's last accomplished batsman Jim Parks joining him, Dexter knew he had to keep his head down, repel the Kent bowling attack and re-find his touch before progressing to his lordly repertoire. Dexter leant well forward in playing Underwood, with a deftly relaxed grip to avoid edging to the encircling close catchers.

In 1963 I had watched Parks (136) and Dexter (107) destroy the Kent bowling with a flurry of elegant and punishing drives, cuts, glances and pulls, but the partnership they formed here was of a different order. With Underwood turning the ball spitefully, watchful defence was called for. Scoring was largely confined to discreet nudges and deflections.

Underwood seemed an unlikely assassin. Flat and splay-footed, he waddled to the wicket with the menace of a reclusive accountant bewildered by the dazzling daylight. But appearances were deceptive. He had a smooth, gliding, repeatable action with which he delivered heavily spun or cut balls of probing pace and nagging accuracy. On wet or crumbling wickets, he was often lethal, hence Underwood's sobriquet 'Deadly'. His fielding was also sounder than his laboured movement suggested, being a reliable catcher away from the wicket. And while his batting seemed rudimentary, he was a brave battler as he demonstrated after Griffith felled him with a vicious bouncer during the 1966 Test series. Having worked hard at his batting, he became a proficient night watchman, eventually recording a first-class century, coincidentally at Hastings, in 1985. In fact, the Central Cricket Ground proved a very happy hunting ground. It was here where he achieved his career-best innings haul of nine wickets for 28 runs in 1964; his career-best match figures, in England, of 14 wickets for 82 runs in 1967; and a startling second innings return of 8-9 runs, recording match figures of 13 wickets for 52 runs, in 1973. He was liberally compensated for the drubbing given by Dexter and Parks in 1963.

In measured fashion, Dexter and Parks took the Sussex score past 60 at lunch, a sounder position than an hour before, but still perilous. But with the ground bathed in warm afternoon sunshine, the wicket lost its former bite, although Underwood and the brisk off-spinner Dixon were occasionally troubling. Then, just as the Sussex pair thought they had entered serene waters, Parks was dismissed by Underwood for 18 runs, caught by future England opener, Bob Woolmer (85/5).

Next batsman, Mike Griffith was content to play second fiddle while Dexter decided it was time to seize control. Tiring at the shackles imposed by Dixon and Underwood, he began cover driving both bowlers with increasing assuredness. Growing in confidence, he started varying his shots, sending the ball scuttling to the boundary straight, through midwicket and square, confounding the fielders with his precise placement and savage power. At the other end, Griffith steadily accumulated runs with a mixture of swipes and swats. Although his bat was not always straight, the Kent bowlers failed to find a chink in his armour as Dexter progressed effortlessly into the 90s. But having reached 99, he was detained temporarily by a sharp shower that resulted in an early tea.

I wondered whether this unfortunate interruption might upset his focus or interfere with his momentum – not a bit of it. On resumption, Dexter calmly knocked his first ball into an unguarded area and claimed his hundred. Moving into overdrive, Dexter smote the ball with rare ferocity, almost oblivious of length or line, although he never relapsed into unruly slogging. The ball seemed to be forever skimming over the lush outfield to the boundary rope where it would be retrieved by an exhausted fielder.

Before lunch Underwood's miserly bowling had conceded less than two runs per over, but by the final session he was being slammed to all quarters as the run rate climbed into double figures. With Dexter hoisting one of his deliveries on to the town hall roof, a monstrous blow, Dixon brought back Sayer and Graham. But shorn of their early menace, their extra pace only ensured that Dexter's shots flashed to the boundary with even greater brutality. Training my binoculars upon Dexter's face, it bore a supercilious sneer. No longer content with defeating his Kent adversaries, he appeared intent upon humiliating them.

Alan Dixon was a sound county pro. He batted usefully and bowled both seam up and off breaks at a hurried pace, with a juddering action which hinted at rusted parts. Realising that there was no stopping Dexter's sizzling assault, Dixon admirably tried to protect his fellow bowlers by taking much of the flack himself. His 18 overs cost 77 runs, but these figures would have been so much worse had he, like Underwood, not stifled Dexter so successfully during the morning session. Underwood's figures had not looked so clever by the time Dexter had departed.

Amid this mayhem, Sayer bowled Mike Griffith for 69 (246/6). It was one of Griffith's best innings for Sussex, having added 162 runs with Dexter for the sixth wicket. Sussex all-rounder Graham Cooper, who replaced Griffith, then eased towards a personal score of 41 runs before he fell to the persevering Sayer. By this time Dexter was a man in a hurry. Determined to claim a second century, but wrongly supposing that close of play was at 6:30pm, he launched a blistering 'aerial' attack, reaching his goal with 23 runs taken off one over from Dixon, including two sixes and a brace of fours. By the time Dexter had holed out to extra cover, off a relieved and very weary Underwood, Sussex had 313 runs on the board, almost two-thirds of which were made by Dexter (203). Underwood's 44 overs had cost him 144 runs.

Dexter had proved his point and was duly selected for the Leeds and Oval Tests. However, he was unable to repeat his Hastings form in either match, although he had the consolation of ending his Test career as a member of a winning England side. Victory was achieved with only minutes left, after a cloudburst had swamped the outfield, prompting a frenzied drying operation, involving ground staff and spectators. Alas, Australia once again retained the Ashes.

1968 Farewell to Sussex

'All Along the Watchtower'

THE YEAR 1968 was a turbulent one. Martin Luther King was gunned down in Memphis, triggering race riots across the United States. Soviet tanks ground Dubcek's liberal reforms into the Prague dust. The Palestinian, Sirhan Sirhan, assassinated Bobby Kennedy. Paris seethed with revolt and South African prime minister Vorster angrily cancelled the 1968/69 MCC tour of South Africa upon hearing of Basil D'Oliveira's selection. There were two anti-Vietnam War demonstrations outside the US Embassy in Grosvenor Square, the first of which turned ugly, although the violent scenes here seemed trivial after the Kent State University shootings of 1970.

It was the year in which I went north, arriving at Lancaster University in a damp, glum autumn. The campus was like a 'Klondike town' minus the gold. With the college buildings only half-constructed, mud was spattered everywhere. Isolated in rural splendour, our stay was one of experimental living. Joss sticks abounded if only to subdue the rancid smell of our clothing. Vitamins were at a premium. A better diet was had on the *Bounty*. Christmas was celebrated with scurvy. Those arriving with short back and sides, horn-rimmed glasses and sports jackets went home with flowing locks, John Lennon specs and beaded buckskin. Student relationships with the nearby city seemed less like 'town and gown' than 'town and clown'. *Withnail and I* had come to Lancaster.

Here I met Liz, who became my wife. Jimi Hendrix's cover of Dylan's 'All Along the Watchtower' defined our early days together. I first heard it on BBC's *Pick of the Pops* one Sunday afternoon, while enjoying her tower room view. Outside was a grazed winter sky, the fading sunset mirrored by Morecambe Bay's gleaming sandbanks, set before a faint wash of Lakeland fells. Just play me Hendrix's strummed acoustic intro; his four-part solo; the bottle sliding improvisations; the 'wah wah' interlude and the apocalyptic climax, and I am instantly whisked back to the couple Liz and I once were, half a century ago. I sometimes wonder whether our much younger selves would have liked the people we have become.

I fell in love with the North, too, with its people, its moors, fells and lakes, even its petrifying cold and insurgent damp. So, it wasn't altogether surprising that I became captivated by one of its struggling football teams in a declining town in a secluded Pennine valley. My initial welcome was hardly warm. Upon arrival, icy rain stung my screwed-up face. I was surrounded by dereliction – the rusted sidings, the boarded-up mills, the empty terraced housing, the filthy canal, and a partially demolished football ground. Yet I warmed to the locals' chirpy resilience, their gallows humour. These qualities were reflected in their football club scrapping to beat an inevitable retreat. After watching Burnley come from behind to beat West Bromwich in March 1970, in front of a pitifully small crowd, my head was turned, despite my enduring fondness for the football teams of my boyhood. This born-again allegiance has followed me everywhere I have worked and lived – in Rochdale, Halifax, Leicester, Bristol and London.

Now retired and living in the North, once more I'm free to watch my team without the exhausting journeys I made for most of my working life, and yet I continue to watch Sussex

County Cricket Club, home and away, whenever possible, and still follow the fortunes of Hastings United and Brighton & Hove Albion.

1968–2019 What Came After

IN CLOSING my youthful recollections of the three Sussex clubs I once followed, in this section I provide a selective and subjective account of how their fortunes panned out subsequently, focusing upon a few key figures who caught my eye.

I begin by looking at two Brighton strikers, Kit Napier and Willie Irvine, who helped Brighton stave off relegation in 1971 and restored them to the Second Division a year later. While Irvine's career began at the top, Napier established himself in humbler surroundings, notably at Workington, but their brand of brotherhood played an important part in Brighton's brief revival.

Having waited ten years to return to the second tier, it was very disappointing that Albion could manage only a brief stay. Neither Brian Clough nor Peter Taylor could restore them, but Alan Mullery did, and his contribution is considered in the third review which looks at how he lifted Brighton into the First Division in May 1979, an amazing feat for a club that had never played in the top flight before.

Like Brighton, Hastings United endured a roller-coaster ride of triumph and despair but, unlike Brighton, gave up the ghost in 1985. This review is not a morbid story, though, for it considers the successes achieved by former Chelsea and

England right-back Peter Sillett as manager of Hastings during the early 80s, making him one of the best managers to serve the club.

Sussex Cricket Club were not, and are not, immune to chaotic fluctuations. Having come within a whisker of winning the County Championship for the first time in 1981, by 1996 the club became embroiled in a 'winter of discontent' which threatened its continued existence. Here, I provide a whistle-stop account of Sussex's bumpy upward journey that took them from 'zeroes' to 'heroes' in the space of five years.

Interspersing these reviews are brief subjective summaries of the times in which these stories unfolded, by way of context-setting, for sport often reflects the times in which it is played.

Kit Napier: Brighton & Hove Albion 1966–72

AFTER LEAVING Hastings I rarely saw Brighton play, although I have watched them at least once at each of the four grounds that they used for home games since 1968. I occasionally saw them when playing away, mostly at Brentford. I also confess to watching their dire second FA Cup replay against Walsall, played at Fulham in December 1969. On that drab, dank evening, I stood among the Brighton fans congregated at the Hammersmith End. I hoped that burly Alex 'Boom, Boom' Dawson might produce one of his famous barnstorming performances, but I was to be disappointed. As the game dragged inconclusively into extra time, the Brighton fans began chanting, to the tune of Hari Krishna, 'Walsall duck pond, Walsall duck pond, Walsall duck pond, Walsall duck pond; Quacker, Quack, Quack, Quacker, Quack Quack, Quacker, Quack Quack, Quacker Quack Quack', accompanying this cerebral celebration with hand pecking gestures. It is my most surreal experience at a football ground.

The next time I saw them play was at the Goldstone on Good Friday, 9 April 1971, when my friend Roger King and I watched a Brighton v Aston Villa game, which the Albion won with a Kit Napier goal. Roger, who remembers this occasion better than I, maintains that the game was played in front of a season-best crowd of over 22,000. As a Villa fan, Roger was very disappointed with his side's performance. He said, 'At the end, the chill reality was that it almost certainly meant another season in Division Three. Brighton at that time were just putting together a run of better results which staved off the threat of relegation. This prospect had looked very real in late winter and early spring. I saw them again just 12 days later when they banged the fatal nail into Reading's relegation coffin, with a 3-0 win at Elm Park, much to the dismay of our family friends.'

Kit Napier's strike partner on Good Friday 1971 was ex-Burnley star and Northern Ireland international Willie Irvine. Irvine said in his biography *Together Again*, written with Burnley author Dave Thomas, 'Kit Napier was the cornerstone of our success. He was brave, with pace. He had bursts of acceleration and was two-footed.' I saw Napier play several times in my final year on the south coast. I admired his neat first touch, his ability in running directly at retreating defenders, with the ball at his feet, and his precise finishing, with his feet and head. Bringing him to Brighton in 1966 was an inspired decision by Archie Macaulay, particularly at a ridiculously low transfer fee of £8,500. In six years at the Goldstone, Napier scored 84 goals in 256 league appearances, a very respectable strike rate of one in three. Napier was an unselfish striker who consistently brought others into the game.

Former Workington full-back John Ogilvie recalled Napier's part in a major giant-killing feat by the now diminished Cumbrian side: 'We were up against Blackburn in the 1964/65 League Cup competition and Kit was in that side. We were lucky to get a draw in the home game. First Division Rovers had ten internationals. They were a good team. We went to Blackburn for the replay on Bonfire Night 1964. It was pouring down. Our trainer, George Aitken, said to us before the game, "Remember they said the *Bismarck* couldn't be sunk?" Well, we just paralysed them. We would have beaten anyone that night. Kit Napier scored twice. He was a very quiet lad, very dry and didn't like being roughed up but he had a hell of a shot. If you gave him any space, he'd get goals.'

Workington followed up this incredible result by thumping Second Division Norwich 3-0 in round four. Although their run was eventually ended by Chelsea in a quarter-final replay, Docherty's King's Road swingers were given an almighty shock. Former Chelsea star Peter Osgood was sat in the dug-out during the first game at Borough Park, Workington. Osgood remembered, 'Out on the field little Workington were working the Chelsea stars over. We fought to leave with a 2-2 draw but not before a nail-biting finale when Workington had a goal disallowed.' But Kit Napier's equaliser earned the 'Reds' a second chance. Although this doughty Cumbrian team lost the replay at Stamford Bridge, Kit and his colleagues had no cause for dismay. They had represented their small industrial town with great distinction.

The catalyst for Workington's triumphant resurgence was the appointment of Ken Furphy as the club's player-manager. According to former 'Reds' full-back John Ogilvie, Furphy was 'one of the best tacticians the club ever had. He'd give you the lowdown on our opponents. He'd tell you which player went this way or that and who'd go down. He must have had Blackburn and Chelsea closely watched.' One of Furphy's last signings for Workington was among his best. This was Kit Napier, a 20-year-old Scot, who had previously failed to settle at Blackpool and Preston. He quickly became a crowd pleaser at Borough Park, though, scoring 25 times in 58 appearances before moving to Newcastle for an £18,000 fee, probably worth around £18m today. After joining Brighton in 1966, he became their leading goalscorer in all but one of the six seasons he spent on the south coast. After falling out with subsequent Brighton boss Pat Saward, he rejoined Ken Furphy at Blackburn, the club he had once humiliated eight years before.

1972–73 'In Place of Strife'?

'I Can See Clearly Now'

IT WAS a bleak mid-winter. As Conservative prime minister Heath slugged out a losing battle with the miners, we had to contend with daily power cuts. Frustrated by primitive conditions at the coalfaces, and lower pay and holiday allowances than other workers, the National Union of Miners was ready to do battle. In January 1972 a new and decisive tactic of industrial action was introduced – the 'flying picket'. The dispute at Saltley power station, Birmingham, was its crowning glory. But if this was Arthur Scargill's 'Battle of the Bull Run', what transpired at Orgreave 12 years later was probably Mrs Thatcher's 'Gettysburg'. Meanwhile, the Northern Irish 'Troubles' were multiplying in the advent of the 'Bloody Sunday' massacre, and so was terrorism abroad perpetrated by the likes of Black September and Red Army Faction.

With electricity supplies subject to strict rotas, thousands of factories were forced into three-day weeks. Millions were laid off. During the regular four-hour blackouts, Liz and I emulated John and Yoko and took to our bed. It was not so much a love-in as an eat-in, though, as we hesitantly consumed the leftovers Liz brought home from her canteen work.

It was then when I began work in a children's home. A laconic, brooding, Jamaican boy stood apart from the scrum.

His interests, in so far as he revealed anything about himself, did not extend much beyond reggae and cricket. No one penetrated his aloof moroseness. But we would often spend half an hour together silently watching the Ashes Test matches on TV or listening to his reggae singles, of which Johnny Nash's 'I Can See Clearly' was his favourite. Did he really see his situation as clearly as his few words and jaded maturity suggested? I would never know.

1973 was the year of Watergate and a major international oil crisis. With the Arabs sore about a successive defeat by Israel, Britain was also made to pay for US Zionist sympathies. There may have been oil in the North Sea, but it would be a difficult task extracting it, requiring expensive imported technology, thereby worsening the UK's troubling trade deficit. Oil yields remained insignificant until the end of the decade; so much for Scotland's 'great black hope'. A scramble for petrol ensued. For several months, petrol rationing seemed inevitable. To add to our winter woes, the coal miners, the railwaymen and the power workers inflicted yet more power cuts and three-day weeks. Without enough investment in the long-neglected British manufacturing sector, the Conservative chancellor of the exchequer's 'dash for growth' did little to raise British economic prospects, merely raising demand for a glut of foreign goods that pushed up inflation further. Even before Britain felt the full weight of the Arabs' wrath, Tory chancellor Tony Barber had to scale back public spending severely and raise interest rates.

Willie Irvine: Brighton & Hove Albion 1971–73

IN THE soggy autumn of 1968 I met Baz, possibly Willie Irvine's most fervent fan. Baz was an evangelist, a voice growling in the college wilderness. He wanted to share his homage of Willie with everyone. Like a zealous, bigoted, Bible Belt preacher, he saw no reason to recognise others' privacy or priorities, never picking his moments. He was a wild boor. And yet the college women indulged him, as if he was an unruly, licks and paws, young retriever. One day, he lurched drunkenly into the room my girlfriend shared with another female student. He didn't knock. He just barged in clutching his small tin of Nescafe, which he considered to be his swipe card. Seeing me sitting on a bed, he narrowed his eyes, studying me blearily while rocking unsteadily on his heels. He enquired in a gentle Lancashire growl whether I had ever seen Willie Irvine play. I said I had, at Spurs. He contemplated that briefly before continuing in a deeper, louder, gruffer voice, 'Then you'll know … (and here he paused, hitching himself up like a long jumper) how fooking ex-cel-lent he is, won't you?' He bit down on his bottom lip before he swore, spring-loading it, so he could propel his expletive at maximum velocity. It was as if he was vomiting the profanity, stumbling forward with the force of his delivery. It was world-class vulgarity.

Baz once blagged his way on to a London-bound coach transporting anti-apartheid protesters to a demonstration. This was a new departure for him. Strong views he had aplenty, political issues, no. But then we twigged. His purpose was to get to the FA Cup replay at Stamford Bridge. Heaven help those protesters once Baz got going. And on the return journey his gruff voice would have been gruffer still, after 90 minutes of furious invective. It was how Baz became known as 'Deepdale Throat'.

Sadly, Willie's promising career at Preston was curtailed by injury. David Webb of Chelsea caught him in a scissor tackle, rupturing his cruciate ligament. After struggling to recover his once formidable prowess, he was transferred in 1971 to Brighton, then under the management of Pat Saward.

At Burnley, where Irvine began his career, he was a 'will o' the wisp', with a sharp eye for an opening. Irvine reckoned he had 'feet as quick as Cassius Clay' (Muhammad Ali). It was no exaggeration, for Irvine put himself about in a scurry, insinuating himself into the tiniest of spaces to get a shot away, heaving himself above defenders with perfect timing to produce flashing headers. He would get up the noses of his opponents, too, with his cocky strutting and brash, 'gobby' manner. The mind-games matter as well as the quick feet. Like the very best strikers, he was always ready to pounce on the half-chance, eyes keenly alert, primed nerve ends sparking, leg muscles twitching in readiness, coiled to make that explosive spurt, just enough to put him ahead of his markers. It didn't need to be much. At this level, the slightest margins can be decisive.

During his international career, he capitalised upon the brilliant service supplied by his friend George Best in netting eight international goals in 23 appearances. Alf Ramsey regretted Irvine's unavailability for England. The lad who had started life with little looked set for the richest prizes football could bestow. By 1966, Irvine was a big name in British football, but his future promised even greater acclaim.

But, on 31 January 1967 Irvine's world caved in. His leg was broken in a petulant FA Cup tie at Everton. One witness said, 'It was a horror tackle. The crack was audible even at the back of a packed Goodison stand.' Irvine was aged just 23. After the game, Harry Catterick, the Everton manager, came into the Burnley dressing room. Willie expected an apology. He didn't get one. Irvine said, '[Catterick] told me that it served me right, that I'd got what I'd been asking for.' There had been much bad blood between the teams. With both Lochhead and Irvine then sidelined by injury, Burnley's European Fairs Cup campaign faltered.

Gradually, the break healed but Willie began to limp half an hour into a game. He fretted, fearing for his future. This spoilt things at home. The team wasn't doing so well, either, letting in a lot more goals. There was a spat between chairman Bob Lord and his team-mate Gordon Harris, resulting in Harris being moved on. The fracas poisoned the air. Willie began to bridle at Burnley's exacting coach Jimmy Adamson. As his confidence fell, the niggling got worse. Irvine claimed, 'Adamson just gnawed away at me. It festered in the back of my head … I couldn't play for him … His coaching was excellent, studious, thoughtful and creative. As a tactician he was outstanding … but I just couldn't relate to him.' The goals began to dry up – down to one in three, a good rate for many strikers, not for Willie. He was no longer an automatic selection. He looked for a way out. But in Willie's desperation to leave, he didn't look before he jumped. He said he had no idea how badly placed Division Two Preston were, but he still signed for them. This was in March 1968. Preston paid Burnley £45,000 for him. Willie received a £5,000 signing-on fee and a regular £75 per week wage plus appearance money. This was £15 more a week than he had received at top-flight Turf Moor. Preston could barely afford this, but they couldn't afford a further relegation either. Willie offered a 'get-out-of-jail-free card'. He delivered quickly with a hat-trick against Huddersfield. Preston survived.

Willie enjoyed his Indian summer on the south coast. He recovered his scoring ability, too, netting 21 goals in 55 league appearances, helping Kit Napier to power Brighton to promotion from Division Three in May 1972. It was his crucial goal which, once again, defeated then-promotion rivals Aston Villa. It came about like this: Brighton midfielder Brian Bromley picked up the ball deep inside his own half and released Templeman, who made a thrusting run towards the Shoreham Road End, nonchalantly brushing aside his markers. Upon reaching the Villa box, he exchanged a sharp one-two with Ken Beamish, who was surrounded by opposing defenders, and, with a lunging effort, found Irvine lurking to his left. Irvine immediately cut in, shaking off the attention of a solitary centre-back, and let fly from 18 yards. The ball flashed into the top right-hand corner, leaving Worcestershire county cricketer Jim Cumbes helpless in the Villa goal. The Goldstone Ground erupted with glee. This magnificent goal deserved to win this tight promotion contest, and to be venerated on *Match of the Day* and on YouTube for decades after.

Alas, promotion was a one-year wonder. Recriminations followed. Irvine said in his biography *Together Again*, written with Dave Thomas, 'Kit, my strike partner, was another to fall out with Pat Saward after promotion and went to Blackburn. The euphoria of promotion hadn't lasted long. Pat Saward had changed. He seemed unapproachable. I seemed to have to book an appointment two or three days in advance. We all had to. Saward decided Barry Bridges was the player he wanted to bring in. Saward insisted, "Bridges would bring success and the team will be fashioned around him." The old maxim "If it ain't broke, don't fix it" was sadly ignored. Kit, with whom I had such a good partnership, went. Others went as well. The supporters became disgruntled and in November a losing streak of 12 games began. Bridges didn't arrive anyway until the season started and by the end of the season was mostly on the bench having scored four goals. I have nothing against him but if Bridges was the answer then nobody could quite fathom what the question was. After eight games in the 1972/73 season, I was up among the top scorers but from early October I was the old model. By the time that losing run had ended, Brighton were in bottom place and I had gone to Halifax. Saward was sacked before the end of the season when he made a memorable remark: "I have no more answers. I am in a fog.'"

1977–79: 'Labour Isn't Working'

'Pretty Vacant'

WITH THE economy spluttering and the pound falling sharply, Labour chancellor of the exchequer Denis Healey looked to the International Monetary Fund for financial help. The price was punitive. The crisis was not as bad as first feared, though. But if the patient was not terminally ill, it was still ailing. It gave prime minister Callaghan the leverage to turn off the subsidy tap for unproductive commercial ventures, such as at British Leyland. The Leyland bosses laid down the gauntlet to 'Red Robbo' and his striking car workers: 'End the strike or face plant closures.' It was about time.

The tawdry, decrepit, seedy image of late-70s Britain spawned a 'bleak chic'. Apart from punk rock and fashions, there were nihilistic films such as *Radio On, O Lucky Man!* and *Jubilee*. There were novels, too, describing emotionally frozen lives as in *The Ice Age, High Rise, Dead Babies* and *The Cement Garden*.

Kerry Packer was the bumptious chairman of Australian TV Channel 9. He was furious that the Australian Cricket Board would not do business with him. His answer was to set up World Series Cricket. This was an affront to cricket authorities accustomed to calling the shots. Packer's impact upon the cricketing establishments was like the impact of 'punk' upon conservative Britain.

With Packer and punk stirring febrile moral panics, prompting cries of folk devilry, MCC's Robin Marlar confronted the allegedly villainous Packer with righteous indignation. Whereas ITV *Today* presenter Bill Grundy confronted the supposedly notorious Sex Pistols with scoffing disdain. And both came a cropper. The Pistols' front man John Lydon (aka 'Johnny Rotten') knew which buttons to press to pump up the outrage. Mocking Olivier's risible version of *Richard the Third*, Lydon sneered in 'Pretty Vacant' that they were totally clueless. Steve Jones's caustic riff, nicked improbably from ABBA hit 'SOS', underscored their sardonic point. It was 'all too much' for London's river police, too. Halting the Pistols' Thames boat gig as it reached Westminster, they deemed the punks' iconoclastic cruise to be disrespectful to Her Majesty's 1977 Jubilee. Had they mistaken 'Anarchy in the UK' for the real thing? Punk, both edgy and confrontational, probably gave rock music its last rebel yell. Thereafter, that distinction would belong increasingly to hip-hop.

The 1970s began with 'glam' rock but ended with the 'glum' variety. Bands such as The Fall, Bauhaus, Joy Division, Public Image Ltd, Gang of Four and Killing Joke produced jagged, jarring, desolate sounds. In one of Britain's coldest winters, doom-laden rock provided a fitting soundtrack as the rubbish piled up, operations were cancelled and the dead remained unburied. Industrial dereliction abounded. 'Labour isn't working,' insisted the Saatchi brothers. It was hard to disagree. There was little surprise about Mrs Thatcher's rise to power. In times of despair, nothing seems to roll so fast through the vacuum as a bandwagon. Her bandwagon was fuelled by mounting exasperation with union activists, and with fear and loathing of Britain's desolate towns and cities. In decaying Britain, punk had articulated disaffection, but it was the escape offered by the flamboyant 'new romantics' and their pretty-boy synthesiser bands that commanded a greater allure. With the growth of MTV, vision began to trump sound as the most prominent pop vehicle. 'Video Killed the Radio Star'.

Alan Mullery: Brighton & Hove Albion 1976–81

ABOVE THE office desk of Brighton chairman Mike Bamber was a picture of a seagull in flight. It featured a motto that was clearly visible to all visitors. It read, 'They can, because they think they can.' Bamber had high expectations. That had been made clear with his appointment of Brian Clough and Peter Taylor in 1973. While their results were disappointing, Bamber had magnified Brighton's profile. When Taylor left in 1976 to join Clough at Nottingham Forest, Bamber was left looking for a replacement capable of taking Brighton out of the Third Division and onwards and upwards.

Bamber did not need to study Alan Mullery's CV too closely to see that he was the man to take Brighton forward. Mullery had enormous experience at the highest level, as a combative midfielder with Fulham, Spurs and England. He was quick-witted, intelligent but down-to-earth. He was generally affable and enjoyed a joke but was also intensely focussed, with an explosive temper when crossed. Mullery was a natural leader, shrewd and consumed with driving ambition, but despite his moments of volatility he knew how to relax his players before big games, taking them to out-of-town hotels, away from the glare of publicity, where they could play golf and chill out.

Mullery was very loyal to his staff but wouldn't stand any nonsense.

Mullery told a national press reporter, 'I was out of work for three months after finishing my playing career with Fulham and had begun to give up hope of getting a job. Mike Bamber did me a favour by offering me the manager's job here. I'm going to repay him by really helping this club to take off. And it's a dead cert they will. They are going up in a big way – higher than the roof of the stand.'

As a new manager, Mullery acknowledged his debt to his mentors: Sir Alf Ramsey, Bill Nicholson, Bedford Jezzard and Alec Stock. Mullery described Ramsey as very studious, who spoke sparingly, but wisely. Ramsey was said to trust his players to do the job he had designated. Spurs boss Bill Nicholson was said to be the same, a brilliant coach with an encyclopaedic knowledge of the game and its players. Having a superb tactical brain, Nicholson was eulogised for his winning game plans. Fulham manager Bedford Jezzard was applauded for raising his players' confidence. He was said to hug and compliment those who performed well. Alec Stock was praised for his disciplinary skill, knowing when a reprimand was necessary but ensuring these were delivered in private. He was said to be very media savvy, always placing a positive spin on his team performances.

Upon taking the Brighton job, Alan Mullery concluded that the rudiments of a successful side already existed. He had a reliable keeper in Peter Grummitt and a skilful, attacking winger in Peter O'Sullivan. The surprise package was young Peter Ward. Previous manager Peter Taylor had bought Ward from Burton Albion for £4,000. Ward was an unknown quantity to Mullery until he began scoring freely in the pre-season practice games. It didn't matter which defenders Mullery set up against Ward, he would get past them. Ward had a sharp eye for a half-chance; quick reactions and quicker feet. Give him an inch and he was 'in like Flint'. He had the look of a natural predator – the strut, the bristling intensity, the zest, the pace and the composure when in on goal. Ward was a huge, unexpected bonus.

But Mullery knew that he needed to trim his squad. When he arrived at the Goldstone, he had 36 professionals. At least a third of them were surplus to requirements. That left him with his first difficult decisions. Among those lined up for the chop were two close mates – Joe Kinnear and Phil Beal – former Spurs colleagues. They were past their best and sitting on lucrative contracts. He couldn't show favouritism. That would compromise him with the full squad. After discussing the situation with Bill Nicholson, Kinnear and Beal were given the bad news. Beal was philosophical. Kinnear wasn't. Kinnear wouldn't talk to Mullery for years, but Mullery knew he'd done the right thing.

The next difficult decision was to drop crowd favourite Fred Binney. Supporters are particularly hard on managers who drop top guns. During the 1975/76 season, Binney had scored 23 times. In his first six league games under Mullery he scored three more. When he was dropped, the crowd were perplexed and so was Binney. Cheekily, Binney offered Mullery his advice: 'Wardy is not strong enough for the Third Division. You should play me. I got over 20 goals last season.' Mullery thanked Binney for his advice but continued to play Peter Ward, partnering him with Ian Mellor, who was pushed up from midfield. Ward and Mellor shared 44 league goals during the 1976/77 promotion season – 32 of them coming from the young, wild-haired, former Rolls-Royce apprentice. As for Binney, he was sent to Exeter. Alan Mullery clocked what he saw, spoke as he found and was as good as his word.

Mullery was delighted to find a natural leader on his books. This was Brian 'Nobby' Horton. Horton had indisputable authority. Leading by example, he won almost every 50-50 ball. He never stopped urging his team on. He loathed losing. Even in five-a-side games he threw himself into tackles as if his life depended on it.

Being a new manager, Mullery missed the dressing room banter he enjoyed as a player. But he realised that he could no longer be 'one of the boys'. He had to preserve a degree of distance from his men. His job was to select the team; organise the training and coaching; and sort out the travel arrangements. He found the coaching sessions he arranged to be the most enjoyable part of his new job. Here, he could demonstrate the technique, the tactics, the moves and positioning that he expected to see from his players.

Mullery's first season went like a dream – promotion to the Second Division in April 1977, behind champions Mansfield. But chairman Mike Bamber wanted more. He had set his heart on First Division football at the Goldstone and indicated that he was prepared to pay the price.

If Bamber's ambition was to be achieved, Mullery knew he needed more quality at the back. Preston's 19-year-old central defender Mark Lawrenson appeared to fit the bill. Mullery knew Lawrenson was sound, having a calm, strong temperament. He had never caused any problems at Deepdale and his performance levels were consistently high. When Bamber saw Lawrenson in action, he was impressed, too. Liverpool were also interested in him but were prepared to bid only £100,000 for him. Brighton offered £12,000 more for Lawrenson and Gary Williams. However, Lawrenson failed his medical. Lawrenson recalled, 'I was fit and healthy and very enthusiastic about playing under Mullery. So, it came as a nasty shock when I was told that I had failed. The doctor thought I was a diabetic because my sugar levels were soaring. The problem was that I had been downing a lot of Guinness and blackcurrant while on holiday in Spain. But the problem was sorted quickly, and I joined Brighton's pre-season training.'

Mullery was permitted to make other purchases, too, including highly promising, young midfielder Paul Clark, sturdy centre-forward Teddy Maybank, winger or midfielder Peter Sayer, striker Malcolm Poskett and loping Irish winger Gerry Ryan. But the stellar signing was Lawrenson.

Meanwhile, local boy Tony Towner and pint-sized winger Eric Potts were transferred to Millwall and Preston respectively. The 1977/78 season ended in huge disappointment, as Spurs were promoted instead of Brighton on goal difference.

The 1978/79 season started erratically, but by Saturday, 3 March Brighton were in second place. Burnley, their opponents on this day, were out of the race, having had many of their games postponed because of the arctic conditions gripping the North.

3 March was a sombre day. Killing time, my wife and I strolled along the empty promenade, unconcerned by the fine rain wafting into our faces on a ruffling wind. There was an indolent feel to the day. Mucky waves staggered listlessly to the shore, collapsing on to the shingle with resigned sighs. With the club trading in its future to preserve its past, we were sceptical of our chances. It felt like an invitation to the *Last Waltz* for Jimmy Adamson's supposed 'team of the 70s'.

Despite their onerous workload in catching up with a long list of postponements, Burnley began the game brightly. Leighton James frequently outpaced Brighton's experienced full-back Chris Cattlin, while Steve Kindon was a swift battering ram in the centre. Eric Steele in the Brighton goal was kept very busy. Had he not been in such superb form, denying successive headers from Fletcher with breathtaking agility, Burnley might well have been in front at the break. It was reported that Alan Mullery tore strips off his players at half-time, berating them for their complacency and lethargy. This verbal assault must have done the trick because Brighton began the second half truly fired up. Adopting a higher defensive line, Horton and Clark began to express themselves in the centre of the park. Ryan and O'Sullivan had more of the ball. As a result, Maybank and Ward were able to push up closer against Burnley's slow-turning central defenders. Now it was Burnley's turn to feel the heat. They were unable to commit so many men forward. Their suspect defence became sorely stretched.

Within five minutes of the restart, a penalty was conceded which Horton put away decisively. But Burnley didn't buckle. Within a minute they were back on terms as Billy Ingham stole into Brighton's box, unseen, to poke home a loose ball. The game then turned into a nip-and-tuck affair but one which began tipping Brighton's way. The contest was settled in the 69th minute by a goal of sublime quality.

No longer shackled by urgent defensive needs, Lawrenson started making probing runs. It was no wonder that Mullery was so keen to bring him to the Goldstone. Lawrenson's superb technique and composure were underpinned by throbbing power. He proceeded to turn the game. Seizing the ball in midfield, he strode forward effortlessly, gliding through the Burnley defence as if it was an apparition. Upon reaching the edge of the box, he easily evaded Jim Thomson's desperate lunge and let fly with a skimming shot that evaded Stevenson's dive and struck the back of the net at the speed of light. A huge roar went up.

My wife and I looked at one another in resignation. How could we compete with quality of this kind? We reluctantly agreed that a goal as good as this deserved to win any game. It was a moment of parting. While Burnley embarked upon a catastrophic slide, taking them to the brink of oblivion in May 1987, Brighton were destined for the First Division, which they achieved with a 3-1 victory at Newcastle in their final game of this season.

However, Mullery would remain at Brighton for only two more seasons. He resigned in June 1981 having disagreed with Bamber's decision to transfer Mark Lawrenson to Liverpool for a £900,000 fee and reduce the club's coaching staff. Mullery had set his heart upon an alternative transfer deal negotiated with Manchester United. This included a player exchange. This row was the culmination of his deteriorating relationship with Bamber, which had soured during a celebratory trip to the USA in the spring of 1979. Charlton manager Mike Bailey replaced him, although he lasted just 17 months before being dismissed after a string of heavy defeats. Ex-Liverpool playmaker Jimmy Melia then took over, guiding Brighton to the 1983 FA Cup Final, where the Albion first held and almost defeated Manchester United, before capitulating in the replay.

Unfortunately, Melia was unable to prevent Brighton's relegation at the end of this season. Although coming near to a First Division return in 1991, when they lost a Wembley play-off final to Notts County, they were about to enter their dark ages, seriously threatening the club's existence. Fortunately, through the intensive labours of all committed to the club, Brighton rose again triumphantly, eventually winning promotion to the Premier League in 2017.

Mullery admitted later that he had been too impetuous in leaving the club in 1981. Although he returned five years later, he lasted only seven months before being sacked, saying ruefully, 'You love the game, then it kicks you in the guts.'

With a child on the way, my wife and I found there was less time and money for football. Saturdays became consumed by morose meanderings around packed supermarkets, heaving shopping centres or, worst of all, MFI, where we bought affordable flat packs to bless with our incompetence. For the first time in my life football became expendable, a financially constrained choice rather than an obsessive necessity, often heard or seen peripherally, until our daughter became old and wise enough to want to go. The addiction doesn't expire, though. It is merely suppressed by the weight of parental duty, waiting for the moment when the trailing guilt of parenthood thins sufficiently for the urge to pop up again. That prospect was hard to imagine while sat on those penal MFI benches waiting to collect our chipboard ensembles. There, my unseeing eyes would be fixed on the cartoon channel, but my attention would be elsewhere; possibly speculating on events at The Shay or Spotland or wherever lowly Burnley were then playing. I would have to wait. The radio was always a car park away. Setting aside the contradictions in warmth, I felt like a beached expat, comatosed by Spanish wine and Tenerife sun, indulging maudlin home thoughts from abroad.

1981–83 'Put Out More Flags'

'Ghost Town'

COVENTRY'S MULTIRACIAL, reggae/ska band The Specials released their 2 Tone single, 'Ghost Town' in the spring of 1981. This hit the top 20 in June just as riots hit the streets of Peckham. There had already been serious outbreaks of violence in nearby Brixton during April. Copycat inner-city disturbances in Toxteth and Birmingham would follow, but Mrs Thatcher remained resolute. She insisted, 'The lady is not for turning … We have paid ourselves 22 per cent more for producing four per cent less.' With high interest rates and an overvalued pound savaging British manufacturing industries, she was adamant that commercial salvation lay in the growth of financial services and tourism and not in our ailing heavy industries. For the first time since the Industrial Revolution we were importing more manufactured goods than we were making. Prosperity, we were told, lay in arranging things.

Mrs Thatcher's popularity had fallen to 25 per cent, the lowest satisfaction rating achieved by any British prime minister. And yet she seemed unchallengeable. Labour was still not working, riven with internecine squabbling and a doctrinaire left-wing agenda few would buy. As for the new party at the centre, the SDP, it appealed only to footloose privileged types with pricking consciences. Despite the efforts of the estimable Shirley Williams, the new party seemed imbued with an image of suave wealth.

It was no surprise that the 80s should have spawned a rapid growth in self-help and action groups. Frustrated by the perceived inadequacies of the democratic process, the allure of direct action was grasped by environmentalists, animal rights activists, nuclear disarmament protesters and a variety of anti-discriminatory campaigners.

There was a brief, if bloody, resurrection of British Imperialism in 1982. The occasion was the recovery of the British Falkland Islands after an armed Argentinian invasion. The tabloids had a field day, with *The Sun* appealing to the basest of football terrace instincts by distributing t-shirts emblazoned with straplines such as 'Stick it Up Your Junta' and worse. *Private Eye* mocked its puerility by running a spoof competition: 'Kill an Argie and Win a Metro'. This grotesque parody of patriotism was appropriated by the English football fans yomping aggressively around northern Spain, before the 1982 World Cup finals, high on booze and 'ere we go' pub jingoism. A leading member of this ragged group told a press reporter, 'When you boil down to it, the British are a violent people. We've always been outnumbered by whoever we fought, whether in India, the Germans, whatever.'

Mrs Thatcher took a mighty risk. Had the task force failed, her political prospects would have sunk faster than the *General Belgrano*. But thanks to acts of outstanding bravery and flawed enemy fuse timings, the task force prevailed – just. No wonder Mrs Thatcher was exultant. 'Rejoice,' she exclaimed once victory was assured. Many Britons thought she had put the 'Great' back into Britain. Her reward for a decisive response over the Falkland Islands invasion was a landslide victory at the polls in June. Labour was almost wiped out as an electoral force in the south of England with the Liberal/Social Democratic Alliance runners-up in two-thirds of these southern constituencies. No matter how much Conservative values were condemned by their detractors, such as the makers of the Emmy award-winning film *The Ploughman's Lunch*, Mrs Thatcher's stock could not have been higher.

Peter Sillett Hastings United
1979–83

PETER SILLETT began his football career at Southampton but moved in 1953, together with his brother John, to Chelsea for a combined fee of £12,000. The then ailing south-coast club was desperate for the cash. Burly Sillett adjusted quickly to top-flight football. His distribution was exemplary, his positional play astute and his tackling robust but assured. Stanley Matthews rated him as one of the best full-backs he had played against. Sillett was never flustered under pressure and possessed one of the most explosive shots in the game. Such was the menace of his dead ball shooting that opponents often positioned a defensive 'wall' whenever a free kick was awarded against them 40 yards or more from goal. His imperturbable demeanour and firm resolution recommended him as a leader of authority. It was no surprise that manager Ted Drake chose him as Chelsea's captain when his side surprisingly won the First Division championship for the first time, at the end of the 1954/55 season.

Fittingly, it was Sillett who struck the crucial blow when Chelsea beat their closest rivals Wolverhampton Wanderers during the final lap of the title race. With only 15 minutes remaining and the game locked in stalemate, Chelsea were awarded a penalty. The 75,000 Stamford Bridge crowd was hushed as Peter Sillett strode forward purposefully, an apparent personification of coolness, although quaking inside. Sillett ran forward and smashed the ball past the diving England goalkeeper Bert Williams. The Bridge erupted. No longer the subject of music-hall derision, Chelsea would be crowned champions.

A month later, Sillett was selected for his international debut against France. Although he conceded the penalty that enabled France to win the game, he played well enough to retain his place for the remaining two matches against Spain and Portugal. He did not look out of place in a team including Billy Wright, Duncan Edwards and Stanley Matthews. Billy Wright once said to Peter's brother John, 'If I was a 100 cap player, then so was Peter.' Alas, his increasing age and reducing speed meant that these were his last appearances in an England shirt. Nevertheless, Juventus recognised his superb technical skills, rating him among the highest-ranked international full-backs. Although Juventus offered him a deal, Peter rejected it saying, 'Italy is too bloody hot for football.' He continued to play First Division football for Chelsea until his late 20s, becoming the elder statesman among 'Drake's Ducklings'. I first saw him play on a scorching afternoon in August 1958 when Chelsea murdered Wolves, then the reigning league champions. With Jimmy Greaves running the Wolves defence ragged, scoring five of Chelsea's six goals, Peter was not hard-pressed, but he remained a steadying figure at the back while his front men ran riot. The game showcased Chelsea's unpredictability. Vibrant victories were juxtaposed with dismal defeats. Had it not been for Greaves's brilliance, Chelsea would have been relegated several years before 1962, when Greaves had already departed for Italy.

Sillett's top-flight career was ended by a broken leg. Although he recovered by the end of the 1961/62 season, he was unable to oust gifted rookie Ken Shellito. He joined Guildford City before becoming player-manager of Ashford Town, Kent, in 1965. He remained there for nine years, mostly as manager. Such were his man–management skills, that he took his tiny club up to the Southern League Premier Division and to an FA Trophy semi-final place. While at Ashford, Sillett signed future England boss Roy Hodgson for the 1972/73 season. He also managed Folkestone Town before becoming a chief scout at Hereford, where brother John was in charge.

In February 1979 Sillett returned to management with Hastings United. According to Hastings fan and writer Roger Sinden, Sillett was not immediately appreciated, not helped by the preceding turmoil after Bobby Drake's sacking, just eight games into the 1978/79 season.

Bobby had been liked for his honesty and enthusiasm, but Hastings chairman Keith Wratten believed he was too lenient. When Cyril Jeans, a former Hastings player and manager, was appointed in Drake's place, albeit in a caretaking role, the team did not greet the news favourably. Captain Kevin Barry spoke of proposing a vote of no confidence in the directors who had supported Jeans's appointment. This direct challenge to their authority was not taken kindly. Barry was banned and sadly left the club. Amid a string of poor results, Cyril Jeans resigned after three months, paving the way for Sillett's appointment. Sillett arrived during the coldest winter since 1962/63, which left Hastings caught up in frenzied fixture congestion during April and May. Sillett tried to bolster his relegation-bound team by bringing in Maidstone striker Ernie Batten, who would score more than 120 goals for the club over the next four seasons. Wayne Peacock, son of 1950s favourite George, went to Maidstone in Batten's place, although he would return for the following season. Hastings fan Roger King remembers, 'The average home attendance was down to 320, including the lowest-ever gate, I think, for a Southern League match – just 125 for a midweek game against Yeovil in early May. Hastings lost their final ten games, including a defeat at Witney in which Hastings could only field ten players.'

Roger and I suspected the worst when we watched Hastings at Nuneaton on 28 April, standing on Manor Park's cinder bank beneath a funereal sky. Hastings seemed too feeble to survive, even with Batten and prolific goalscorer Steve Gill up front. They hardly fired a shot in anger in an ineffectual 0-3 defeat.

John Lambert, one of several players who Sillett inherited, was at first dubious about him, telling Roger Sinden some years later, 'While I found Peter likeable, it was difficult to see what he did to earn his money. His style was deceptively laid back, offering little tactical direction, but just expecting his team to play.' It was a formula that worked well enough for Sir Matt Busby though! Experienced midfielder Dave Crush had a more positive view. He told Roger Sinden that Sillett was someone 'who commanded instant respect, who was knowledgeable'. Being older than most of his team-mates, Dave probably had a better knowledge of Sillett's illustrious playing career.

Sillett made it clear to Crush that he signed him for his aggressive qualities in the forward line. Sillett had told Sinden, 'No one likes playing against Crushie. I'd rather have him in my team than play against him.' But Crush agreed with John Lambert about Sillett's 'laid-back' manner. Crush recalled, 'I called at Peter's house one night to find him spread horizontally on the sofa eating his meal. That's taking the quality to a new extreme.'

As many managers have found, players perform at their best when liberated from excessive tactical ideology. Sillett's approach gained popularity, especially with his commitment to exciting, attacking football. Fast-striding winger Wayne Peacock admitted feeling disconcerted by Sillett's appointment, partly because of the turbulence that preceded his arrival. However, Peacock recognised it was natural that a new manager might cause him and others to feel unsure of their places but confirmed that he and Peter soon established a good mutual understanding, assisted by their shared love of cribbage, particularly on long coach journeys. A new broom does not have to sweep away all before it.

In addition to inherited players such as goalkeeper Gerry Armstrong, defenders Malcolm Streeter and Peter Petkovic and returning winger Wayne Peacock, Sillett recruited a prolific goalscorer in Batten; a sound centre-half, Micky Crowe; a gifted playmaker, Matt Stock and versatile defender Bob Glozier. While Crowe and Glozier added beef, Stock gave additional flair to what became a winning formula.

In Sillett's first three full seasons in charge, Hastings United achieved tenth, third and second positions in the newly created Southern Division of the Southern League. Although Wealdstone beat them to promotion by one point in 1981/82, Hastings joined the restored Southern League Premier Division for the 1982/83 season, following Wealdstone's promotion to the Conference. Not only was there a promotion to celebrate in 1981/82, Hastings also reached the FA Cup first round proper for the first time since November 1960. Alas, on 21 December 1981 Batten missed a penalty as Hastings lost 2-0 at Enfield.

I drove from Bristol to Yeovil on a sunny 31 January 1981 to watch Hastings take on their illustrious opponents in an FA Trophy second-round tie. In those cash-strapped days it was a rare treat for me to go to a game. Since leaving Hastings I had seen them no more than a handful of times, although I followed their progress in back issues of the *Hastings & St Leonard Observer,* which mum kept for me. At the game I met fanatical Hastings supporter Roger Sinden with his wife and their new baby. I thought this was taking the Jesuit principle a bit far but confessed to feeling shamed by his undying loyalty. I readily forgave myself on the drive home, after hearing that third-tier Burnley had dropped to seventh after losing 0-3 at Chesterfield.

The Yeovil tie had attracted considerable local interest on account of Malcolm Allison's temporary stint as their coaching advisor. Urged on by their vocal West Country support,

Yeovil began dominantly, forcing Hastings to defend deep and denying them any outlets. It was no surprise when Yeovil took the lead.

However, during the second half Hastings found a way back into the game and began to exert considerable pressure on the Yeovil goal. It was fully merited when David Crush drove in an equaliser. Whereupon Hastings began to play with a swagger, their crisp passing and darting movement causing increasing consternation on and off the pitch, with Allison hollering a stream of incomprehensible instructions. It was not just me who was perplexed, judging by the bewildered, hang-dog expressions of some of the Yeovil players. It made no difference. Hastings comfortably held on to their hard-won parity.

The replay took place in Hastings on Tuesday, 3 February. Unfortunately, I couldn't be there, but Mum sent me a cutting of the *Hastings & St Leonards Observer*'s report by Phil Elms. It was given the heading: 'MAGICAL NIGHT FOR 2,000'.

Phil wrote, 'Amazing scenes from an age past were recreated on Tuesday night when the Pilot Field's biggest crowd for 14 years saw Hastings United into the last 16 of the FA Trophy at the expense of fancied Yeovil, winning 2-1. The gate of 1,997, boosted no doubt by the presence of Malcolm Allison, generated a fantastic atmosphere and turned a football match into a real sporting occasion. Allison, the sacked Crystal Palace manager, looked tired and dejected after four days as Yeovil's temporary coaching consultant. He spent Tuesday evening bellowing at his players from the touchline but all to no avail. Yeovil's best chance to ditch Hastings had been lost in the first half of Saturday's game on Somerset soil. Having forced a replay, Hastings needed no second bidding. They attacked the Yeovil defence relentlessly and their secret weapon remained a secret for just a matter of minutes. That was Wayne Peacock, a flu victim on Saturday but restored to his favourite right-wing position for the replay.

'Seven times the fast-striding Peacock was sent clear of his marker. His exploits set up the opening goal. Micky Westburgh released Peacock at the halfway line. Peacock lost and regained possession before centring to Matt Stock. Stock performed a little dance and squeezed the ball through a gap for versatile defender Peter Petkovic to slide past Brian Parker, the England non-league international keeper. Fourteen minutes gone and United had made a dream start. Five minutes later, Yeovil replied with a simple goal by classy Dave Green. Gerry Armstrong could only palm away Steve Hayward's header and the former Portsmouth striker drilled a low shot inside the near post.

'The deciding goal came as early as the 30th minute. Terry Cottle completely misjudged Kevin Wallis's upfield header and Ernie Batten burst through, keeping close control and putting away his 33rd goal of the season.

'Yeovil began the second half like men possessed. Perhaps Allison's potion might work after all? They had Hastings pinned back for quarter of an hour, during which time the dissenting Stock joined Bob Glozier on the booking list. As Yeovil's efforts went unrewarded – Armstrong was in immaculate form – Dave Platt was booked for a crunching tackle on Dave Crush. Full credit to Micky Crow, United's centre-half who concealed a neck injury until the game was over, and to Chris Hamshare, whose midfield skills were so important.'

Unfortunately, Hastings progressed no further. Worcester defeated them with a last-minute goal in a replay (1-2), after the first game at the Pilot Field was drawn 0-0.

Phil Elms reflected, 'Success, however, had its price. The players' wage bill reflected the standard of football to which supporters had become accustomed.' Sillett was also offered a new contract by new chairman Bernard Sealy. Meanwhile tension was building within the United boardroom because of the low income and high outgoings. Although 1,977 attended the exciting Yeovil tie, the equally riveting two-horse race with Wealdstone in the following 1981/82 season drew an average home gate of 582, with the highest attendance of 977 coming in the final leg. The 1981/82 average gate of 582 was 168 or 22 per cent lower than achieved in the second worst season in United's history, 1961/62, when only 14 points were accumulated. How was it possible to run a club on so little revenue? Chairman Sealy was ousted soon after as the club's financial situation became evermore critical. Sealy had played for Hastings as a goalkeeper during the 1970s, taking part in Kent Floodlight Cup and friendly games. It seemed ironic that he was appointed to the board with the specific role of financial advisor.

With Hastings spluttering once again in the Southern League Premier Division, Peter Sillett was dismissed in November 1983 with 19 months of his contract remaining, and no prospect of being paid off. New club chairman Mick Piper informed Sillett of the board's decision in a letter delivered by hand in the small hours of the morning. It seemed a shoddy way to treat anyone, let alone a respected servant, who had done so much to revive interest in the club. Long-standing supporter Roger King remarked, 'Having lifted Hastings's home gates by over 50 per cent, Peter Sillett probably achieved the greatest improvement in attendance levels that United had made, since the days of Ted Ballard who brought about a similar rise between 1961/62 and 1962/63. For the average Southern League South gate in the 1979/80 season, Sillett's first full season with the club, was 327. This was when Hastings finished in tenth place. But by the 1980/81 season, the average attendance had risen to 501, when Hastings came third with the Sillett magic beginning to work.' The unpalatable truth was that a regular crowd of 501 was insufficient to balance the books. Hastings had been spending beyond its means. Investing in better players had not come cheaply. By 1985 the club's debts were ruinous.

Roger King reflected, 'I saw few games in the 1980s. I was aware, though, how that wonderful 1981/82 season was, regrettably, followed by disaster. At the end of the 1981/82 season, 1,435 people watched a final showdown between the leading contestants Wealdstone and United. Wealdstone were the deserved winners, therefore beating Hastings to the championship. The 1,435 gate was a huge one for those unhappy times. The last programme of the season underlined the many positives achieved by Sillett's impressive team. Despite the disappointment at not getting into the Alliance, now known as the Vanarama National League Premier Division, Hastings won three-quarters of the points available to them in the 1981/82 season. At that time, no runner-up at this level had gained such a high proportion of points. This was the scale of Sillett's team's achievement. However, had Hastings been promoted to the Alliance then, this might have led to earlier liquidation rather than solvency.' With Burnley about to embark upon a tailspin that would leave them hurtling towards the Alliance in 1987 – then known as the Football Conference – it was the nearest I came to watching my first love play my subsequent love at an equal level.

Roger King continued, 'Yet within 18 months Bernard Sealey had left the board, Peter Sillett had gone, in November 1983, and so had most of the better players, Ernie Batten being more long-lasting than most, but was also gone before May 1984. Wayne Peacock, Malcolm Streeter and Peter Petkovic stayed to the bitter end, though.'

Jack Tresadern, Ted Ballard and Peter Sillett were United's greatest managers, although Dave Underwood and Bobby Drake deserve much credit, as does Gerry Boon for keeping the show on the road while desperately trying to 'beat the retreat'.

Sillett had not renounced Hastings, though. He returned to the Pilot Field in 1988 after guiding Ashford once again to the Southern League Premier Division in 1987 – a truly remarkable feat. Sillett then went on to lead Hastings Town to promotion in the Beazer Homes League Southern Division in 1992. When Sillett took over at Hastings United in 1979, he reckoned it would take him three full seasons to return his side to the Southern League Premier Division. He was true to his word. At Hastings Town it took him just one year more to achieve the same. His team began to falter in the higher division, though, leading to his dismissal in November 1992, a precipitate action, perhaps, for Town comfortably avoided the drop. Peter Sillett died of cancer six years later. He is deservedly remembered with great respect and much fondness.

As for the demise of Hastings United, chairman Mick Piper said in 1983, the year of Sillett's sacking, 'If the directors looked at the club purely as a hard-headed business venture, we'd close down the football side tomorrow and just run the squash.' Twice Hastings survived winding-up threats from the Inland Revenue, while Hastings Borough Council, denied sight of the club's accounts since 1982, took steps to withdraw the Pilot Field lease unless commitments totalling £5,000 were honoured. Reports set before the council early in 1985 said that United needed £59,000 to wipe the slate clean. That is around £300,000 in today's values. This figure comprised a £52,000 bank loan on the five-year-old Pilot Field squash complex. This project was meant to deliver solvency, with enough over to facilitate playing success.

A desperate attempt was made by the directors and supporters to raise £30,000. Mick Piper said £5,000 had been raised to pay off the council and that there were plans to sell the squash complex to a consortium of members for £75,000. But clearing the debts offered no gain, leaving the club without any means of generating future income. In this maelstrom it was amazing that Sillett's successor, Gerry Boon, managed to keep Hastings United in the Southern League Premier Division, although their average home gate for the 1984/85 season was a pathetic 275.

Roger King concluded, 'Amazingly, Hastings survived relegation in May 1983 when all had looked lost. Conveniently, Enderby lost their last five games, but United still needed a last-day win at Corby to overtake them. Then, in 1983/84, a Hastings team, looking more like an early-season reserve

XI with every passing month, found themselves once again in real danger by the spring. And yet they produced a 3-0 victory in their must-win game against Gosport at the start of April, and followed that with an unbeaten eight-match run, comprising six wins and two draws. No one quite believed it. Congratulations must go to manager Gerry Boon. But with the club just days from closure, in March 1984 the directors, under Mick Piper, put in a lot of their own cash to ensure one final season.

'At the start of the 1984/85 season I went to Division One Ashford for a Southern League Cup game just prior to the league programme. It was quite literally shocking. Hastings were defeated 0-3 in a performance of such ineptitude that I came away thinking that relegation was certain, and that avoiding bottom place would be a real achievement. But I had counted without the Leamington meltdown, and enough United performances of sheer hard graft, as opposed to skill, plus good fortune at the end in that Crawley beat Witney twice in the final five days. Once again, though, United needed to win a vital last-day game, versus Welling, to overhaul Witney and reach the safety of 16th place. At the end, the people who ran the club were talking optimistically about the next season, but in three more weeks it was all over.'

Lest we forget, the 80s were particularly bad for English football. Repugnant hooliganism accounted for 39, mostly Italian, deaths at Heysel Stadium, Brussels, in May 1985. And an innocent teenager, at his first match, lost his life at St Andrew's, Birmingham, when an unruly stampede by Leeds 'fans' caused a wall to collapse. There was also the enraged riot led by Millwall supporters at Luton, resulting in substantial damage to Kenilworth Road seats, and to the British Rail trains carrying them. The Heysel disaster led to the banning of English clubs from European competitions. The outrages in England led to the Thatcher government introducing compulsory identity cards, although before implementation there was a belated change of heart over this impractical measure. Many English grounds were in poor states of repair, with crumbling concrete allowing the hooligans copious ammunition. The introduction of penal wire cages to prevent pitch invasions was the last straw for many genuine supporters out of love with the so-called 'beautiful game'.

Although a vast majority of English fans behaved in an exemplary fashion inside and outside football grounds, the government and the popular press generally regarded them as pariahs. Perhaps this was why the police at Hillsborough in April 1989 fatally confused distress signals with disorder. The prevalent disaffection affected gates at all levels, both at professional and semi-professional clubs. Hastings's attempts at encouraging better local support came at a time of rising UK unemployment. Whether because of cost or other disinclination, a vast majority of Hastings people had forsaken the U's, except, perhaps, for the odd 'big game'.

It was kismet that United and Town should meet one another in the FA Cup first-qualifying round in September 1984. Then there was hope, no matter how improbable, that United could still survive. A brilliant goal from Wayne Peacock enabled United to defeat their neighbours 2-1. United's embattled manager Gerry Boon remarked, 'This game was so important to the club. We had everything to lose and I mean everything. If we had lost it would have meant we didn't have the best players in the area.' His loyalty as manager matched that when he was a player at Hastings United. He deserved a better fate and yet, having battled successfully against the drop in 1985, his United side were allowed one last triumph, a victory in the Gilbert Price Floodlight Cup over Banstead.

The rapid rise of Hastings Town played a significant part in Hastings United's demise. As the *Hastings & St Leonards Observer* reporter put it, 'Town had the ideas and the money; United had golden memories and debts.' The club was silently put to sleep with Hastings Town assuming its place in the Southern League, though not in the upper division. Ironically, Hastings Town was the direct descendant of Hastings and

St Leonards FC, the club displaced by the nascent Hastings United in 1948.

A club bearing the name of Hastings United continues to play at the Pilot Field. Like its predecessor, the new club struggles to make ends meet in a cash-strapped place in cash-strapped times. Whenever supporters of much bigger clubs claim that they are the most passionate and loyal fans, I am sceptical. It's hard to imagine more dedicated fans than the few supporters of these little non-league clubs. Not only do they bellow their minnows on, week in, week out, in inhospitable places, with only a few hundred others, if that, for company, many of these zealots work tirelessly to help their clubs remain afloat. Instead of being derided as mad or sad, these committed fans should be applauded for their loyalty. As fans, we can and, perhaps, should be more than consumers. Lest we forget, many professional club membership schemes offer as much of a stake as a Tesco loyalty card. Should that be the sum of our involvement?

1989–2000 Babel Belt

'I am the Resurrection'

IN 1989 the world was in a state of flux. The fall of the Berlin Wall signified a sudden end of the Cold War, with Soviet leader Mikhail Gorbachev announcing a radical policy of *perestroika* or reconstruction. A rapid, if fractious, dissolution of Soviet and Iron Curtain states followed. Meanwhile, US nuclear missiles were withdrawn at Greenham Common, vociferously cheered by the women protesters encamped there. Greater threats to Western security were posed by religious fundamentalist regimes or bandit states that condoned, incubated and sponsored terrorism. In 1989 Britain and the USA were still reeling at the December downing of a Pan Am jetliner over Lockerbie. Author Salman Rushdie was threatened by an Iranian fatwa with Muslims at home and abroad vilifying his *The Satanic Verses*, while the genocide atrocities of the Balkan and Rwandan wars flouted international peace keeping.

Repressive regimes were challenged and some overthrown. In Beijing's Tiananmen Square there were tragic consequences, while in Romania the hated Ceausescu administration was ended. Even the previously impregnable Thatcher government tottered, thrown into turmoil by Mrs Thatcher's sacking of foreign minister Geoffrey Howe over a disputed European monetary policy. The angry resignation of her chancellor of the exchequer, Nigel Lawson, cast further doubt about her durability. The anti-poll tax riots and cabinet disaffection brought her down. British health and safety standards came under scrutiny after a spate of fatal rail accidents and the Hillsborough crush, captured live on TV.

In 1991 rioting re-emerged in British towns and cities. These were the snarling underdogs of an underclass, stripped of purpose, ambition, conscience or inhibition. Canary Wharf seemed like a latter-day Babel, presiding over the disadvantaged communities around it, built in blind homage to the voracious demands of high finance. How ironic it should be constructed where working men and women once toiled, where commerce was measured in tangible commodities. Here, there and everywhere, 80s regeneration seemed closer to gentrification.

In 1999 Britain was largely sustained by a thriving global financial sector, but its manufacturing base, the basis for its world power, had largely withered. England's bottom place in the world's cricket hierarchy seemed a symbolic reflection of what had been lost since the end of World War Two: industrial might, military strength and imperial power.

The 90s seemed book-ended by two major demolitions. It began with the fall of the Berlin Wall and concluded with an horrific assault upon Manhattan's 'Twin Towers'. The fall of the Berlin Wall denoted the demise of the Iron Curtain, the end of the Cold War and the start of greater freedoms, whereas the horrific attack in Manhattan returned us to the politics of fear. Fundamentalist insurgency became the new global threat, stalking areas of political instability, notably those where collapsing oppressive regimes released toxic racial and religious animosities.

The new millennium arrived with pomp and angst. Although the Dome did not pull or the river catch fire, or the Eye go around, at least the 'Bug' did not bite. Airliners did not crash to earth and we could still use the ATM the next day.

'Dust and Diamonds': Sussex CCC 1968–2019

'Sussex by the Sea'

EPILEPTIC SEIZURES brought me back to Sussex County Cricket Club after a 36-year gap. I had been working too hard. Having lost my right to drive, I realised I needed to slow down. Spending a day or so at the cricket each month seemed a good idea. There was much to catch up on while I had been away. Much had changed, notably the fielding which was sharper and more agile. The batting was more aggressive, too. In a County Championship game I watched in 2005, involving Sussex and Glamorgan, a scoring rate of four or five runs an over was maintained throughout the first two days. Whereas, the same fixture in 1966 produced an average run-rate of no more than 2.3 runs per over until a run-chase on the final afternoon lifted this rate to the 2005 level.

While Dexter and Parks were dashers during the 60s, most of the County Championship cricket I watched tended to be attritional. That was why Tony Greig was such a welcome shot in the arm when he joined Sussex in 1967. The gangling South African all-rounder tossed aside the manual of careful accumulation. In his County Championship debut, against Lancashire, in May 1967, he came to the wicket with Sussex in the mire at 34/3. Greig showed scant regard for reputation or prudence, as he blasted 15 fours and two sixes in a ferocious innings of 156. I was wide-eyed with astonishment as he carved a typically accurate delivery from the venerable Statham for six, the ball sailing high over the extra cover boundary and scattering some alarmed members in the main stand. Two months later, Greig took 8-25 against Gloucestershire, with a bewildering concoction of medium-paced seamers and off spin.

Greig passed 1,000 runs and 50 wickets in each of his first three seasons with Sussex, exhibiting unshakable confidence in his ability to dominate the best opponents. He was 6ft 6in tall, strikingly blond and bubbling with enthusiasm. He captivated all who met him. His team-mate Peter Graves once said, 'He was just so different. He had that boyish exuberance, irrepressible charisma. He was noisy too.'

Several years after moving North, I watched Greig in an Ashes Test match at Headingley. He began the day's play by spanking Jeff Thomson's first three thunderbolts to the cover boundary. How the Headingley crowd roared its approval. The carnage Thomson and Lillee had wreaked 'Down Under' was still fresh in our memories. Defying Thommo's armoury of foot-crushing yorkers and rib-breaking bouncers, he counter-attacked belligerently. He regarded anything in his half as potentially there to be hit, deploying a giant stride forward to put him in a position to drive on the rise. Anything in the bowler's half was contemptuously ignored or evaded, if the hook or pull were out of the equation. As each of his crashing cover drives flashed to the boundary, he provocatively parodied the umpire by waving his right arm back and forth. He knew how to disarm his opponents by getting up their noses.

Although Sussex won the Gillette Trophy for the third time in September 1978, beating Somerset by five wickets, a game I saw on TV, they did so without Greig. He was no stranger to controversy. He had incensed the West Indian side of 1976 by boasting that he would make them 'grovel'. After Richards, Greenidge, Holding and Roberts had rammed this offensive word down his throat, he apologised abjectly at the Oval by prostrating himself in front of hundreds of Windies fans. Greig was not a racist, just too pumped up for his own good at times. When Kerry Packer's World Series 'circus' threatened to usurp Test cricket, amid bitter recriminations of the non-participants, Greig paid the price for becoming the Australian tycoon's recruiting officer while serving as England's captain. He was soon lost to English cricket.

As much as Sussex and I regretted Greig's departure, they regrouped and prospered once more. Their Gillette Cup victory in 1978 seemed evidence of that. I recall how well 22-year-old Paul Parker (62 not out), 24-year-old John Barclay (44) and 23-year-old Gehan Mendis (44) batted, in taking Sussex to a five-wicket victory over a strong Somerset side containing Viv Richards, Ian Botham and giant West Indian fast bowler, Joel Garner. In Imran Khan, though, Sussex had an even better all-rounder than Greig. Imran, who was capable of bowling at around 90mph, clean bowled Botham for 80 in that Lord's final, just when the young Somerset and England star was threatening to take the game away from Sussex.

A year later Sussex came fourth in the County Championship, their best ranking since 1963. South African Kepler Wessels was back from national service, contributing 1,800 runs at an average of 52.49. Parker with an average of 42.96 and Imran Khan with one of 35 ensured Sussex achieved telling totals, supported by the technically correct Barclay (32.14). Imran was devastating with the ball, too, taking 72 wickets at an average of 13.70, ably supported by Geoff Arnold (52 at 18.26) and Barclay with deceptively innocuous off-breaks (52 at 24.3). In the summer of 1980, 20-year-old Colin Wells from Newhaven made a splash also, scoring 1,024 runs at an average of 44.52 in support of the aforementioned stalwarts. With Imran now backed by hefty South African speed merchant, Garth Le Roux, Sussex eyed a Championship prize, a triumph that had hitherto eluded them. Disappointingly, Sussex came fourth again without any consolatory one-day rewards.

Under Barclay's shrewd and thoughtful captaincy, Sussex kicked on in 1981, but frustratingly fell two points short in their Championship bid. Title winners Nottinghamshire were boosted massively by the all-round strength of Clive Rice and Richard Hadlee, while Derek Randall was a prolific run-scorer. Nevertheless, this was Sussex's highest Championship position since David Sheppard led them to second place in 1953. Thereafter, Sussex's fortunes receded although Barclay led them to victory in the Sunday John Player League in 1982.

The late eighties were not kind to Sussex, as their previously powerful squad became depleted by injury and departures. Tony Greig's younger brother, Ian, another gifted all-rounder, left in 1985. Barclay resigned a year later having failed to recover from a badly damaged finger. Imran and Le Roux left in 1988 while Dermot Reeve, 'man of the match' in Sussex's triumph in the NatWest Final of 1986, left in 1989. To cap it all, in 1987 Sussex finished bottom of the County Championship. While the loss of Imran was a colossal blow, Le Roux's departure hit Sussex almost as hard. Like Imran, his bowling was often venomous and his batting, explosive. He scored 3,341 runs in first-class games for Sussex with an average score of 28.31, while also taking 393 wickets at an average of 23.16. Had South Africa not been excluded from Test match cricket on account of their apartheid policy, Le Roux would have played many more international games for his country than the 15 he belatedly managed. Sussex were extremely fortunate to have had the services of these mighty all-rounders.

However, Alan Wells, younger brother of Colin, led a spirited revival in 1992, scoring 1,465 runs at an average of 48.83. With James Hall, Martin Speight, nomadic opener David Smith, Neil Lenham, wicketkeeper Peter Moores and all-rounder Franklyn Stephenson also averaging over 30 runs, Sussex's fortunes took a turn for the better, finishing the 1992

Championship season in seventh position. Meanwhile, Ian Salisbury enjoyed considerable success with his leg spin, after taking 79 wickets at a commendable average of 27.02. Ed Giddins's medium-fast swing bowling secured 31 wickets at a similar average.

In September 1993, Sussex returned to Lord's for the NatWest Bank Final where they met Warwickshire in arguably one of the best one-day finals in English cricket. It was a beautiful late summer day. Nevertheless, Warwickshire captain Dermot Reeve, formerly of Sussex, elected to field first upon winning the toss. Sussex skipper Alan Wells admitted that the wicket had a tinge of green. Not that this inhibited the Sussex batsmen, who played with such freedom that anyone watching on either side of the wicket might have assumed that this was a flat track. Reeve was so convinced of its perils, though, that he posted two slips for the first hour. By then Sussex were off to a flier. Fifty-seven runs came off the first ten overs and 100 off only 16.

Although Bill Athey perished quickly for nought, badly miscuing a hook off a climbing delivery from 6ft 5in Tim Munton with only four on the board, the incoming batsman, Martin Speight, set about the Warwickshire attack with relish. Gladstone Small produced several fizzing leg-cutters that had Speight groping outside his off stump, but the Sussex batsman was not to be deterred. He began by slogging successive balls from Munton to the midwicket boundary before producing an elegant cover drive off Small for four more. Then skipping down the wicket, he smashed a Munton delivery back over the bowler's head for yet another four. Not content with that, he repeated the shot, this time lifting the ball higher for six. Proving he was no slouch, David Smith crunched a wider delivery from Small through point, setting aside his early scare when he nearly castled himself with an inside edge. With caution thrown to a non-existent wind, this pair wreaked carnage. While Small persisted with a testing line just outside off stump, believing his command of seam would eventually succeed, Munton was all over the place in line and length, not helped by the ferocity of the Sussex strokeplay. Speight seemed sure of his invincibility, continuing to play premeditated drives and swats.

Amazingly, Reeve chose not to position sweepers on the cover and midwicket boundaries which were peppered by Speight and Smith. Reeve was content to deploy his fielders on the edge of the square in anticipation of a false shot. With no long-off or long-on, Speight continued to dance down the track and hoist balls in these directions. Belatedly, Reeve decided that Munton was taking too much punishment and substituted him with Paul Smith. Smith was also over six feet tall. His bowling style suggested a like-for-like replacement. Smith was cannier than Munton, though, producing three well-disguised slower balls that completely bewildered Smith. But the whacking went on. Speight sped to his fifty at a rate of a run a ball. In a post-Twenty20 world this may seem unremarkable, but one-day cricket then was typified by its obduracy as much as its long hitting. Meanwhile, David Smith showcased the virtues of both, while his powerful driving remained productive.

Reeve finally twigged that while Small had the guile to beat the bat, he was not going to roll over the Sussex batting as his captain had hoped. He decided to bring himself on with his medium-paced, boomerang swing. This did the trick. Speight's eyes lit up at a tempting delivery, and he lashed out without recognising the degree of swing, smearing the ball skywards from a top edge. The Bears' wicketkeeper settled under the ball's swirling fall and safely snaffled it. Sussex were 107/2. The scorecard read 'caught Piper bowled Reeve' but it might well have said 'bowled hubris'.

Alan Wells came to the wicket, opening with a cultured cover drive for four, then repeated the shot for anyone not appreciating his perfect timing. Reeve decided that it was time for spin and brought on Neil Smith. It was a wise choice. Smith bowled a niggardly spell, conceding only 37 runs in

GOOD OLD SUSSEX BY THE SEA

his 12 overs. Importantly, he brought Wells' fluent innings of 33 runs to an end when the Sussex captain attempted a premeditated sweep and failed to connect, the ball trapping him on the full. Nevertheless, Wells and Smith added 76 runs, although the scoring rate had dropped, thanks to the better control exercised by spinners Twose and Smith.

All-rounder Franklyn Stephenson arrived at the wicket, determined to hit the spinners off their line. However, his thumping shot off Twose was brilliantly caught by spin twin Smith. Stephenson (3) barely troubled the scorers. Neil Lenham was a different proposition though, slamming a couple of fours off the appropriately named Twose. Although Lenham was dropped at deep square leg by Dominic Ostler when hooking Small, his subsequent pull off the same bowler flashed to the boundary. Not to be left out, Smith bashed a gigantic six over long-on off Neil Smith. Sussex reached 200/4 off 43.2 overs. They needed to step on the gas, though, and did so, reaching 266/4 off 54 overs. Smith duly reached his century, sprinkled with seven fours and a six, while Lenham reached his fifty. The rate of scoring became frenzied. The 300 mark was passed in 57.3 overs. This was only the second time this figure had been reached in NatWest or the preceding Gillette finals, Sussex eventually posted a record total of 321/6.

Surely, this was a winning score? The bookies thought so, putting Sussex 7/1 on to take the title. When the Warwickshire openers, Moles and Ratcliffe, were dismissed quickly by Tony Pigott and Franklyn Stephenson, leaving the Bears in huge trouble at 18/2, I was certain that Sussex had this in the bag. Asif Din and Paul Smith had other ideas. Coming together at 93/3 after Salisbury had spun out Ostler, this pair put on 71 for the fourth wicket. And when Paul Smith left for 60 having been caught at the wicket by Moores off Stephenson, Reeve played a captain's innings of 81, full of scurried singles, accompanying Asif Din (104) ably as142 runs were added.

Warwickshire hero Asif Din, now a Warwickshire committee member, recalled: 'It is a very special memory. It created so much interest. Because it was so late finishing, club games all over the West Midlands had ended and people, some not even changed out of their whites, were glued to the telly in clubhouses watching it with a pint. There are many highlights in life; your marriage, your first child – and as a cricketer your first century and first "five-for". But to score a hundred in a Lord's final, and in that Lord's final, for the county you have played for all your career – well, it doesn't get better than that.'

Before the advent of the Twenty20 competition, 250 was considered a demanding 60-over score.

Asif continued: '321 was a formidable score. It was like we were 4-0 down at half-time in a football match but we just said to ourselves let's just relax, go out there and be positive and see where it takes us. We lost a couple of early wickets but then Dominic Ostler and Paul Smith put on a partnership. I had been due to go in at seven but when we lost those two quick wickets Dermot Reeve, the captain, told me to pad up. I did that and went and lay on the bench in the dressing-room and watched the game on the telly. Then Ossie got out.

'It was just a case of trying to keep us in the game. I was so hyped up. I remember going down to talk to Paul between overs and using my native language. I'd go and say something to him in Punjabi and he would just nod and go back to his end and we'd carry on! It helped us that Sussex, with a big total in the bank, were happy to give us singles. We took plenty of them and added the odd two and four and just kept ourselves in the game. I think it was when the PA announcer gave the score after 40 overs, and ours was exactly what Sussex's had been, that we thought this was "game on".

'All we were focused on was the 321 we needed. It was as though I was in a shell, shutting out the crowd noise, so it came as a big surprise when I suddenly saw I was in the 90s. I had got to 60 mostly in singles but went from 60 to 90 quite quickly.

Sussex started to panic. We had been going along quite comfortably at six an over and were still right in the game.

Then I got out in the penultimate over to the sweetest hit I made all day! That left 16 off the last and Dermot [Reeve] played it brilliantly against Franklyn Stephenson who, with his slower balls, was one of the best in the world at the time. I remember Dermot hitting one to cover and Bill Athey misfielded it, so they got back for two and kept Dermot on strike which was huge. Then it came down to two off the last ball and Twosey did it off the first ball he received. What a finish!'

Sussex's opening bowler, Ed Giddins, recalled: 'They needed 21 off the last two overs and I went for five. I had Asif Din caught out on the boundary by Martin Speight. Warwickshire needed to get 16 off the final over in the dark and I thought that we were home and dry, I must admit. But Dermot Reeve was one of the most mentally strong cricketers in the world at that time. I think he was named man of the match in three of the six finals he played. And he got the better of the great Franklyn Stephenson that day for sure. One thing I always remember about that game was looking up at the digital scoreboard. It gave the runs per over and when Warwickshire went out to bat it was just a little over 5.30 per over and they always kept within that. It's now the equivalent of 450. I believe it gave the chasing team a psychological edge because a lot of people don't quickly do maths in their head but at just over five an over you can keep the board ticking over.'

He added: 'The bookmakers appeared to have got the odds spot on when Warwickshire needed 21 runs off the final two overs. I thought that the trophy was heading back to Sussex. It was until Roger Twose took two through the covers off the last ball.'

He admitted he is still haunted by that game, commenting that it took a hugely talented Sussex side two seasons to get over this result while Warwickshire, who signed Brian Lara during the following season, went from strength to strength.

Giddins thought it would have been better to have lost that game by 150 runs than to lose it off the final ball. He added: 'Warwickshire went on to win three of the four trophies in the following year. Whereas, we at Sussex had a hangover that stayed with us through the following season, it was that much of a disappointment.'

In conclusion, Ed thought he and his team-mates might have dealt with their disappointment better had there been a few Championship games left to play. Instead, they had to incubate that demoralising defeat over the winter. But Ed exaggerated the defeat's negative impact upon Sussex's subsequent performance for they came eighth in the Championship of 1994, a respectable achievement. But amid increasing turmoil within the club, Sussex declined thereafter, stumbling into bottom place in 1997.

Realising all was not well at the club he had stoutly represented, Tony 'Lester' Pigott came to their rescue in 1996. During his 16-year first-class career, Harrovian Pigott played for Sussex and, briefly, Surrey. As a wholehearted fast-medium bowler, he captured 672 first-class wickets at an average of just below 31, with his first three victims, in 1978, claimed in a hat-trick against Surrey. As a biffing lower-order batsman, he once lustily smote a first-class century (104 not out). Incredibly, he played for England, too, during their disastrous 1983/84 winter tour of New Zealand. Pigott was 'Johnny on the spot', contracted to play for Wellington, when a calamitous list of injuries brought about his selection for the Christchurch Test. The match was humiliating for England who were bowled out for 82 and 93, losing in under 12 hours, although Pigott performed satisfactorily, taking 2-75 with his brisk seamers.

Pigott became increasingly hampered by back injuries, though, and his career fizzled out after moving to Surrey. He then took over coaching the Surrey second XI, before returning to Sussex during their 'winter of discontent' in 1996. With Sussex struggling to remain viable, Pigott swung into action, tabling a motion of no confidence in the committee. When a members' revolt forced the committee out in 1997, he became the club's chief executive. He then set about recruiting high-profile players such as Derbyshire's

Chris Adams and Australian Test player Michael Bevan and pioneered floodlit cricket.

However, this rebuilding proved expensive. Sussex lost nearly £200,000 in 1998, having spent £40,000 on a failed TV marketing campaign. There was a confusion of roles and responsibilities between him and general manager Dave Gilbert, a former Australian Test fast bowler. Gilbert remarked: 'You can't help but like Tony. He was always popular with the members and the committee because he always wore his heart on his sleeve as a player, giving absolutely everything, and then he was the catalyst for change when the club changed direction. But he was simply not up to the job. His spending was irrational and largely unaccountable, and I was getting increasingly fed up clearing up the wreckage. It was very unfair on Tony to give him a job for which he was entirely unsuited.' Whether this is fair comment or not, there is no denying that Pigott put Sussex back on the road to health and prosperity. His signing of Chris Adams was inspirational in reviving Sussex's cricketing fortunes. Adams arrived after a catastrophic season which ended with Sussex bottom of the Championship table having been thrashed by just about every other side, a humiliating malaise not helped by the departure of six capped players.

Pigott resigned in 1999, citing personal reasons. He now runs a pub in Hurstpierpoint. But he should be proud of what he helped achieve at Hove. For, in that year of his departure, green roots of recovery were evident, despite Sussex narrowly missing out on a place in the upper echelon of the newly divided Championship. Sussex won the Second Division National League in 2001, their first trophy in 13 years. Captain Adams and coach Peter Moores had brought about a substantial upgrade in their Championship side. Adams led from the front, scoring almost 2,000 runs in all competitions in 1999, earning a place on England's winter tour of South Africa. Michael Di Venuto was a splendid replacement for fellow Australian, Bevan, scoring over 1,000 runs in the Championship. Batsmen Richard Montgomerie from Northants and Tony Cottey from Glamorgan, were excellent additions. Adams was also delighted with his seam attack, comprising James Kirtley, Jason Lewry, all-rounder Robin Martin-Jenkins and Mark Robinson, who would form the backbone of the club's subsequent rise. Although Adams was initially sceptical of Peter Moores's value, the pair formed a relationship of mutual respect which powered Sussex to a succession of triumphs.

Sussex stormed out of the Second Division as champions. Having consolidated their top division status in sixth place in 2002, hailed by Adams as a bigger achievement than promotion, Sussex seized their long sought-after prize, the Championship title, in 2003. This came just three years after 'receiving' the wooden spoon. A vital component in their triumph was the signing of Pakistani leg-spinner Mushtaq Ahmed, who had been widely considered to be over the hill. Mushtaq proved the folly of that assessment by taking 103 Championship wickets, the first Sussex bowler to achieve that since Tony Buss and John Snow in 1966. There was little time wasted in awarding Mushtaq a second two-year contract. Adams described Mushtaq's achievement as 'awesome', adding that 'the most important signings we made were world-class overseas players', the other being Murray Goodwin of Zimbabwe, who headed Sussex's batting averages with 1,496 runs at an average of 59.84.

It was Goodwin's powerful pull for four off Leicestershire's Phillip DeFreitas that seized the Championship title at 1.44pm on a glorious sunny day at Hove on 18 September 2003. Goodwin proceeded, in carnival mode, to an unbeaten triple century (335), full of powerful yet cultured drives, deft deflections and mighty pulls, hooks and cuts. His feat exceeded Duleepsinhji's 73-year-old county record. Although Goodwin dominated Sussex's batting as much as Mushtaq dominated their bowling, this was far from a two-man show. Prior and Cottey accumulated over 1,000 runs each and as proof of

Sussex's batting depth eight players averaged in excess of 30 runs. Meanwhile, the Sussex seam quartet of Lewry, Kirtley, Martin-Jenkins and Taylor aggregated 142 wickets. Kirtley also bowled England to victory over the South Africans at Nottingham.

In his elegant victory speech, Adams declared, 'We wanted it more than any of the others,' but added, thoughtfully, that he wished 'to share this triumph with all those Sussex players who have gone before.'

I returned to Hove two years after to begin my 'prescribed' down time. Sussex were playing Surrey, hoping to beat their opponents and Kent to the runners-up spot, behind champions-elect Warwickshire. It was a sombre autumn day with just brief interruptions of wan sunlight within the prevalent gloom. A chilly breeze wafted around the ground as the wheeling gulls above cawed and cackled. Between two tractors stretched a long rope, a lasso to remove the residual dew.

Sussex were chasing Surrey's challenging total of 283, after the visitors had stumbled to 14/4 and then 60/5 before being rescued by a belligerent partnership between Rikki Clarke (112) and Martin Bicknell (40). Clarke's century was made in only 83 balls with 18 fours and three sixes. He was particularly harsh on Mushtaq before the Sussex leg-spinner clean bowled him. In reply, Sussex reached 129/3 at the close of play. I picked up proceedings at the start of the second day. While Adams played expansively, Yardy, who resumed on 69 not out, progressed cautiously, often removing his bat from deliveries pitched outside his off stump with a curious curtain-pulling mannerism. Occasionally, a fuller-pitched ball would tempt him to drive. While left-handed Yardy lacked the elegance of Gower, his drives emitted a pleasing 'puck' that resonated around the thinly populated ground, with the ball, more often than not, racing to the cover boundary. There were two Sussex stalwarts sat close to me in their Panama hats and windcheaters. Watching another Yardy drive, the taller, leaner man commented in a plummy voice: 'It's hardly a thing of beauty, is it.' One of his companions responded: 'I think it would be safer to say he is more of an artisan than an artist.' I longed for Yardy to reach his first Championship century to silence these snobbish detractors. To his delight and mine, he did, with Yardy celebrating by waving his bat excitedly towards the Sussex dressing room.

Unfortunately, his side collapsed from 210/3 to 271 all out, with Jimmy Ormond making significant inroads in the seamer-friendly conditions. Surrey then built upon their slender advantage to win the game by 37 runs. Despite the uncomfortable conditions for cricket-watching I was hooked once more, subsequently watching Sussex play not only at Hove, Arundel and Horsham, but further afield, whenever a 'time out day' coincided with a reachable fixture.

Shortly before my retirement I ducked out of a county council managers' conference and travelled to Nottingham to watch Sussex win their second Championship trophy. I felt confident I would not be rumbled until a camera-holding Sky reporter made for me with the intention of gaining a fan's view of Sussex's triumph. To my relief another Sussex supporter crossed his path before I reached the interviewer, meaning that he was reeled in instead. Now, I can watch Sussex play in heavenly peace, no longer interrupted by work calls. While their glorious Championship victories of 2003, 2006 and 2007 are now distant history, with their young side struggling to achieve traction in the lower Championship division, their one-day sides continue to compete attractively. Now my parents have passed away, watching Sussex County Cricket Club remains as my closest association with my East Sussex boyhood and my much-loved home county.

Last Words

I SUPPOSE that our choice of favourite team says a lot about how we view ourselves. As much as I enjoy my teams' triumphs, I feel more comfortable being pleasantly surprised at their achievements as I do with mine. I have never considered supporting a large, wealthy club. I don't think I could sustain the weight of ego required. I wouldn't be able to do 'the talk', let alone 'the walk'. Besides, great expectations sit too heavily on my shoulders, although this has never diminished my efforts. I'm sure it's a legacy of my invaluable Sussex education.

It's strange that football, a game that carries few certainties and leaves many disappointments, should have become my sanctuary when other aspects of my life were in chaos. Yet all those years ago, that is what football delivered. My industrial production of scrapbooks and creation of card and programme collections have served me very well in this exercise. Strangely, my daughter came to football via personal loss, too, in her case the terminal illness and death of her much-loved grandmother. Like me, long before her, she accumulated vast quantities of football trivia, including pin-ups as I had done, and committed endless football facts to memory. Obsessions have their uses.

My dad, who introduced me to football, succumbed to dementia in his later years, stripping him of his talents, independence, personality and dignity, leaving him agitated by almost every aspect of daily life, which had become strange and unpredictable. And yet whenever I took him to football games, especially at Griffin Park, where he once had many happy times as a young man, he seemed to find an elusive sense of calm, notwithstanding the baying voices around us. I wondered whether the contented smile that sometimes played briefly upon his lips, lighting up his pallid, watery eyes, was prompted by his imagined sight of his past. Perhaps he thought he saw his former mates, standing in their favourite corner, in their open-necked shirts and baggy flannels, puffing on their untipped Woodbines in the late summer warmth, ghosts of a generation decimated by war.

Cricket, too, settled his anxieties. We spent many summer weekends revisiting grounds at which he had played. He loved the resonant sound of ball on bat, the swishy breeze in the trees, the scent of cut grass and the humming insects in the tall heat. Most of all he loved the lunches we had at country pubs. It was the last sense of pleasure to desert him.

I lament the reduction in inherited support, by which I mean families passing on their loyalty to a particular club through the generations, from father or mother to son and daughter and so on. This was much more familiar in my youth than appears now. Watching football and cricket was once a celebration of family and local identity. Now this tradition has become weakened by a consumerist perspective in which teams are wantonly embraced or rejected according to their results. I admit that my choice of Burnley did not arise from any family loyalties because, as much as Dad loved football, he did not pass on to me his former passion for Brentford. I was left to make my own selection. But having made my final choice, Burnley, my daughter followed me, enjoying the town and its people as well as its football team.

Cricket was a sport too far, though. And yet I still hanker for Sussex, and its past associations, which my county cricket watching helps with. This book is a testament to that enduring love.

Tim Quelch

Sports books and journals consulted

Mullery, Alan with Tony Norman, *Alan Mullery: the autobiography* (Headline, 2006).

Camillin, Paul, *Brighton & Hove Albion Miscellany* (Pavilion, 2006).

Tester, Dan, *Brighton & Hove Albion on This Day* (Pitch Publishing, 2007).

Brighton & Hove Albion programmes 1958–1972.

Elms, Philip, *Claret and Blue: The Story of Hastings United* (1066 Newspapers Publications, 1988).

Empire News and News Chronicle Football Annual (1958–1963 annuals, Thomson & Co.).

Glanville, Brian, *England Managers: The Toughest Job in Football* (Headline, 2007).

Harrison, Paul, *FA Cup Giant Killers* (Stadia/Tempus, 2007).

Giller, Norman, *Footballing Fifties* (JR Books, 2007).

Watts, Derek, *Football's Giant Killers: 50 Great Cup Upsets* (Book Guild, 2010).

Prole, David, *Football in London* (Sportsman's Book Club, 1964).

Young, Percy M., *Football in Sheffield* (Sportsman's Book Club, 1964).

Mercer, Joe, *The Great Ones* (Sportsman's Book Club, 1966).

Greaves, Jimmy, *Greavsie: The Autobiography* (Little, Brown Books, 2003).

Harrison, Paul, *Gravesend & Northfleet FC* (Stadia/Tempus, 2006).

Sinden, Roger, *Hastings United Through Time: A Collection of Football Recollections* (Flying Free Management Ltd).

Sinden, Roger *Hastings Reunited: A Collection of Football Recollections* (Flying Free, 2005).

Hastings United Sports & Social Club Official Handbook First Issue January/February 1967 First Issue, (Sports Publications, Watford, 1967).

Hastings United programmes 1960–1968.

Horner, Matthew, *He Shot, He Scored: The Official Biography of Peter Ward* (Sea View Media, 2009).

Wilson, Jonathan, *Inverting the Pyramid: The History of Football Tactics* (Orion, 2008).

Hadgraft, Rob, *Ipswich Town: Champions of England 1961–62* (Desert Island Books, 2002).

Taylor, Rogan and Andrew Ward, *Kicking and Screaming: an oral history of football in England* (Robson Books, 1996).

McDonald, Tony, *Leyton Orient: The Untold Story of the O's Best-Ever Team* (Football World, 2006).

Whittell, Peter, *The Life Story of Doncaster Rovers Legend Alick Jeffrey* (Chronicle Publishing, 2003).

Camillin, Paul, *Match of My Life: Brighton & HA* (Know the Score Books, 2008).

Smith, Martyn, *Match of the Day: 40th Anniversary* (BBC Books, 2004).

Dougan, Derek and Patrick Murphy, *Matches of the Day 1958–1983* (Dent, 1984).

Osgood, Peter with Martin King and Martin Knight, *Ossie: King of Stamford Bridge* (Mainstream Sport, 2002).

News of the World Football Annuals 1964 to 1995.

Swan, Peter with Nick Johnson, *Peter Swan: Setting the Record Straight* (Stadia, 2006).

Playfair Cricket Annuals 1954–2008 Edited by Gordon Ross until 1985, thereafter by Bill Frindall. 1954–1962 Playfair Books Ltd. 1964, The Dickens Press, 1977–1985 Queen Anne Press, 1986–1992 MacDonald Queen Anne Press, 1993–2008 Headline.

Greaves, Jimmy with Norman Giller, *The Sixties Revisited* (Queen Anne Press, 1992).

Green, Geoffrey, *Soccer in the Fifties* (Ian Allan, 1974).

The Sportsview Book of Soccer: 1958–1963 annuals (Vernon Holding & Partners Ltd).

Hill, Jimmy, *Striking for Soccer* (Peter Davies, 1961).

Irvine, Willie with Dave Thomas, *Together Again* (Sports Books, 2005).

Rowland, George (Ed), *The Ultimate Drop* (Tempus, 2001).

Vinicombe, John, *Up, Up, And Away: Brighton & Hove Albion's Rise to the 1st Division* (George Nobbs, 1979).

Wisden Cricketers' Almanac 1954–2008: Edited by Norman Preston until 1978, Sporting Handbooks Ltd; Edited by Matthew Engel until 2007, Wisden & Co Ltd; Edited by Scyld Berry in 2008, John Wisden & Co Ltd.

Plus football match reports and additional material from: Brighton *Argus, Daily Mail, Daily Mirror, Four Four Two, The Guardian, Hastings & St Leonards Observer, the Independent, Mail on Sunday, News of the World, Daily Herald, The Times, Mail on Sunday, Northampton Chronicle & Echo, The People, The Observer & Observer magazines; Sunday Express, Sunday Times, When Saturday Comes* and Hastings United & Brighton & Hove Albion programmes & websites. Particular thanks go to the help offered by freelance journalist with Cumbrian papers, John Walsh and club and supporter websites, notably Workington's Workipedia site. Thanks also to Phil Snow, Barnet FC supporter, for extract of his interview with Ricky George.

Non-football reference works consulted

Sampson, Anthony, *Anatomy of Britain* (Hodder & Stoughton, 1962).

Mercer, Derrik (Ed), *Chronicle of the 20th Century* (Longman, 1998).

Turner, Alwyn W., *Crisis? What Crisis?: Britain in the 1970s* (Aurum, 2008).

Palmer, Tony, *Dancing in the Street* (BBC Books, 1996).

Crossman, Richard, *The Diaries of a Cabinet Minister: Volume 1* (Book Club Associates, 1975).

Heylin, Clinton, *From the Velvets to the Voidoids: A Pre-Punk History for a Post-Punk World* (Helter Skelter Publishing, 2005).

Marr, Andrew, *A History of Modern Britain* (Macmillan, 2007).

Hodgson, Geoffrey, *The People's Century Vol. 2* (BBC Books, 1996).

Booker, Christopher, *The Neophiliacs* (Collins, 1969).

Sandbrook, Dominic, *Never Had It So Good: A History of Britain from Suez to The Beatles* (Little, Brown, 2005).

Booker, Christopher, *The Seventies* (Penguin, 1980).

Marwick, Arthur, *The Sixties* (Oxford, 1998).

McAleer, Dave (Ed) *The Ultimate Hit Singles Book* (Carlton Books, 1998).

Beckett, Andy, *When the Lights Went Out: What Really Happened to Britain in the Seventies* (Faber & Faber, 2009).

Sandbrook, Dominic, *White Heat: A History of Britain in the Swinging Sixties* (Abacus/Little, Brown Books, 2006).

Opie, Robert, *The 1950s & 1960s Scrapbooks* (Global Publishing, 1998).

Lewis, Peter, *The 50s* (Cupid Press, 1978).